The Thinker's Library, No. 53.

THE LIFE OF JESUS

BY

ERNEST RENAN

COMPLETE EDITION

LONDON:

WATTS & CO.,

5 & 6 JOHNSON'S COURT, FLEET STREET, E.C.4

First published in this form 1935

Printed and Published in Great Britain by C. A. Watts & Co. Limited,
5 & 6 Johnson's Court, Fleet Street, London, E.C.4

Dost thou recall, from the bosom of God where thou reposest, those long days at Ghazir, in which, alone with thee, I wrote these pages, inspired by the places we had visited together? Silent at my side, thou didst read and copy each sheet as soon as I had written it, while the sea, the villages, the ravines, and the mountains were spread at our feet. When the overwhelming light had given place to the innumerable army of stars, thy shrewd and subtle questions, thy discreet doubts, led me back to the sublime object of our common thoughts. One day thou didst tell me that thou wouldst love this book—first, because it had been composed with thee, and also because it pleased thee. Though at times thou didst fear for it the narrow judgments of the frivolous, yet wert thou ever persuaded that all truly religious souls would ultimately take pleasure in it. In the midst of these sweet meditations, the Angel of Death struck us both with his wing : the sleep of fever seized us at the same time—I awoke alone ! . . . Thou sleepest now in the land of Adonis, near the holy Byblus and the sacred stream where the women of the ancient mysteries came to mingle their tears. Reveal to me, O good genius, to me whom thou lovedst, those truths which conquer death, deprive it of terror, and make it almost beloved.

PREFACE

LIKE many another " infidel," Ernest Renan grew up in an atmosphere of piety. He was born in the Breton fishing-town of Tréguier in 1823. When he was only five years old his father, a ship-outfitter, was drowned at sea. Henceforth the home influence of a sensitive and impressionable child was exercised by two women, Renan's mother and his sister, Henriette, who was twelve years his senior. The latter was the bread-winner of the family and proved a second mother to the young Ernest. In his manhood she became his most trusted counsellor and friend.

Renan's mother remained a Catholic to the end of her life, but Henriette lost all belief in the Supernatural long before her brother had entertained a single doubt of his hereditary faith. Yet she put no obstacle in the way of his cherished ambition to become a priest. His first school was the ecclesiastical college at Tréguier, where he soon showed such brilliancy that, through the kind efforts of Dupanloup (afterwards Bishop of Orleans), he was sent to a superior college in Paris. Thence he passed to the Seminary of Issy, and afterwards to St. Sulpice and St. Stavistas (the lay college of the Oratorians). It was during his stay in the last of these establishments that Renan reluctantly came to the conviction that he could never enter the Catholic priesthood. According to his own account, the critical study of the Bible was the main factor of his change. His bias was strongly pietistic, and he loved and admired his clerical teachers. Bad priests never seem to have come his way.

When he announced his decision—he was now twenty-two—the older men among his instructors sought to dis-

suade him, hoping that his faith might return when he had
settled down to his clerical duties. Dupanloup, however,
agreed that he ought to choose a lay career and offered to
help him with money.

He was encouraged to take the final step by Henriette,
who sent him 500 francs while he was looking for employ-
ment. It was not long before Renan obtained a post as
usher in a boys' school, where he started a lifelong friendship with Berthelot, the famous chemist, who was then
eighteen. His duties occupying only the evenings, Renan
had plenty of time at his disposal for reading during the
day.

In 1849 the French Government sent Renan on a scientific
mission to Italy. On his return to Paris he received a small
post in the Bibliothèque Nationale, which, together with
the savings of Henriette, who had now come to live with
him, kept the two alive. In 1852 was published Renan's
work on the most renowned Islamic philosopher of the
Middle Ages, Averroes. This brought him his doctor's
degree and established his reputation as a thinker. He
married two years later, and in 1859 he published new
translations, with commentaries, of the Book of Job and
the Song of Songs.

The chair of Hebrew and Chaldaic at the Collège de
France now became vacant, and Renan offered himself as
a candidate. Naturally, he was bitterly opposed by the
Catholics. Napoleon III was then the ruler of France
and his wife, the Empress Eugénie, supported the Catholic
reactionaries. The Emperor was bound to conciliate so
powerful a body of his subjects, without whose support
he could not hope to retain his precarious authority. But
he did not lack admiration for Renan and wished to do
something for him. So he sent him on an archæological
mission to Syria.

Renan sailed for the East with the devoted Henriette as
his companion, and they made their first stay at Beyrout.
A few months later his wife joined him, but was compelled

by her home duties to return to France in the following
summer. Henriette remained behind and shared, as
far as she could, her brother's investigations of Phœnician
antiquities.

In July, 1861, Renan had finished his work, and the two
paid a visit to the Upper Lebanon. Renan was now
engaged in making his first draft of the *Vie de Jésus*, his
sister copying it out for him page by page.

The brother and sister went back to Beyrout, in order to
prepare for a journey to Cyprus, where the mission was
to reach its end. Time, however, was found for excavations
at Gebeil (the ancient Byblus), in the fabled land of
Adonis. Here Renan and Henriette were struck down
with a severe attack of fever. Henriette's case proved
fatal. They buried her in the land of Adonis, as Renan
tells us in his beautiful dedication to her soul, which
prefaces the book by which all the world knows him.
Renan returned to France. The mission bore fruit in the
important *Corpus Inscriptionum Semiticarum*, of which
he was the editor. A richly illustrated report of the
mission's achievements was published in 1864. The
previous year had seen the appearance of the *Vie de Jésus*.

Shortly before the issue of his most popular work Renan
had obtained the chair of Hebrew and Semitic languages
in the University of Paris, which had been left vacant
through the death of Quatremère, under whom he had
studied. The Catholics were furious. Even among the
Liberals there was suspicion of the new professor, and it
was feared that Renan was sympathetic to the Imperial
régime.

His inaugural address provoked more than one interruption, the climax coming when he referred to Jesus as " a
man so great that . . . I should not wish to contradict those
who, impressed by the unique character of his movement,
call him God." This damning with faint praise, as they
were bound to consider it, gave offence to the Catholics.
Four days later Renan was suspended from his professiorial

A 2

duties, although he retained his salary and for two years
taught Hebrew in his own house to those students who
desired it. The publication of the *Vie de Jésus* prevented
his reinstatement. The French ministry offered him a
post in the Bibliothèque Impériale, which he declined with
scorn.

The *Vie de Jésus* was only the first of a series dealing
very fully with Christian origins. Three years later
appeared *The Apostles*. To this were subsequently added
*The Gospels and the Second Christian Generation, Saint
Paul, The Antichrist, The Christian Church*, and *Marcus
Aurelius*. The last brought the story down to the last
quarter of the second century. It is perhaps the most
remarkable of the series. Few have depicted so vividly,
and with such a wealth of erudition, the social and intellectual life of Pagans and Christians in the days of the
last of the great Stoic Emperors as did Ernest Renan.

The great French scholar's *New Studies of Religious
History* (collected in 1884) show the catholicity of his
interests, dealing as they do with such themes as the
Islamic mystery play of the martyrdom of Hussein, the
growth of the legend of the Buddha, and the life of St.
Francis of Assisi. His *History of Israel*, which was published in 1887–91, revealed Renan's competency to handle
Old Testament problems with the same skill and learning
that he applied to those of the New.

It will always be gratifying to Englishmen of broad
sympathies and culture to remember that Renan delivered
in London the Hibbert course of lectures for the year 1880.
His subject was the influence of Roman institutions on the
development of Catholicism. The liberal-minded Dean
Stanley was among those who showed their cordiality to
the famous heretic.

Renan's exquisite *Recollections of My Youth* (1883), which
is perhaps his best known work after the *Vie de Jésus*,
must have endeared him to the hearts of millions. Seldom
has a more touching story been told, or one so candid and

dignified, of the struggle of a soul thirsty for truth and ready to sacrifice everything in its service.

The political fluctuations of Renan, at one time suspicious of democracy as a possible foe of culture and finally reconciled to it and hopeful of its future evolution, hardly concern us here. Nor need we dwell on his experiments in drama, which would never have won him fame.

The Chair of Semitic Languages, which Renan forfeited, through his own indiscretions and the bigotry of his orthodox enemies, under the Second Empire was ultimately restored to him under the Third Republic. He had become one of the most celebrated men of letters in France, and his sympathetic courtesy and geniality of temper had gained for him the respect, if not the affection, of many to whom his religious opinions were repugnant. When he died in the autumn of 1892, at the age of nearly sixty-nine, he was still busy with his classes at the Collège de France, whither he had returned after a very short holiday in his native Brittany, which he loved so well.

Seventy-two years have passed since Ernest Renan's *Vie de Jésus*, the first biography of Jesus to present him as entirely human, was launched on a world already much troubled with doubts about the Supernatural. In less than six months 60,000 copies of this momentous work were sold. Edition quickly followed edition, no less than twenty-three appearing within the space of twenty years.

Although thousands welcomed the *Vie de Jésus* for its lucidity and charm, as well as for the tenderness and sympathy with which Jesus and the great movement he is reputed to have started were delineated, the rage of Orthodoxy against the book and its author was at least as great as that provoked by Strauss's *Leben Jesu* nearly thirty years earlier.

Here for the first time was a purely naturalistic biography of one whom Christendom had so long adored as God manifest in the flesh. The *Leben Jesu* by Strauss can hardly be called a biography ; it is a searching criticism of the Gospels, and makes scarcely an attempt to construct a history in the place of the legend, which Strauss did more perhaps than any previous critic to demolish. To much the same category belong the works of those Biblical scholars who preceded Strauss—Herder, Reimarus, Evanson, Bahrdt, Venturini, Paulus, and others. Arguments about the mutual relations of the Gospels, their trustworthiness and their probable dating; conjectures (sometimes fantastic) about what might have happened in Galilee and Jerusalem some nineteen hundred years ago—all this the earlier Higher Critics of the New Testament gave. But none before Renan drew a real portrait of a man who could be loved as a man and judged as a man.

The charm and the skill with which Renan handles his theme may well serve to hide the critical and literary blemishes of his work. His Jesus is a young carpenter of Nazareth, who was at first one of the disciples of the fiery revivalist, John the Baptiser, and took up his slogan, " The Kingdom of Heaven is at hand." Later he broke away from the group and formed his own body of disciples. " The Kingdom of Heaven " meant nothing less than the restoration of the ancient theocracy in all its glory, as Jewish piety imagined it to have once existed, involving the overthrow of Roman rule and, in the opinion of many Jews, the re-establishment of the dynasty of David in Jerusalem. To the future king the name of Messiah (Heb. *Moshiah* = " Anointed ") was given. Jesus did not at first claim to be the Messiah. He preached an ethic of love and justice, of pity and self-renunciation, of humility and purity of heart, which should prepare his fellow-countrymen—foreigners were outside the scope of his propaganda—for the wonderful era that was shortly coming. Jesus enforced his teaching with simple parables, stories drawn from natural happenings, observable by all, and from the everyday life of the people—the sower scattering his seed on different soils, the mustard-seed that grew into a stately tree, the net breaking under the weight of the fish it enclosed, the shepherd hunting for the lost sheep, the merchant selling all his goods to buy the precious pearl. The Rabbis often used parables in their expositions. Parables with similar themes to those of the Gospels appear in the Talmud.

Simple folk loved Jesus and eagerly listened to his discourses. Among them he wrought many faith-cures. But his popularity with the Galilean peasants, whose attachment to Jewish Orthodoxy was rather loose, drew on him the keen resentment of the Pharisees, who, like Jesus, were Messianic in their outlook and much of whose ethical teaching resembled his, and still more the hostility of the Sadducees, who were pro-Roman and unfriendly to Messianic visions, and from whose ranks came the great hierarchy of the Temple. Popularity with the multitude and opposition from their religious and political leaders spurred Jesus to greater boldness. He was no longer content with the rôle of a prophet of the Kingdom, a wandering " Son of Man " (Ezekiel had borne that title). He claimed to be himself the Messiah. He even foretold his death by violence, his ascent to God his Father's right hand, and his eventual return in triumph on the clouds of heaven, accompanied by a host of angels. His character underwent a measure of degeneration. " The Galilean idyll," which graced his earlier career, disappeared, and the gentle, persuasive teacher was turned into an angry denunciator, and his mind became obsessed with apocalyptic horrors. Even fraud now assisted his propaganda. According to Renan, the raising of Lazarus was a trick, planned by the subject of the pretended miracle with the aid of Martha and Mary.

The end was inevitable. With the aid of a treacherous disciple the enemies of Jesus tracked him down and, after a mock trial before the High Priest on a blasphemy charge, dragged him before Pontius Pilatus, procurator of Judea, who reluctantly sentenced him to crucifixion as a rebel against Roman rule. Jesus was buried by a wealthy

Jewish sympathiser in his own family tomb. The story of his resurrection a day or two later was started by the hallucinations of a frenzied devotee, Mary of Magdala. A woman's love and folly had given to the world a risen God !

Renan's reconstruction of the story of Jesus does not lack plausibility in many of its features, but he has certainly failed to present a figure worthy of any great respect. This deluded visionary and fanatic, even stooping to fraud, has no claim to the glowing panegyric with which Renan closes his narrative. That Jesus was not only lovable, but, in a sense, worshipful, Renan truly felt and would have his readers feel. Was it not his Catholic upbringing that induced this frame of mind rather than the calm survey of the facts which he believed a critical study of the Gospels substantiated ?

At times Renan is even weakly sentimental. From an æsthetic viewpoint, if from no other, one must condemn his surmise that Jesus in the Garden of Gethsemane cast a thought on the girls he might have wooed in Galilee. No wonder a young French lady put down the *Vie de Jésus* with the remark : " What a pity it does not end with a marriage ! "

Renan, of course, did not accept without qualification the traditional views on the dating and authorship of the Gospels. But his conservatism would be hard to match to-day outside the ranks of the theologians. Bernard Shaw is hardly more uncritical than he sometimes is. Renan adhered to the opinion, first broached by Lachmann in the eighteenth century, that *Mark* was the earliest Gospel and, broadly speaking, reliable as a biographical source— an opinion which is still the prevailing one among Protestant scholars (Catholics are forbidden by the Papal Biblical Commission to maintain *Mark's* priority), though it is disputed by some eminent critics, like Raschke, who regards *Mark* as a late document. Renan's treatment of the Fourth Gospel is strangely arbitrary. Although not attributing it to John the son of Zebedee, he sees in it a valuable source of biographical data for the life of Jesus. His offensive interpretation of the story of Lazarus has no justification whatever, and is on a par with the vagaries of Paulus and Venturini, on which Strauss expended his scorn. The story is, in all probability, a didactic fiction, which the Fourth Evangelist may have built up on a basis of popular conjectures, gathering round a legendary or historic name.

To-day the question is being seriously mooted whether any materials exist for a life of Jesus, even conceding his historicity. No more drastic criticism of previous attempts at biographical reconstruction has been written than Dr. Albert Schweitzer's *Von Reimarus zu Wrede* (translated under the title of *The Quest of the Historical Jesus*), " that cemetery of departed hypotheses," as the late Prof. W. B. Smith so amusingly described it. Circumspect readers of Dr. Schweitzer's lengthy work will regard his own efforts in the way of Jesuine biography as open to the same charge of arbitrariness which he shrewdly and wittily makes against so many other critics.

It is not surprising that, in view of " such quantities of sand," the belief has been steadily growing during the last twenty-five years that Jesus belongs wholly to the realm of myth. Ingenious attempts, sometimes bewilderingly erudite, have been made by many scholars— Arthur Drews, W. B. Smith, J. M. Robertson, Kalthoff, Jensen, Couchoud, Bergh van Eysinga, and others—to explain the rise of Christianity without an historical Jesus. But there has been so far little measure of agreement among the Mythicists, beyond denial of the reputed founder's existence. The alleged traces of a pre-Christian cult of a sacrificed and resurrected Saviour God, named Jesus or Joshua, seem very dubious. The final victory may well lie with the Historicists. And yet it cannot be said that their position is rationally unchallengeable. The history of the numerous and often contradictory defences of the Gospels

is a history of continual critical surrenders. Did Jesus
claim to be the Messiah? Wrede and many other Historicists say no. Guignebert believes that an hallucination of Peter was the source, not only of the myth of the
resurrection, but of the doctrine of the Messiahship of
Jesus, though this seems to militate against all psychological
probability. Wrede, Harnack, and the Liberal School
generally, regard Jesus as an ethical teacher, whose views
of the Kingdom of Heaven were mystical rather than
political. He was a prophet of the inner life. On the other
hand, Schweitzer discovers in Jesus an apocalyptic seer,
preaching an " interim ethic," whose value can hardly be
detached from those forecasts of catastrophe and millennial
glory in which time has proved him mistaken. According
to Eisler, the Galilean propagandist was an aspirant to
David's crown, though piously refusing to enforce his rights
till God should intervene.

Many evangelical data, once proclaimed unassailable,
are now seriously questioned even by opponents of the
Mythicists. Among these are the Twelve Apostles, the
treachery of Judas, and the Sermon on the Mount. Where
do we reach the bottom-rock of historical fact? Some will
say that the Crucifixion is at least certain. The late
Canon Cheyne, however, expressed doubts even of this
event, and it seems possible to give an explanation of it
in terms of myth. The interesting thesis of Mr. J. M.
Robertson that a mystery play underlies the story of the
Passion seems to receive support from the discovery of
some cuneiform tablets relating to the Babylonian god
Marduk, whose death and resurrection were dramatically
represented long before the Christian era. Marduk, the
son of Ea and intercessor with his father for mankind,
was tried, condemned to death, slain, buried in a mountain
cave, and raised to life. He is also said to have visited
" the spirits in prison " (a curious parallel to 1 Peter iii. 19).
Possibly some form of this dramatic mystery was known
in certain heterodox circles of Judaism. Prof. Zimmern in

Germany and Dr. S. Langdon in England, both Assyriologists of repute, hold that the Marduk Passion-myth has some bearing on the problem of Christian origins. The Witness of Paul, which has been cited again and again as one of the unshakeable pillars of the tradition, has become at least questionable. Not only is the formidable attack by Van Manen on the authenticity of the whole of the Pauline Epistles to be reckoned with, but also the fact that the defence of them to-day generally involves the surrender of several as non-Pauline and the admission of large interpolations in the rest. At any rate, the theology of Paul, or of those who wrote under his name, seems to demand a longer growth of propaganda preceding it than the Orthodox tradition assumes.

A. D. HOWELL SMITH.

CONTENTS

INTRODUCTION

IN WHICH THE SOURCES OF THIS HISTORY ARE PRINCIPALLY TREATED

A HISTORY of the " Origin of Christianity " ought to embrace all the obscure and, if one might so speak, subterranean periods which extend from the first beginnings of this religion up to the moment when its existence became a public fact, notorious and evident to the eyes of all. Such a history would consist of four books. The first, which I now present to the public, treats of the particular fact which has served as the starting-point of the new religion; and is entirely filled by the sublime person of the Founder. The second would treat of the Apostles and their immediate disciples, or, rather, of the revolutions which religious thought underwent in the first two generations of Christianity. I would close this about the year 100, at the time when the last friends of Jesus were dead, and when all the books of the New Testament were fixed almost in the forms in which we now read them. The third would exhibit the state of Christianity under the Antonines. We should see it develop itself slowly, and sustain an almost permanent war against the empire, which had just reached the highest degree of administrative perfection, and, governed by philosophers, combated in the new-born sect a secret and theocratic society, which obstinately denied and incessantly undermined it. This book would cover the entire period of the second century. Lastly, the fourth book would show the decisive progress which Christianity made from the time of the Syrian emperors. We should see the learned system of the Antonines crumble, the decadence of the ancient civilisation become irrevocable, Christianity profit from its ruin, Syria conquer the whole West, and Jesus, in company with the gods and the deified sages of Asia, take possession of a society for which philosophy and a purely civil government no longer sufficed. It was then that the religious ideas of the races grouped around the Mediterranean became profoundly modified; that the Eastern religious everywhere took precedence; that the Christian Church, having become very numerous, totally forgot its dreams of a millennium, broke its last ties with Judaism, and entered completely into the Greek and Roman world. The contests and the literary labours of the third century, which were carried on without concealment, would be described only in their general features. I would relate still more briefly the persecutions at the commencement of the fourth century, the last effort of the empire to return to its former principles, which denied to religious association any place in the State. Lastly, I would only foreshadow the change of policy which, under Constantine, reversed the position, and made of the most free and spontaneous religious movement an official worship, subject to the State, and persecutor in its turn.

I know not whether I shall have sufficient life and strength to complete a plan so vast. I shall be satisfied if, after having written the Life of Jesus, I am permitted to relate, as I understand it, the history of the Apostles, the state of the Christian conscience during the weeks which followed the death of Jesus, the formation of the cycle of legends concerning the resurrection, the first acts of the Church of Jerusalem, the life of Saint Paul, the crisis of the time of Nero, the appearance of the Apocalypse, the fall of Jerusalem, the foundation of the Hebrew-Christian sects of Batanea, the compilation of the Gospels, and the rise of the great schools of Asia Minor originated by John. Everything pales by the side of that marvellous first century. By a peculiarity rare in history, we see much better what passed in the Christian world from the year 50 to the year 75 than from the year 100 to the year 150.

Those who will consult the following excellent writings[1] will there find explained a number of points upon which I have been obliged to be very brief :—

Etudes Critiques sur l'Evangile de saint Matthieu, par M. Albert Réville, pasteur de l'église Wallonne de Rotterdam.

Histoire de la Théologie Chrétienne au Siècle Apostolique, par M. Reuss, professeur à la Faculté de Théologie et au Séminaire Protestant de Strasbourg.

Des Doctrines Religieuses des Juifs pendant les Deux Siècles Antérieurs à l'Ere Chrétienne, par M. Michel Nicolas,

---

[1] While this work was in the press, a book has appeared which I do not hesitate to add to this list, although I have not read it with the attention it deserves—*Les Evangiles*, par M. Gustave d'Eichthal. Première Partie : *Examen Critique et Comparatif des Trois Premiers Evangiles.* Paris, Hachette, 1863.

professeur à la Faculté de Théologie Protestante de Montau-ban.

Vie de Jésus, par le Dr. Strauss; traduite par M. Littré, Membre de l'Institut.

Revue de Théologie et de Philosophie Chrétienne, publiée sous la direction de M. Colani, de 1850 à 1857.—*Nouvelle Revue de Théologie*, faisant suite à la precédénte depuis 1858.

The criticism of the details of the Gospel texts especially has been done by Strauss in a manner which leaves little to be desired. Although Strauss may be mistaken in his theory of the compilation of the Gospels; and although his book has, in my opinion, the fault of taking up the theological ground too much, and the historical ground too little, it will be necessary, in order to understand the motives which have guided me amid a crowd of minutiæ, to study the always judicious, though sometimes rather subtle, argument of the book, so well translated by my learned friend, M. Littré.

I do not believe I have neglected any source of information as to ancient evidences. Without speaking of a crowd of other scattered data, there remain, respecting Jesus, and the time in which he lived, five great collections of writings—1st, The Gospels, and the writings of the New Testament in general; 2nd, The compositions called the " Apocrypha of the Old Testament "; 3rd, The works of Philo; 4th, Those of Josephus; 5th, The Talmud. The writings of Philo have the priceless advantage of showing us the thoughts which, in the time of Jesus, fermented in minds occupied with great religious questions. Philo lived, it is true, in quite a different province of Judaism to Jesus, but, like him, he was very free from the littlenesses which reigned at Jerusalem; Philo is truly the elder brother of Jesus. He was sixty-two years old when the Prophet of Nazareth was at the height of his activity, and he survived him at least ten years. What a pity that the chances of life did not conduct him into Galilee! What would he not have taught us!

Josephus, writing specially for pagans, is not so candid. His short notices of Jesus, of John the Baptist, of Judas the Gaulonite, are dry and colourless. We feel that he seeks to present these movements, so profoundly Jewish in character and spirit, under a form which would be intelligible to Greeks and Romans. I believe the passage respecting Jesus[1] to be authentic. It s perfectly in the style of Jose-

---

[1] *Ant.*, XVIII. iii. 3.

phus, and, if this historian has made mention of Jesus, it is
thus that he must have spoken of him. We feel only that
a Christian hand has retouched the passage, has added
a few words—without which it would almost have been
blasphemous [1]—has perhaps retrenched or modified some
expressions. It must be recollected that the literary
fortune of Josephus was made by the Christians, who
adopted his writings as essential documents of their sacred
history. They made, probably in the second century,
an edition corrected according to Christian ideas. At all
events, that which constitutes the immense interest of
Josephus on the subject which occupies us is the clear light
which he throws upon the period. Thanks to him, Herod,
Herodias, Antipas, Philip, Annas, Caiaphas, and Pilate are
personages whom we can touch with a finger, and whom we
see living before us with a striking reality.

The Apocryphal books of the Old Testament, especially
the Jewish part of the Sibylline verses, and the Book of
Enoch, together with the Book of Daniel, which is also really
an Apocrypha, have a primary importance in the history of
the development of the Messianic theories, and for the
understanding of the conceptions of Jesus respecting the
kingdom of God. The Book of Enoch especially, which
was much read at the time of Jesus, gives us the key to the
expression " Son of Man," and to the ideas attached to it.
The ages of these different books, thanks to the labours of
Alexander, Ewald, Dillmann, and Reuss, are now beyond
doubt. Every one is agreed in placing the compilation of
the most important of them in the second and first centuries
before Jesus Christ. The date of the Book of Daniel is
still more certain. The character of the two languages in
which it is written, the use of Greek words, the clear,
precise, dated announcement of events which reach even to
the time of Antiochus Epiphanes, the incorrect descriptions
of Ancient Babylonia there given, the general tone of the
book, which in no respect recalls the writings of the captivity,
but, on the contrary, responds, by a crowd of analogies,
to the beliefs, the manners, the turn of imagination of the
time of the Seleucidæ; the Apocalyptic form of the visions,
the place of the book in the Hebrew canon, out of the
series of the prophets, the omission of Daniel in the panegyrics
of chapter xlix. of Ecclesiasticus, in which his position is
all but indicated, and many other proofs which have been
deduced a hundred times, do not permit of a doubt that

---

[1] " If it be lawful to call him man."

the Book of Daniel was but the fruit of the great excitement produced among the Jews by the persecution of Antiochus. It is not in the old prophetical literature that we must class this book, but rather at the head of Apocalyptic literature, as the first model of a kind of composition, after which come the various Sibylline poems, the Book of Enoch, the Apocalypse of John, the Ascension of Isaiah, and the Fourth Book of Esdras.

In the history of the origin of Christianity, the Talmud has hitherto been too much neglected. I think, with M. Geiger, that the true notion of the circumstances which surrounded the development of Jesus must be sought in this strange compilation, in which so much precious information is mixed with the most insignificant scholasticism. The Christian and the Jewish theology, having in the main followed two parallel ways, the history of the one cannot well be understood without the history of the other. Innumerable important details in the Gospels find, moreover, their commentary in the Talmud. The vast Latin collection of Lightfoot, Schœttgen, Buxtorf, and Otho contained already a mass of information on this point. I have imposed on myself the task of verifying in the original all the citations which I have admitted, without a single exception. The assistance which has been given me for this part of my task by a learned Israelite, M. Neubauer, well versed in Talmudic literature, has enabled me to go further, and to clear up the most intricate parts of my subject by new researches. The distinction of epochs is here most important, the compilation of the Talmud extending from the year 200 to about the year 500. We have brought to it as much discernment as is possible in the actual state of the studies. Dates so recent will excite some fears among persons habituated to accord value to a document only for the period in which it was written. But such scruples would here be out of place. The teaching of the Jews from the Asmonean epoch down to the second century was principally oral. We must not judge of this state of intelligence by the habits of an age of much writing. The Vedas, and the ancient Arabian poems, have been preserved for ages from memory, and yet these compositions present a very distinct and delicate form. In the Talmud on the contrary, the form has no value. Let us add that before the *Mishnah* of Judas the Saint, which has caused all others to be forgotten, there were attempts at compilation, the commencement of which is probably much earlier than is commonly supposed. The style of the

Talmud is that of loose notes; the collectors did no more probably than classify under certain titles the enormous mass of writings which had been accumulating in the different schools for generations.

It remains for us to speak of the documents which, presenting themselves as biographies of the Founder of Christianity, must naturally hold the first place in a Life of Jesus. A complete treatise upon the compilation of the Gospels would be a work of itself. Thanks to the excellent researches of which this question has been the object during thirty years, a problem which was formerly judged insurmountable has obtained a solution which, though it leaves room for many uncertainties, fully suffices for the necessities of history. We shall have occasion to return to this in our Second Book, the composition of the Gospels having been one of the most important facts for the future of Christianity in the second half of the first century. We will touch here only a single aspect of the subject, that which is indispensable to the completeness of our narrative. Leaving aside all which belongs to the portraiture of the Apostolic times, we will inquire only in what degree the data furnished by the Gospels may be employed in a history formed according to rational principles.

That the Gospels are in part legendary is evident, since they are full of miracles and of the supernatural; but legends have not all the same value. No one doubts the principal features of the life of Francis d'Assisi, although we meet the supernatural at every step. No one, on the other hand, accords credit to the *Life of Apollonius of Tyana*, because it was written long after the time of the hero, and purely as a romance. At what time, by what hands, under what circumstances, have the Gospels been compiled? This is the primary question upon which depends the opinion to be formed of their credibility.

Each of the four Gospels bears at its head the name of a personage known either in the Apostolic history or in the Gospel history itself. These four personages are not strictly given us as the authors. The formulæ, " according to Matthew," " according to Mark," " according to Luke," " according to John," do not imply that, in the most ancient opinion, these recitals were written from beginning to end by Matthew, Mark, Luke, and John; they merely signify that these were the traditions proceeding from each of these Apostles and claiming their authority. It is clear that, if these titles are exact, the Gospels, without ceasing to be in part legendary, are of great value, since they enable us to go back to the half-century which followed the death of Jesus, and, in two instances, even to the eye-witnesses of his actions.

Firstly, as to Luke, doubt is scarcely possible. The Gospel of Luke is a regular composition, founded on anterior documents. It is the work of a man who selects, prunes, and combines. The author of this Gospel is certainly the same as that of the Acts of the Apostles. Now, the author of the Acts is a companion of St. Paul, a title which applies to Luke exactly. I know that more than one objection may be raised against this reasoning; but one thing, at least, is beyond doubt—namely, that the author of the third Gospel and of the Acts was a man of the second Apostolic generation, and that is sufficient for our object. The date of this Gospel can, moreover, be determined with much precision by considerations drawn from the book itself. The 21st chapter of Luke, inseparable from the rest of the work, was certainly written after the siege of Jerusalem, and but a short time after. We are here, then, upon solid ground; for we are concerned with a work written entirely by the same hand, and of the most perfect unity.

The Gospels of Matthew and Mark have not nearly the same stamp of individuality. They are impersonal compositions, in which the author totally disappears. A proper name written at the head of works of this kind does not amount to much. But if the Gospel of Luke is dated, those of Matthew and Mark are dated also; for it is certain that the third Gospel is posterior to the first two, and exhibits the character of a much more advanced compilation. We have, besides, on this point, an excellent testimony from a writer of the first half of the second century—namely, Papias, bishop of Hierapolis, a grave man, a man of traditions, who was all his life seeking to collect whatever could be known of the person of Jesus. After having declared that on such matters he preferred oral tradition to books, Papias mentions two writings on the acts and words of Christ: first, a writing of Mark, the interpreter of the Apostle Peter, written briefly, incomplete, and not arranged in chronological order, including narratives and discourses (λεχθέντα ἢ πραχθέντα), composed from the information and recollections of the Apostle Peter; second, a collection of sentences (λόγια) written in Hebrew by Matthew, " and which each one has translated as he could." It is certain that these two descriptions answer pretty well to the general physiognomy of the two books now called " Gospel according to Matthew," "Gospel according to Mark"; the first characterised by its long discourses; the second, above all, by anecdote—much more exact than the first upon small facts, brief even to dryness, containing few discourses, and indifferently composed.   That these two works, such as we now read them, are absolutely similar to those read by Papias, cannot be sustained : firstly, because the writings of Matthew were to Papias solely discourses in Hebrew of which there were in circulation very varying translations; and, secondly, because the writings of Mark and Matthew, were to him profoundly distinct, written without any knowledge of each other, and, as it seems, in different languages.   Now, in the present state of the texts, the "Gospel according to Matthew" and the "Gospel according to Mark" present parallel parts so long and so perfectly identical, that it must be supposed, either that the final compiler of the first had the second under his eyes, or *vice versâ*, or that both copied from the same prototype. That which appears the most likely is that we have not the entirely original compilations of either Matthew or Mark, but that our first two Gospels are versions in which the attempt is made to fill up the gaps of the one text by the other.   Every one wished, in fact, to possess a complete copy.   He who had in his copy only discourses wished to have narratives, and *vice versâ*.   It is thus that "the Gospel according to Matthew" is found to have included almost all the anecdotes of Mark, and that "the Gospel according to Mark" now contains numerous features which come from the *Logia* of Matthew.   Every one, besides, drew largely on the Gospel tradition then current.   This tradition was so far from having been exhausted by the Gospels that the Acts of the Apostles and the most ancient Fathers quote many words of Jesus which appear authentic, and are not found in the Gospels we possess.

It matters little for our present object to push this delicate analysis further, and to endeavour to reconstruct in some manner on the one hand the original *Logia* of Matthew, and on the other the primitive narrative such as it left the pen of Mark.   The *Logia* are doubtless represented by the great discourses of Jesus which fill a considerable part of the first Gospel.   These discourses form, in fact, when detached from the rest, a sufficiently complete whole.   As to the narratives of the first and second Gospels, they seem to have for basis a common document, of which the text reappears sometimes in the one and sometimes in the other, and of which the second Gospel, such as we read it to-day, is but a slightly modified reproduction. In other words, the scheme of the Life of Jesus, in the Synoptics, rests upon two original documents—first, the discourses of Jesus collected by Matthew; second, the collection of anecdotes and personal reminiscences which Mark wrote from the recollections of Peter. We may say that we have these two documents still, mixed with accounts from another source, in the two first Gospels, which bear, not without reason, the name of the " Gospel *according* to Matthew " and of the " Gospel *according* to Mark."

What is indubitable, in any case, is that very early the discourses of Jesus were written in the Aramean language, and very early also his remarkable actions were recorded. These were not texts defined and fixed dogmatically. Besides the Gospels which have come to us, there were a number of others professing to represent the tradition of eye-witnesses. Little importance was attached to these writings, and the preservers, such as Papias, greatly preferred oral tradition. As men still believed that the world was nearly at an end, they cared little to compose books for the future; it was sufficient merely to preserve in their hearts a lively image of him whom they hoped soon to see again in the clouds. Hence the little authority which the Gospel texts enjoyed during one hundred and fifty years. There was no scruple in inserting additions, in variously combining them, and in completing some by others. The poor man who has but one book wishes that it may contain all that is dear to his heart. These little books were lent, each one transcribed in the margin of his copy the words, and the parables he found elsewhere, which touched him. The most beautiful thing in the world has thus proceeded from an obscure and purely popular elaboration. No compilation was of absolute value. Justin, who often appeals to that which he calls " The Memoirs of the Apostles," had under his notice Gospel documents in a state very different from that in which we possess them. At all events, he never cares to quote them textually. The Gospel quotations in the pseudo-Clementinian writings, of Ebionite origin, present the same character. The spirit was everything; the letter was nothing. It was when tradition became weakened, in the second half of the second century, that the texts bearing the names of the Apostles took a decisive authority and obtained the force of law.

Who does not see the value of documents thus composed of the tender remembrances, and simple narratives, of the first two Christian generations, still full of the strong impression which the illustrious Founder has produced, and which seemed long to survive him? Let us add, that the Gospels in question seem to proceed from that branch of the Christian family which stood nearest to Jesus. The last work of compilation, at least of the text which bears the name of Matthew, appears to have been done in one of the countries situated at the north-east of Palestine, such as Gaulonitis, Auranitis, Batanea, where many Christians took refuge at the time of the Roman war, where were found relatives of Jesus even in the second century, and where the first Galilean tendency was longer preserved than in other parts.

So far we have only spoken of the three Gospels named the Synoptics. There remains a fourth, that which bears the name of John. Concerning this one, doubts have a much better foundation, and the question is further from solution. Papias—who was connected with the school of John, and who, if not one of his auditors, as Irenæus thinks, associated with his immediate disciples, among others, Aristion, and the one called *Presbyteros Joannes*—says not a word of a "Life of Jesus" written by John, although he had zealously collected the oral narratives of both Aristion and *Presbyteros Joannes*. If any such mention had been found in his work, Eusebius, who points out everything therein that can contribute to the literary history of the Apostolic age, would doubtless have mentioned it.

The intrinsic difficulties drawn from the perusal of the fourth Gospel itself are not less strong. How is it that, side by side with narration so precise and so evidently that of an eye-witness, we find discourses so totally different from those of Matthew? How is it that, connected with a general plan of the life of Jesus, which appears much more satisfactory and exact than that of the Synoptics, these singular passages occur in which we are sensible of a dogmatic interest peculiar to the compiler, of ideas foreign to Jesus, and sometimes of indications which place us on our guard against the good faith of the narrator? Lastly, how is it that, united with views the most pure, the most just, the most truly evangelical, we find these blemishes, which we would fain regard as the interpolations of an ardent sectarian? Is it indeed John, son of Zebedee, brother of James (of whom there is not a single mention made in the fourth Gospel), who is able to write in Greek these lessons of abstract metaphysics, to which neither the Synoptics nor the Talmud offer any analogy? All this is of great importance; and, for myself, I dare not be sure that the fourth

Gospel has been entirely written by the pen of a Galilean
fisherman. But that, as a whole, this Gospel may have
originated towards the end of the first century from the
great school of Asia Minor, which was connected with John,
that it represents to us a version of the life of the Master,
worthy of high esteem, and often to be preferred, is demonstrated in a manner which leaves us nothing to be desired,
both by exterior evidences and by examination of the
document itself.

And, firstly, no one doubts that, towards the year 150,
the fourth Gospel did exist, and was attributed to John.
Explicit texts from St. Justin, from Athenagoras, from
Tatian, from Theophilus of Antioch, from Irenæus, show
that henceforth this Gospel mixed in every controversy, and
served as corner-stone for the development of the faith.
Irenæus is explicit; now, Irenæus came from the school of
John, and between him and the Apostle there was only
Polycarp. The part played by this Gospel in Gnosticism,
and especially in the system of Valentinus, in Montanism,
and in the quarrel of the Quartodecimans, is not less decisive.
The school of John was the most influential one during the
second century; and it is only by regarding the origin of
the Gospel as coincident with the rise of the school that the
existence of the latter can be understood at all. Let us add
that the first Epistle attributed to St. John is certainly by
the same author as the fourth Gospel; now, this Epistle is
recognised as from John by Polycarp, Papias, and Irenæus.

But it is, above all, the perusal of the work itself which
is calculated to give this impression. The author always
speaks as an eye-witness; he wishes to pass for the Apostle
John. If, then, this work is not really by the Apostle, we
must admit a fraud, of which the author convicts himself.
Now, although the ideas of the time respecting literary
honesty differed essentially from ours, there is no example
in the Apostolic world of a falsehood of this kind. Besides,
not only does the author wish to pass for the Apostle John,
but we see clearly that he writes in the interest of this
Apostle. On each page he betrays the desire to fortify his
authority, to show that he has been the favourite of Jesus;
that in all the solemn circumstances (at the Lord's supper,
at Calvary, at the tomb) he held the first place. His
relations on the whole fraternal, although not excluding a
certain rivalry with Peter; his hatred, on the contrary, of
Judas, a hatred, probably anterior to the betrayal, seems to
pierce through here and there. We are tempted to believe
that John, in his old age, having read the Gospel narratives,

on the one hand remarked their various inaccuracies, on the other was hurt at seeing that there was not accorded to him a sufficiently high place in the history of Christ; that then he commenced to dictate a number of things which he knew better than the rest, with the intention of showing that in many instances, in which only Peter was spoken of, he had figured with him and even before him. Already during the life of Jesus, these trifling sentiments of jealousy had been manifested between the sons of Zebedee and the other disciples. After the death of James, his brother, John remained sole inheritor of the intimate remembrances of which these two Apostles, by the common consent, were the depositaries. Hence his perpetual desire to recall that he is the last surviving eye-witness, and the pleasure which he takes in relating circumstances which he alone could know. Hence, too, so many minute details which seem like the commentaries of an annotator—" it was the sixth hour"; " it was night "; " the servant's name was Malchus "; " they had made a fire of coals, for it was cold "; " the coat was without seam." Hence, lastly, the disorder of the compilation, the irregularity of the narration, the disjointedness of the first chapters, all so many inexplicable features on the supposition that this Gospel was but a theological thesis, without historic value, and which, on the contrary, are perfectly intelligible, if, in conformity with tradition, we see in them the remembrances of an old man, sometimes of remarkable freshness, sometimes having undergone strange modifications.

A primary distinction, indeed, ought to be made in the Gospel of John. On the one side this Gospel presents us with a rough draught of the life of Jesus, which differs considerably from that of the Synoptics. On the other, it puts into the mouth of Jesus discourses of which the tone, the style, the treatment, and the doctrines have nothing in common with the *Logia* given us by the Synoptics. In this second respect the difference is such that we must make choice in a decisive manner. If Jesus spoke as Matthew represents, he could not have spoken as John relates. Between these two authorities no critic has ever hesitated, or can ever hesitate. Far removed from the simple, disinterested, impersonal tone of the Synoptics, the Gospel of John shows incessantly the pre-occupation of the apologist— the mental reservation of the sectarian, the desire to prove a thesis, and to convince adversaries. It was not by pretentious tirades, heavy, badly written, and appealing little to the moral sense, that Jesus founded his divine work. If even Papias had not taught us that Matthew wrote the sayings of Jesus in their original tongue, the natural, ineffable truth, the charm beyond comparison of the discourses in the Synoptics, their profoundly Hebraistic idiom, the analogies which they present with the sayings of the Jewish doctors of the period, their perfect harmony with the natural phenomena of Galilee—all these characteristics, compared with the obscure Gnosticism, with the distorted metaphysics, which fill the discourses of John, would speak loudly enough. This by no means implies that there are not in the discourses of John some admirable gleams, some traits which truly come from Jesus. But the mystic tone of these discourses does not correspond at all to the character of the eloquence of Jesus, such as we picture it according to the Synoptics. A new spirit has breathed; Gnosticism has already commenced; the Galilean era of the kingdom of God is finished; the hope of the near advent of Christ is more distant; we enter on the barrenness of metaphysics, into the darkness of abstract dogma. The spirit of Jesus is not there, and, if the son of Zebedee has truly traced these pages, he had certainly, in writing them, quite forgotten the Lake of Gennesareth, and the charming discourses which he had heard upon its shores.

One circumstance, moreover, which strongly proves that the discourses given us by the fourth Gospel are not historical, but compositions intended to cover with the authority of Jesus certain doctrines dear to the compiler, is their perfect harmony with the intellectual state of Asia Minor at the time when they were written. Asia Minor was then the theatre of a strange movement of syncretical philosophy; all the germs of Gnosticism existed there already. John appears to have drunk deeply from these strange springs. It may be that, after the crisis of the year 68 (the date of the Apocalypse) and of the year 70 (the destruction of Jerusalem), the old Apostle, with an ardent and plastic spirit, disabused of the belief in a near appearance of the Son of Man in the clouds, may have inclined towards the ideas that he found around him, of which several agreed sufficiently well with certain Christian doctrines. In attributing these new ideas to Jesus, he only followed a very natural tendency. Our remembrances are transformed with our circumstances; the ideal of a person that we have known changes as we change. Considering Jesus as the incarnation of truth, John could not fail to attribute to him that which he had come to consider as the truth.

If we must speak candidly, we will add that probably

B

John himself had little share in this; that the change was made around him rather than by him. One is sometimes tempted to believe that precious notes, coming from the Apostle, have been employed by his disciples in a very different sense from the primitive Gospel spirit. In fact, certain portions of the fourth Gospel have been added later; such is the entire twenty-first chapter, in which the author seems to wish to render homage to the Apostle Peter after his death, and to reply to the objections which would be drawn, or already had been drawn, from the death of John himself (ver. 21–23). Many other places bear the traces of erasures and corrections. It is impossible at this distance to understand these singular problems, and without doubt many surprises would be in store for us, if we were permitted to penetrate the secrets of that mysterious school of Ephesus, which, more than once, appears to have delighted in obscure paths. But there is a decisive test. Everyone who sets himself to write the life of Jesus without any predetermined theory as to the relative value of the Gospels, letting himself be guided solely by the sentiment of the subject, will be led in numerous instances to prefer the narration of John to that of the Synoptics. The last months of the life of Jesus especially are explained by John alone; a number of the features of the passion, unintelligible in the Synoptics, resume both probability and possibility in the narrative of the fourth Gospel. On the contrary, I dare defy anyone to compose a Life of Jesus with any meaning from the discourses which John attributes to him. This manner of incessantly preaching and demonstrating himself, this perpetual argumentation, this stage-effect devoid of simplicity, these long arguments after each miracle, these stiff and awkward discourses, the tone of which is so often false and unequal, would not be tolerated by a man of taste compared with the delightful sentences of the Synoptics. There are here evidently artificial portions, which represent to us the sermons of Jesus, as the dialogues of Plato render us the conversations of Socrates. They are, so to speak, the variations of a musician improvising on a given theme. The theme is not without some authenticity; but in the execution the imagination of the artist has given itself full scope. We are sensible of the factitious mode of procedure, of rhetoric, of gloss. Let us add that the vocabulary of Jesus cannot be recognised in the portions of which we speak. The expression, "kingdom of God," which was so familiar to the Master, occurs there but once. On the other hand, the style of the discourses attributed to Jesus by the fourth

Gospel presents the most complete analogy with that of the
Epistles of St. John; we see that, in writing the discourses,
the author followed not his recollections, but rather the
somewhat monotonous movement of his own thought.
Quite a new mystical language is introduced, a language of
which the Synoptics had not the least idea ("world,"
"truth," "life," "light," "darkness," etc.). If Jesus
had ever spoken in this style, which has nothing of Hebrew,
nothing Jewish, nothing Talmudic in it, how, if I may thus
express myself, is it that but a single one of his hearers
should have so well kept the secret?

Literary history offers, besides, another example, which
presents the greatest analogy with the historic phenomenon
we have just described and serves to explain it. Socrates,
who, like Jesus, never wrote, is known to us by two of his
disciples, Xenophon and Plato; the first corresponding to
the Synoptics in his clear, transparent, impersonal compilation; the second recalling the author of the fourth
Gospel, by his vigorous individuality. In order to describe
the Socratic teaching, should we follow the "dialogues"
of Plato or the "discourses" of Xenophon? Doubt, in
this respect, is not possible; everyone chooses the "discourses," and not the "dialogues." Does Plato, however,
teach us nothing about Socrates? Would it be good
criticism, in writing the biography of the latter, to neglect
the "dialogues"? Who would venture to maintain this?
The analogy, moreover, is not complete, and the difference
is in favour of the fourth Gospel. The author of this
Gospel is, in fact, the better biographer; as if Plato, who,
while attributing to his master fictitious discourses, had
known important matters about his life, which Xenophon
ignored entirely. Without pronouncing upon the material
question as to what hand has written the fourth Gospel,
and while inclined to believe that the discourses, at least, are
not from the son of Zebedee, we admit still that it is indeed
"the Gospel according to John," in the same sense that the
first and second Gospels are the Gospels "according to
Matthew" and "according to Mark." The historical sketch
of the fourth Gospel is the Life of Jesus, such as it was
known in the school of John; it is the recital which Aristion
and *Presbyteros Joannes* made to Papias, without telling
him that it was written, or rather attaching no importance
to this point. I must add that, in my opinion, this school
was better acquainted with the exterior circumstances of
the life of the founder than the group whose remembrances
constituted the Synoptics. It had, especially upon the

sojourns of Jesus at Jerusalem, data which the others did not possess. The disciples of this school treated Mark as an indifferent biographer, and devised a system to explain his omissions. Certain passages of Luke, where there is, as it were, an echo of the traditions of John, prove also that these traditions were entirely unknown to the rest of the Christian family.

These explanations will suffice, I think, to show, in the course of my narrative, the motives which have determined me to give the preference to this or that of the four guides whom we have for the Life of Jesus. On the whole, I admit as authentic the four Canonical Gospels. All, in my opinion, date from the first century, and the authors are, generally speaking, those to whom they are attributed; but their historic value is very diverse. Matthew evidently merits an unlimited confidence as to the discourses; they are the *Logia*, the identical notes taken from a clear and lively remembrance of the teachings of Jesus. A kind of splendour at once mild and terrible—a divine strength, if we may so speak—emphasises these words, detaches them from the context, and renders them easily distinguishable. The person who imposes upon himself the task of making a continuous narrative from the gospel history possesses, in this respect, an excellent touchstone. The real words of Jesus disclose themselves; as soon as we touch them in this chaos of traditions of varied authenticity, we feel them vibrate— they betray themselves spontaneously, and shine out of the narrative with unequalled brilliancy.

The narrative portions grouped in the first Gospel around this primitive nucleus have not the same authority. There are many not well-defined legends which have proceeded from the zeal of the second Christian generation. The Gospel of Mark is much firmer, more precise, containing fewer subsequent additions. He is the one of the three Synoptics who has remained the most primitive, the most original, the one to whom the fewest after-elements have been added. In Mark the facts are related with a clearness for which we seek in vain among the other evangelists. He likes to report certain words of Jesus in Syro-Chaldean. He is full of minute observations, coming doubtless from an eye-witness. There is nothing to prevent our agreeing with Papias in regarding this eye-witness, who evidently had followed Jesus, who had loved him and observed him very closely, and who had preserved a lively image of him, as the Apostle Peter himself.

As to the work of Luke, its historical value is sensibly

weaker. It is a document which comes to us second-hand,
The narrative is more mature. The words of Jesus are
there, more deliberate, more sententious. Some sentences
are distorted and exaggerated. Writing outside of Palestine,
and certainly after the siege of Jerusalem, the author
indicates the places with less exactitude than the other two
Synoptics; he has an erroneous idea of the temple, which he
represents as an oratory where people went to pay their
devotions. He subdues some details in order to make the
different narratives agree; he softens the passages which
had become embarrassing on account of a more exalted idea
of the divinity of Christ; he exaggerates the marvellous;
commits errors in chronology; omits Hebraistic comments;
quotes no word of Jesus in this language, and gives to all the
localities their Greek names. We feel we have to do with
a compiler—with a man who has not himself seen the
witnesses, but who labours at the texts and wrests their
sense to make them agree. Luke had probably under
his eyes the biographical collection of Mark and the *Logia*
of Matthew. But he treats them with much freedom;
sometimes he fuses two anecdotes or two parables in one;
sometimes he divides one in order to make two. He
interprets the documents according to his own idea; he
has not the absolute impassibility of Matthew and Mark.
We might affirm certain things of his individual tastes and
tendencies; he is a very exact devotee; he insists that Jesus
had performed all the Jewish rites; he is a warm Ebionite
and democrat—that is to say, much opposed to property—
and persuaded that the triumph of the poor is approaching;
he likes especially all the anecdotes showing prominently the
conversion of sinners—the exaltation of the humble; he
often modifies the ancient traditions in order to give them
this meaning; he admits into his first pages the legends
about the infancy of Jesus, related with the long amplifications, the spiritual songs, and the conventional proceed-
ings which form the essential features of the Apocryphal
Gospels. Finally, he has in the narrative of the last hours
of Jesus some circumstances full of tender feeling, and
certain words of Jesus of delightful beauty, which are
not found in more authentic accounts, and in which we
detect the presence of legend. Luke probably borrowed
them from a more recent collection, in which the principal
aim was to excite sentiments of piety.

A great reserve was naturally enforced in presence of a
document of this nature. It would have been as uncritical
to neglect it as to employ it without discernment. Luke

has had under his eyes originals which we no longer possess. He is less an evangelist than a biographer of Jesus, a " harmoniser," a corrector after the manner of Marcion and Tatian. But he is a biographer of the first century, a divine artist, who, independently of the information which he has drawn from more ancient sources, shows us the character of the founder with a happiness of treatment, with a uniform inspiration, and a distinctness which the other two Synoptics do not possess. In the perusal of his Gospel there is the greatest charm; for to the incomparable beauty of the foundation, common to them all, he adds a degree of skill in composition which singularly augments the effect of the portrait, without seriously injuring its truthfulness.

On the whole, we may say that the Synoptical compilation has passed through three stages : first, the original documentary state (λόγια of Matthew, λεχθέντα ἢ πραχθέντα of Mark), primary compilations which no longer exist; second, the state of simple mixture, in which the original documents are amalgamated without any effort at composition, without there appearing any personal bias of the authors (the existing Gospels of Matthew and Mark); third, the state of combination or of intentional and deliberate compiling, in which we are sensible of an attempt to reconcile the different versions (Gospel of Luke). The Gospel of John, as we have said, forms a composition of another order, and is entirely distinct.

It will be remarked that I have made no use of the Apocryphal Gospels. These compositions ought not in any manner to be put upon the same footing as the Canonical Gospels. They are insipid and puerile amplifications, having the Canonical Gospels for their basis, and adding nothing thereto of any value. On the other hand, I have been very attentive to collect the shreds preserved by the Fathers of the Church, of the ancient Gospels which formerly existed parallel with the Canonical Gospels, and which are now lost—such as the Gospel according to the Hebrews, the Gospel according to the Egyptians, the Gospels styled those of Justin, Marcion, and Tatian. The first two are principally important because they were written in Aramean, like the *Logia* of Matthew, and appear to constitute one version of the Gospel of this Apostle, and because they were the Gospel of the *Ebionim*—that is, of those small Christian sects of Batanea who preserved the use of Syro-Chaldean, and who appear in some respects to have followed the course marked out by Jesus. But it must be confessed that, in the state in which they have come to us, these Gospels are inferior, as critical authorities, to the compilation of Matthew's Gospel which we now possess.

It will now be seen, I think, what kind of historical value I attribute to the Gospels. They are neither biographies after the manner of Suetonius, nor fictitious legends in the style of Philostratus; they are legendary biographies. I should willingly compare them with the Legends of the Saints, the Lives of Plotinus, Proclus, Isidore, and other writings of the same kind, in which historical truth and the desire to present models of virtue are combined in various degrees. Inexactitude, which is one of the features of all popular compositions, is there particularly felt. Let us suppose that, ten or twelve years ago, three or four old soldiers of the Empire had each undertaken to write the life of Napoleon from memory. It is clear that their narratives would contain numerous errors and great discordances. One of them would place Wagram before Marengo; another would write without hesitation that Napoleon drove the Government of Robespierre from the Tuileries; a third would omit expeditions of the highest importance. But one thing would certainly result with a great degree of truthfulness from these simple recitals, and that is the character of the hero, the impression which he made around him. In this sense such popular narratives would be worth more than a formal and official history. We may say as much of the Gospels. Solely attentive to bring out strongly the excellency of the Master, his miracles, his teaching, the evangelists display entire indifference to everything that is not of the very spirit of Jesus. The contradictions respecting time, place, and persons were regarded as insignificant; for the higher the degree of inspiration attributed to the words of Jesus, the less was granted to the compilers themselves. The latter regarded themselves as simple scribes, and cared but for one thing— to omit nothing they knew.

Unquestionably certain preconceived ideas associated themselves with such recollections. Several narratives, especially in Luke, are invented in order to bring out more vividly certain traits of the character of Jesus. This character itself constantly underwent alteration. Jesus would be a phenomenon unparalleled in history if, with the part which he played, he had not early become idealised. The legends respecting Alexander were invented before the generation of his companions in arms became extinct; those respecting St. Francis d'Assisi began in his lifetime.

A rapid metamorphosis operated in the same manner in the twenty or thirty years which followed the death of Jesus, and imposed upon his biography the peculiarities of an ideal legend. Death adds perfection to the most perfect man; it frees him from all defect in the eyes of those who have loved him. With the wish to paint the Master, there was also the desire to explain him. Many anecdotes were conceived to prove that in him the prophecies regarded as Messianic had had their accomplishment. But this procedure, of which we must not deny the importance, would not suffice to explain everything. No Jewish work of the time gives a series of prophecies exactly declaring what the Messiah should accomplish. Many Messianic allusions quoted by the evangelists are so subtle, so indirect, that one cannot believe they all responded to a generally admitted doctrine. Sometimes they reasoned thus : " The Messiah ought to do such a thing; now, Jesus is the Messiah; therefore Jesus has done such a thing." At other times, by an inverse process, it was said : " Such a thing has happened to Jesus; now, Jesus is the Messiah; therefore such a thing was to happen to the Messiah." Too simple explanations are always false when analysing those profound creations of popular sentiment which baffle all systems by their fullness and infinite variety. It is scarcely necessary to say that, with such documents, in order to present only what is indisputable, we must limit ourselves to general features. In almost all ancient histories, even in those which are much less legendary than these, details open up innumerable doubts. When we have two accounts of the same fact, it is extremely rare that the two accounts agree. Is not this a reason for anticipating many difficulties when we have but one ? We may say that among the anecdotes, the discourses, the celebrated sayings which have been given us by the historians, there is not one strictly authentic. Were there stenographers to fix these fleeting words ? Was there an annalist always present to note the gestures, the manners, the sentiments, of the actors ? Let anyone endeavour to get at the truth as to the way in which such or such contemporary fact has happened; he will not succeed. Two accounts of the same event given by different eye-witnesses differ essentially. Must we, therefore, reject all the colouring of the narratives, and limit ourselves to the bare facts only ? That would be to suppress history. Certainly, I think that, if we except certain short and almost mnemonic axioms, none of the discourses reported by Matthew are textual; even our stenographic reports are scarcely so. I freely admit that the admirable account of the Passion contains many trifling inaccuracies. Would it, however, be writing the history of Jesus to omit those sermons which give to us in such a vivid manner the character of his discourses, and to limit ourselves to saying, with Josephus and Tacitus, " that he was put to death by the order of Pilate at the instigation of the priests " ? That would be, in my opinion, a kind of inexactitude worse than that to which we are exposed in admitting the details supplied by the texts. These details are not true to the letter, but they are true with a superior truth, they are more true than the naked truth, in the sense that they are truth rendered expressive and articulate—truth idealised.

I beg those who think that I have placed an exaggerated confidence in narratives in great part legendary to take note of the observation I have just made. To what would the life of Alexander be reduced if it were confined to that which is materially certain? Even partly erroneous traditions contain a portion of truth which history cannot neglect. No one has blamed M. Sprenger for having, in writing the life of Mohammed, made much of the *hadith* or oral traditions concerning the prophet, and for often having attributed to his hero words which are only known through this source. Yet the traditions respecting Mohammed are not superior in historical value to the discourses and narratives which compose the Gospels. They were written between the year 50 and the year 140 of the Hegira. When the history of the Jewish schools in the ages which immediately preceded and followed the birth of Christianity shall be written, no one will make any scruple of attributing to Hillel, Shammai, Gamaliel, the maxims ascribed to them by the *Mishnah* and the *Gemara*, although these great compilations were written many hundreds of years after the time of the doctors in question.

As to those who believe, on the contrary, that history should consist of a simple reproduction of the documents which have come down to us, I beg to observe that such a course is not allowable. The four principal documents are in flagrant contradiction one with another. Josephus rectifies them sometimes. It is necessary to make a selection. To assert that an event cannot take place in two ways at once, or in an impossible manner, is not to impose an *à priori* philosophy upon history. The historian ought not to conclude that a fact is false because he possesses several versions of it, or because credulity has mixed with them much that is fabulous. He ought in such a case to be very

B 2

cautious, to examine the texts, and to proceed carefully by induction. There is one class of narratives especially to which this principle must necessarily be applied. Such are narratives of supernatural events. To seek to explain these, or to reduce them to legends, is not to mutilate facts in the name of theory; it is to make the observation of facts our groundwork. None of the miracles with which the old histories are filled took place under scientific conditions. Observation, which has never once been falsified, teaches us that miracles never happen but in times and countries in which they are believed, and before persons disposed to believe them. No miracle ever occurred in the presence of men capable of testing its miraculous character. Neither common people nor men of the world are able to do this. It requires great precautions and long habits of scientific research. In our days have we not seen almost all respectable people dupes of the grossest frauds or of puerile illusions? Marvellous facts, attested by the whole population of small towns, have, thanks to a severer scrutiny, been exploded. If it is proved that no contemporary miracle will bear inquiry, is it not probable that the miracles of the past which have all been performed in popular gatherings would equally present their share of illusion, if it were possible to criticise them in detail?

It is not, then, in the name of this or that philosophy, but in the name of universal experience, that we banish miracle from history. We do not say, "Miracles are impossible." We say, "Up to this time a miracle has never been proved." If to-morrow a thaumaturgus present himself with credentials sufficiently important to be discussed, and announce himself as able, say, to raise the dead, what would be done? A commission, composed of physiologists, physicists, chemists, persons accustomed to historical criticism, would be named. This commission would choose a corpse, would assure itself that the death was real, would select the room in which the experiment should be made, would arrange the whole system of precautions, so as to leave no chance of doubt. If, under such conditions, the resurrection were effected, a probability almost equal to certainty would be established. As, however, it ought to be possible always to repeat an experiment —to do over again which has been done once; and as, in the order of miracle, there can be no question of ease or difficulty, the thaumaturgus would be invited to reproduce his marvellous act under other circumstances, upon other corpses, in another place. If the miracle succeeded each time, two things would be proved : first, that supernatural events happen in the world; second, that the power of producing them belongs, or is delegated to, certain persons. But who does not see that no miracle ever took place under these conditions, but that always hitherto the thaumaturgus has chosen the subject of the experiment, chosen the spot, chosen the public; that, besides, the people themselves—most commonly in consequence of the invincible want to see something divine in great events and great men—create the marvellous legends afterwards? Until a new order of things prevails, we shall maintain, then, this principle of historical criticism—that a supernatural account cannot be admitted as such, that it always implies credulity or imposture, that the duty of the historian is to explain it, and seek to ascertain what share of truth, or of error, it may conceal.

Such are the rules which have been followed in the composition of this work. To the perusal of documentary evidences I have been able to add an important source of information—the sight of the places where the events occurred. The scientific mission, having for its object the exploration of ancient Phœnicia, which I directed in 1860 and 1861, led me to reside on the frontiers of Galilee, and to travel there frequently. I have traversed, in all directions, the country of the Gospels; I have visited Jerusalem, Hebron, and Samaria; scarcely any important locality of the history of Jesus has escaped me. All this history, which at a distance seems to float in the clouds of an unreal world, thus took a form, a solidity which astonished me. The striking agreement of the texts with the places, the marvellous harmony of the Gospel ideal with the country which served it as a framework, were like a revelation to me. I had before my eyes a fifth Gospel, torn, but still legible, and henceforward, through the recitals of Matthew and Mark, in place of an abstract being, whose existence might have been doubted, I saw living and moving an admirable human figure. During the summer, having to go up to Ghazir, in Lebanon, to take a little repose, I fixed, in rapid sketches, the image which had appeared to me, and from them resulted this history. When a cruel bereavement hastened my departure, I had but a few pages to write. In this manner the book has been composed almost entirely near the very places where Jesus was born, and where his character was developed. Since my return I have laboured unceasingly to verify and check in detail the rough sketch which I had written in haste in a Maronite cabin, with five or six volumes around me.

Many will regret, perhaps, the biographical form which my work has thus taken. When I first conceived the idea of a history of the origin of Christianity, what I wished to write was, in fact, a history of doctrines, in which men and their actions would have hardly had a place. Jesus would scarcely have been named; I should have endeavoured to show how the ideas which have grown under his name took root and covered the world. But I have learned since that history is not a simple game of abstractions; that men are more than doctrines. It was not a certain theory on justification and redemption which brought about the Reformation; it was Luther and Calvin. Parseeism, Hellenism, Judaism, might have been able to have combined under every form; the doctrines of the Resurrection and of the Word might have developed themselves during ages without producing this grand, unique, and fruitful fact, called Christianity. This fact is the work of Jesus, of St. Paul, of St. John. To write the history of Jesus, of St. Paul, of St. John, is to write the history of the origin of Christianity. The anterior movements belong to our subject only in so far as they serve to throw light upon these extraordinary men, who naturally could not have existed without connection with that which preceded them.

In such an effort to make the great souls of the past live again, some share of divination and conjecture must be permitted. A great life is an organic whole which cannot be rendered by the simple agglomeration of small facts. It requires a profound sentiment to embrace them all, moulding them into perfect unity. The method of art in a similar subject is a good guide; the exquisite tact of a Goethe would know how to apply it. The essential condition of the creations of art is, that they shall form a living system of which all the parts are mutually dependent and related.

In histories such as this, the great test that we have got the truth is to have succeeded in combining the texts in such a manner that they shall constitute a logical, probable narrative, harmonious throughout. The secret laws of life, of the progression of organic products, of the melting of minute distinctions, ought to be consulted at each moment; for what is required to be reproduced is not the material circumstance, which it is impossible to verify, but the very soul of history; what must be sought is not the petty certainty about trifles, it is the correctness of the general sentiment, the truthfulness of the colouring. Each trait which departs from the rules of classic narration ought to warn us to be careful; for the fact which has to be related has been living, natural, and harmonious. If we do not succeed in rendering it such by the recital, it is surely because we have not succeeded in seeing it aright. Suppose that, in restoring the Minerva of Phidias according to the texts, we produced a dry, jarring, artificial whole, what must we conclude? Simply that the texts want an appreciative interpretation; that we must study them quietly until they dovetail and furnish a whole in which all the parts are happily blended. Should we then be sure of having a perfect reproduction of the Greek statue? No; but at least we should not have the caricature of it; we should have the general spirit of the work—one of the forms in which it could have existed.

This idea of a living organism we have not hesitated to take as our guide in the general arrangement of the narrative. The perusal of the Gospels would suffice to prove that the compilers, although having a very true plan of the Life of Jesus in their minds, have not been guided by very exact chronological data; Papias, besides, expressly teaches this. The expressions, "At this time . . . after that . . . then . . . and it came to pass . . ." etc., are the simple transitions intended to connect different narratives with each other. To leave all the information furnished by the Gospels in the disorder in which tradition supplies it, would only be to write the history of Jesus as the history of a celebrated man would.be written, by giving pell-mell the letters and anecdotes of his youth, his old age, and of his maturity. The Koran, which presents to us, in the loosest manner, fragments of the different epochs in the life of Mohammed, has yielded its secret to an ingenious criticism; the chronological order in which the fragments were composed has been discovered so as to leave little room for doubt. Such a rearrangement is much more difficult in the case of the Gospels, the public life of Jesus having been shorter and less eventful than the life of the founder of Islamism. Meanwhile, the attempt to find a guiding thread through this labyrinth ought not to be taxed with gratuitous subtlety. There is no great abuse of hypothesis in supposing that a founder of a new religion commences by attaching himself to the moral aphorisms already in circulation in his time, and to the practices which are in vogue; that, when riper, and in full possession of his idea, he delights in a kind of calm and poetical eloquence, remote from all controversy, sweet and free as pure feeling; that he warms by degrees, becomes animated by opposition, and finishes by polemics and strong invectives. Such are the periods which may plainly be distinguished in the Koran. The order adopted with an extremely fine tact by the Synoptics supposes an analogous progress. If Matthew be attentively read, we shall find in the distribution of the discourses a gradation perfectly analogous to that which we have just indicated. The reserved turns of expression of which we make use in unfolding the progress of the ideas of Jesus will also be observed. The reader may, if he likes, see in the divisions adopted in doing this only the indispensable breaks for the methodical exposition of a profound and complicated thought.

If the love of a subject can help one to understand it, it will also, I hope, be recognised that I have not been wanting in this condition. To write the history of a religion, it is necessary, firstly, to have believed it (otherwise we should not be able to understand how it has charmed and satisfied the human conscience); in the second place, to believe it no longer in an absolute manner, for absolute faith is incompatible with sincere history. But love is possible without faith. To abstain from attaching one's self to any of the forms which captivate the adoration of men is not to deprive ourselves of the enjoyment of that which is good and beautiful in them. No transitory appearance exhausts the Divinity; God was revealed before Jesus—God will reveal himself after him. Profoundly unequal, and so much the more Divine, as they are grander and more spontaneous, the manifestations of God hidden in the depths of the human conscience are all of the same order. Jesus cannot belong solely to those who call themselves his disciples. He is the common honour of all who share a common humanity. His glory does not consist in being relegated out of history; we render him a truer worship in showing that all history is incomprehensible without him.

CHAPTER I

PLACE OF JESUS IN THE HISTORY OF THE WORLD

THE great event of the history of the world is the revolution by which the noblest portions of humanity have passed from the ancient religions, comprised under the vague name of Paganism, to a religion founded on the Divine Unity, the Trinity, and the Incarnation of the Son of God. It has taken nearly a thousand years to accomplish this conversion. The new religion had itself taken at least three hundred years in its formation. But the origin of the revolution in question is a fact which took place under the reigns of Augustus and Tiberius. At that time there lived a superior personage, who, by his bold originality, and by the love which he was able to inspire, became the object and fixed the starting-point of the future faith of humanity.

As soon as man became distinguished from the animal, he became religious—that is to say, he saw in nature something beyond the phenomena, and for himself something beyond death. This sentiment, during some thousands of years, became corrupted in the strangest manner. In many races it did not pass beyond the belief in sorcerers, under the gross form in which we still find it in certain parts of Oceania. Among some, the religious sentiment degenerated into the shameful scenes of butchery which form the character of the ancient religion of Mexico. Among others, especially in Africa, it became pure Fetichism—that is, the adoration of a material object, to which were attributed supernatural powers. Like the instinct of love, which at times elevates the most vulgar man above himself, yet sometimes becomes perverted and ferocious, so this divine faculty of religion during a long period seems only to be a cancer which must be extirpated from the human race, a cause of errors and crimes which the wise ought to endeavour to suppress.

The brilliant civilisations which were developed from a very remote antiquity in China, in Babylonia, and in Egypt, caused a certain progress to be made in religion. China arrived very early at a sort of mediocre good sense, which

prevented great extravagances. She neither knew the
advantages nor the abuses of the religious spirit. At all
events, she had not in this way any influence in directing
the great current of humanity. The religions of Babylonia
and Syria were never freed from a substratum of strange
sensuality; these religions remained, until their extinction
in the fourth and fifth centuries of our era, schools of im-
morality, in which at intervals glimpses of the divine world
were obtained by a sort of poetic intuition. Egypt, notwithstanding an apparent kind of fetichism, had very early
metaphysical dogmas and a lofty symbolism. But doubtless these interpretations of a refined theology were not
primitive. Man has never, in the possession of a clear idea,
amused himself by clothing it in symbols; it is oftener
after long reflections, and from the impossibility felt by the
human mind of resigning itself to the absurd, that we seek
ideas under the ancient mystic images whose meaning is
lost. Moreover, it is not from Egypt that the faith of
humanity has come. The elements which, in the religion
of a Christian, passing through a thousand transformations,
came from Egypt and Syria, are exterior forms of little
consequence, or dross of which the most purified worships
always retain some portion. The grand defect of the
religions of which we speak was their essentially superstitious character. They only threw into the world
millions of amulets and charms. No great moral thought
could proceed from races oppressed by a secular despotism,
and accustomed to institutions which precluded the
exercise of individual liberty.

The poetry of the soul, faith, liberty, virtue, devotion,
made their appearance in the world with the two great
races which, in one sense, have made humanity—viz. the
Indo-European and the Semitic races. The first religious
intuitions of the Indo-European race were essentially
naturalistic. But it was a profound and moral naturalism,
a loving embrace of nature by man, a delicious poetry, full
of the sentiment of the Infinite—the principle, in fine, of
all that which the Germanic and Celtic genius, of that which
a Shakespeare and a Goethe, should express in later times.
It was neither theology nor moral philosophy—it was a
state of melancholy, it was tenderness, it was imagination;
it was, more than all, earnestness, the essential condition
of morals and religion. The faith of humanity, however,
could not come from thence, because these ancient forms
of worships had great difficulty in detaching themselves
from Polytheism, and could not attain to a very clear

symbol. Brahminism has only survived to the present day by virtue of the astonishing faculty of conservation which India seems to possess. Buddhism failed in all its approaches towards the West. Druidism remained a form exclusively national, and without universal capacity. The Greek attempts at reform, Orpheism, the Mysteries, did not suffice to give a solid aliment to the soul. Persia alone succeeded in making a dogmatic religion, almost Monotheistic, and skilfully organised; but it is very possible that this organisation itself was but an imitation, or borrowed. At all events, Persia has not converted the world; she herself, on the contrary, was converted when she saw the flag of the Divine unity as proclaimed by Mohammedanism appear on her frontiers.

It is the Semitic race which has the glory of having made the religion of humanity. Far beyond the confines of history, resting under his tent free from the taint of a corrupted world, the Bedouin patriarch prepared the faith of mankind. A strong antipathy against the voluptuous worships of Syria, a grand simplicity of ritual, the complete absence of temples, and the idol reduced to insignificant *theraphim*, constituted his superiority. Among all the tribes of the nomadic Semites, that of the Beni-Israel was already chosen for immense destinies. Ancient relations with Egypt, whence perhaps resulted some purely material ingredients, did but augment their repulsion to idolatry. A " Law," or *Thora*, very anciently written on tables of stone, and which they attributed to their great liberator Moses, had become the code of Monotheism, and contained, as compared with the institutions of Egypt and Chaldea, powerful germs of social equality and morality. A chest or portable ark, having staples on each side to admit of bearing poles, constituted all their religious *matériel*; there were collected the sacred objects of the nation, its relics, its souvenirs, and lastly the " book," the journal of the tribe, always open, but which was written in with great discretion. The family charged with bearing the ark and watching over the portable archives, being near the book and having the control of it, very soon became important. From hence, however, the institution which was to control the future did not come. The Hebrew priest did not differ much from the other priests of antiquity. The character which essentially distinguishes Israel among theocratic peoples is that its priesthood has always been subordinated to individual inspiration. Besides its priests, each wandering tribe had its *nabi* or prophet, a sort of living oracle who was consulted for the solution of obscure questions supposed to require a high degree of clairvoyance. The *nabis* of Israel, organised in groups or schools, had great influence. Defenders of the ancient democratic spirit, enemies of the rich, opposed to all political organisation, and to whatsoever might draw Israel into the paths of other nations, they were the true authors of the religious pre-eminence of the Jewish people. Very early they announced unlimited hopes, and when the people, in part the victims of their impolitic counsels, had been crushed by the Assyrian power, they proclaimed that a kingdom without bounds was reserved for them, that one day Jerusalem would be the capital of the whole world, and the human race become Jews. Jerusalem and its temple appeared to them as a city placed on the summit of a mountain, towards which all people should turn, as an oracle whence the universal law should proceed, as the centre of an ideal kingdom, in which the human race, set at rest by Israel, should find again the joys of Eden.

Mystical utterances already make themselves heard, tending to exalt the martyrdom and celebrate the power of the " Man of Sorrows." Respecting one of those sublime sufferers, who, like Jeremiah, stained the streets of Jerusalem with their blood, one of the inspired wrote a song upon the sufferings and triumph of the " servant of God," in which all the prophetic force of the genius of Israel seemed concentrated. " For he shall grow up before him as a tender plant, and as a root out of a dry ground : he hath no form nor comeliness. He is despised and rejected of men : and we hid, as it were, our faces from him; he was despised, and we esteemed him not. Surely he hath borne our griefs, and carried our sorrows; yet we did esteem him stricken, smitten of God, and afflicted. But he was wounded for our transgressions, he was bruised for our iniquities : the chastisement of our peace was upon him; and with his stripes we are healed. All we like sheep have gone astray; we have turned everyone to his own way; and the Lord hath laid on him the iniquity of us all. He was oppressed, and he was afflicted, yet he opened not his mouth : he is brought as a lamb to the slaughter, and as a sheep before her shearers is dumb, so he openeth not his mouth. And he made his grave with the wicked. When thou shalt make his soul an offering for sin, he shall see his seed, he shall prolong his days, and the pleasure of the Lord shall prosper in his hand."

Important modifications were made at the same time in

the *Thora*. New texts, pretending to represent the true law of Moses, such as Deuteronomy, were produced, and inaugurated in reality a very different spirit from that of the old nomads. A marked fanaticism was the dominant feature of this spirit. Furious believers unceasingly instigated violence against all who wandered from the worship of Jehovah—they succeeded in establishing a code of blood, making death the penalty for religious faults. Piety brings, almost always, singular contradictions of vehemence and mildness. This zeal, unknown to the coarser simplicity of the time of the Judges, inspired tones of moving prophecy and tender unction, which the world had never heard till then. A strong tendency towards social questions already made itself felt; Utopias, dreams of a perfect society, took a place in the code. The Penta-teuch, a mixture of patriarchal morality and ardent devotion, primitive intuitions and pious subtleties, like those which filled the souls of Hezekiah, of Josiah, and of Jeremiah, was thus fixed in the form in which we now see it, and became for ages the absolute rule of the national mind.

This great book once created, the history of the Jewish people unfolded itself with an irresistible force. The great empires which followed each other in Western Asia, in destroying its hope of a terrestrial kingdom, threw it into religious dreams, which it cherished with a kind of sombre passion. Caring little for the national dynasty or political independence, it accepted all governments which permitted it to practice freely its worship and follow its usages. Israel will henceforward have no other guidance than that of its religious enthusiasts, no other enemies than those of the Divine unity, no other country than its Law.

And this Law, it must be remarked, was entirely social and moral. It was the work of men penetrated with a high ideal of the present life, and believing that they had found the best means of realising it. The conviction of all was that the *Thora*, well observed, could not fail to give perfect felicity. This *Thora* has nothing in common with the Greek or Roman " Laws," which, occupying themselves with scarcely anything but abstract right, entered little into questions of private happiness and morality. We feel beforehand that the results which will proceed from it will be of a social and not a political order, that the work at which this people labours is a kingdom of God, not a civil republic; a universal institution, not a nationality or a country.

Notwithstanding numerous failures, Israel admirably

sustained this vocation. A series of pious men, Ezra, Nehemiah, Onias, the Maccabees, consumed with zeal for the Law, succeeded each other in the defence of the ancient institutions. The idea that Israel was a holy people, a tribe chosen by God and bound to him by covenant, took deeper and firmer root. An immense expectation filled their souls. All Indo-European antiquity had placed paradise in the beginning; all its poets had wept a vanished golden age. Israel placed the age of gold in the future. The perennial poesy of religious souls, the Psalms, blossomed from this exalted piety, with their divine and melancholy harmony. Israel became truly and specially the people of God, while around it the pagan religions were more and more reduced, in Persia and Babylonia, to an official charlatanism, in Egypt and Syria to a gross idolatry, and in the Greek and Roman world to mere parade. That which the Christian martyrs did in the first centuries of our era, that which the victims of persecuting orthodoxy have done, even in the bosom of Christianity, up to our time, the Jews did during the two centuries which preceded the Christian era. They were a living protest against superstition and religious materialism. An extraordinary movement of ideas, ending in the most opposite results, made of them, at this epoch, the most striking and original people in the world. Their dispersion along all the coast of the Mediterranean, and the use of the Greek language, which they adopted when out of Palestine, prepared the way for a propagandism of which ancient societies, divided into small nationalities, had never offered a single example.

Up to the time of the Maccabees, Judaism, in spite of its persistence in announcing that it would one day be the religion of the human race, had had the characteristic of all the other worships of antiquity—it was a worship of the family and the tribe. The Israelite thought, indeed, that his worship was the best, and spoke with contempt of strange gods; but he believed also that the religion of the true God was made for himself alone. Only when a man entered into the Jewish family did he embrace the worship of Jehovah. No Israelite cared to convert the stranger to a worship which was the patrimony of the sons of Abraham. The development of the pietistic spirit, after Ezra and Nehemiah, led to a much firmer and more logical conception. Judaism became the true religion in a more absolute manner; to all who wished, the right of entering it was given; soon it became a work of piety to bring into it the greatest number possible. Doubtless the refined sentiment which elevated John the Baptist, Jesus, and St. Paul above the petty ideas of race did not yet exist; for, by a strange contradiction, these converts were little respected and were treated with disdain. But the idea of a sovereign religion, the idea that there was something in the world superior to country, to blood, to laws—the idea which makes apostles and martyrs—was founded. Profound pity for the pagans, however brilliant might be their worldly fortune, was henceforth the feeling of every Jew. By a cycle of legends destined to furnish models of immovable firmness, such as the histories of Daniel and his companions, the mother of the Maccabees and her seven sons, the romance of the racecourse of Alexandria—the guides of the people sought above all to inculcate the idea that virtue consists in a fanatical attachment to fixed religious institutions.

The persecutions of Antiochus Epiphanes made this idea a passion, almost a frenzy. It was something very analogous to that which happened under Nero two hundred and thirty years later. Rage and despair threw the believers into the world of visions and dreams. The first apocalypse, " The Book of Daniel," appeared. It was like a revival of prophecy, but under a very different form from the ancient one, and with a much larger idea of the destinies of the world. The Book of Daniel gave, in a manner, the last expression to the Messianic hopes. The Messiah was no longer a king, after the manner of David and Solomon, a theocratic and Mosaic Cyrus; he was a " Son of Man " appearing in the clouds—a supernatural being, invested with human form, charged to rule the world, and to preside over the golden age. Perhaps the *Sosiosh* of Persia, the great prophet who was to come, charged with preparing the reign of Ormuzd, gave some features to this new ideal. The unknown author of the Book of Daniel had, in any case, a decisive influence on the religious event which was about to transform the world. He supplied the *mise-en-scène*, and the technical terms of the new belief in the Messiah; and we might apply to him what Jesus said of John the Baptist—Before him, the prophets; after him, the kingdom of God.

It must not, however, be supposed that this profoundly religious and soul-stirring movement had particular dogmas for its primary impulse, as was the case in all the conflicts which have disturbed the bosom of Christianity. The Jew of this epoch was as little theological as possible. He did not speculate upon the essence of the Divinity : the beliefs about angels, about the destinies of man, about the Divine personality, of which the first germs might already be perceived, were quite optional—they were meditations, to which each one surrendered himself according to the turn of his mind, but of which a great number of men had never heard. They were the most orthodox even, who did not share in these particular imaginations, and who adhered to the simplicity of the Mosaic law. No dogmatic power analogous to that which orthodox Christianity has given to the Church then existed. It was only at the beginning of the third century, when Christianity had fallen into the hands of reasoning races, mad with dialectics and metaphysics, that that fever for definitions commenced which made the history of the Church but the history of one immense controversy. There were disputes also among the Jews—excited schools brought opposite solutions to almost all the questions which were agitated; but in these contests, of which the Talmud has preserved the principal details, there is not a single word of speculative theology. To observe and maintain the law, because the law was just, and because, when well observed, it gave happiness—such was Judaism. No *credo*, no theoretical symbol. One of the disciples of the boldest Arabian philosophy, Moses Maimonides, was able to become the oracle of the synagogue, because he was well versed in the canonical law.

The reigns of the last Asmoneans, and that of Herod, saw the excitement grow still stronger. They were filled by an uninterrupted series of religious movements. In the degree that power became secularised, and passed into the hands of unbelievers, the Jewish people lived less and less for the earth, and became more and more absorbed by the strange fermentation which was operating in their midst. The world, distracted by other spectacles, had little knowledge of that which passed in this forgotten corner of the East. The minds abreast of their age were, however, better informed. The tender and clear-sighted Virgil seems to answer, as by a secret echo, to the second Isaiah. The birth of a child throws him into dreams of a universal palingenesis. These dreams were of every-day occurrence, and shaped into a kind of literature which was designated Sibylline. The quite recent formation of the empire exalted the imagination; the great era of peace on which it entered, and t at impression of melancholy sensibility which the mind experiences after long periods of revolution, gave birth on all sides to unlimited hopes.

In Judea expectation was at its height. Holy persons

—among whom may be named the aged Simeon, who, legend tells us, held Jesus in his arms; Anna, daughter of Phanuel, regarded as a prophetess—passed their life about the temple, fasting, and praying that it might please God not to take them from the world without having seen the fulfilment of the hopes of Israel. They felt a powerful presentiment; they were sensible of the approach of something unknown.

This confused mixture of clear views and dreams, this alternation of deceptions and hopes, these ceaseless aspirations, driven back by an odious reality, found at last their interpretation in the incomparable man, to whom the universal conscience has decreed the title of Son of God, and that with justice, since he has advanced religion as no other has done, or probably ever will be able to do.

CHAPTER II

JESUS was born at Nazareth, a small town of Galilee, which before his time had no celebrity. All his life he was designated by the name of " the Nazarene," and it is only by a rather embarrassed and roundabout way [1] that, in the legends respecting him, he is made to be born at Bethlehem. We shall see later the motive for this supposition, and how it was the necessary consequence of the Messianic character attributed to Jesus. The precise date of his birth is unknown. It took place under the reign of Augustus, about the Roman year 750, probably some years before the year 1 of that era which all civilised people date from the day on which he was born.

The name of *Jesus*, which was given him, is an alteration

---

[1] The census effected by Quirinus, to which legend attributes the journey from Bethlehem, is at least ten years later than the year in which, according to Luke and Matthew, Jesus was born. The two evangelists in effect make Jesus to be born under the reign of Herod (Matt. ii. 1, 19, 22; Luke i. 5). Now, the census of Quirinus did not take place until after the deposition of Archelaus—*i.e.*, ten years after the death of Herod, the 37th year from the era of Actium (Josephus, *Ant.*, XVII. xiii. 5, XVIII. i. 1, ii. 1). The inscription by which it was formerly pretended to establish that Quirinus had levied two censuses is recognised as false (see Orelli, *Inscr. Lat.*, No. 623, and the supplement of Henzen in this number; Borghesi, *Fastes Consulaires* [yet unpublished] in the year 742). The census in any case would only be applied to the parts reduced to Roman provinces, and not to the tetrarchies. The texts by which it is sought to prove that some of the operations for statistics and tribute commanded by Augustus ought to extend to the dominion of the Herods, either do not mean what they have been made to say, or are from Christian authors who have borrowed this statement from the Gospel of Luke. That which proves, besides, that the journey of the family of Jesus to Bethlehem is not historical, is the motive attributed to it. Jesus was not of the family of David (see Chap. XV.), and, if he had been, we should still not imagine that his parents should have been forced, for an operation purely registrative and financial, to come to enrol themselves in the place whence their ancestors had proceeded a thousand years before. In imposing such an obligation, the Roman authority would have sanctioned pretensions threatening her safety.

from *Joshua*. It was a very common name; but afterwards mysteries, and an allusion to his character of Saviour, were naturally sought for in it. Perhaps he, like all mystics, exalted himself in this respect. It is thus that more than one great vocation in history has been caused by a name given to a child without premeditation. Ardent natures never bring themselves to see aught of chance in what concerns them. God has regulated everything for them, and they see a sign of the supreme will in the most insignificant circumstances.

The population of Galilee was very mixed, as the very name of the country indicated. This province counted among its inhabitants, in the time of Jesus, many who were not Jews (Phœnicians, Syrians, Arabs, and even Greeks). The conversions to Judaism were not rare in these mixed countries. It is therefore impossible to raise here any question of race, and to seek to ascertain what blood flowed in the veins of him who has contributed most to efface the distinctions of blood in humanity.

He proceeded from the ranks of the people. His father Joseph and his mother Mary were people in humble circumstances, artisans living by their labour, in the state so common in the East, which is neither ease nor poverty. The extreme simplicity of life in such countries, by dispensing with the need of comfort, renders the privileges of wealth almost useless, and makes everyone voluntarily poor. On the other hand, the total want of taste for art, and for that which contributes to the elegance of material life, gives a naked aspect to the house of him who otherwise wants for nothing. Apart from something sordid and repulsive which Islamism bears everywhere with it, the town of Nazareth, in the time of Jesus, did not perhaps much differ from what it is to-day. We see the streets where he played when a child, in the stony paths or little crossways which separate the dwellings. The house of Joseph doubtless much resembled those poor shops, lighted by the door, serving at once for shop, kitchen, and bedroom, having for furniture a mat, some cushions on the ground, one or two clay pots, and a painted chest.

The family, whether it proceeded from one or many marriages, was rather numerous. Jesus had brothers and sisters, of whom he seems to have been the eldest. All have remained obscure, for it appears that the four personages who were named as his brothers, and among whom one, at least, James, had acquired great importance in the earliest years of the development of Christianity, were his

cousins-german. Mary, in fact, had a sister also named
Mary, who married a certain Alpheus or Cleophas (these
two names appear to designate the same person), and was
the mother of several sons who played a considerable part
among the first disciples of Jesus. These cousins-german
who adhered to the young Master, while his own brothers
opposed him, took the title of " brothers of the Lord."
The real brothers of Jesus, like their mother, became
important only after his death. Even then they do not
appear to have equalled in importance their cousins, whose
conversion had been more spontaneous, and whose character
seems to have had more originality. Their names were so
little known that when the evangelist put in the mouth of
the men of Nazareth the enumeration of the brothers
according to natural relationship, the names of the sons
of Cleophas first presented themselves to him.

His sisters were married at Nazareth, and he spent the
first years of his youth there. Nazareth was a small town
in a hollow, opening broadly at the summit of the group
of mountains which close the plain of Esdraelon on the
north. The population is now from three to four thousand,
and it can never have varied much. The cold there is
sharp in winter, and the climate very healthy. The town,
like all the small Jewish towns at this period, was a heap
of huts built without style, and would exhibit that harsh
and poor aspect which villages in Semitic countries now
present. The houses, it seems, did not differ much from
those cubes of stone, without exterior or interior elegance,
which still cover the richest parts of the Lebanon, and
which, surrounded with vines and fig-trees, are still very
agreeable. The environs, moreover, are charming; and
no place in the world was so well adapted for dreams of
perfect happiness. Even in our times Nazareth is still a
delightful abode, the only place, perhaps, in Palestine in
which the mind feels itself relieved from the burden which
oppresses it in this unequalled desolation. The people are
amiable and cheerful; the gardens fresh and green.
Anthony the Martyr, at the end of the sixth century, drew
an enchanting picture of the fertility of the environs, which
he compared to paradise. Some valleys on the western
side fully justify his description. The fountain, where
formerly the life and gaiety of the little town were concentrated, is destroyed; its broken channels contain now only
a muddy stream. But the beauty of the women who meet
there in the evening—that beauty which was remarked
even in the sixth century, and which was looked upon as

a gift of the Virgin Mary—is still most strikingly preserved. It is the Syrian type in all its languid grace. No doubt Mary was there almost every day, and took her place with her jar on her shoulder in the file of her companions who have remained unknown. Anthony the Martyr remarks that the Jewish women, generally disdainful to Christians, were here full of affability. Even now religious animosity is weaker at Nazareth than elsewhere.

The horizon from the town is limited. But if we ascend a little, the plateau, swept by a perpetual breeze, which overlooks the highest houses, the prospect is splendid. On the west are seen the fine outlines of Carmel, terminated by an abrupt point, which seems to plunge into the sea. Before us are spread out the double summit which towers above Megiddo; the mountains of the country of Shechem, with their holy places of the patriarchal age; the hills of Gilboa, the small picturesque group to which are attached the graceful or terrible recollections of Shunem and of Endor; and Tabor, with its beautiful rounded form, which antiquity compared to a bosom. Through a depression between the mountains of Shunem and Tabor are seen the valley of the Jordan and the high plains of Peræa, which form a continuous line from the eastern side. On the north the mountains of Safed, in inclining towards the sea, conceal St. Jean d'Acre, but permit the Gulf of Khaïfa to be distinguished. Such was the horizon of Jesus. This enchanted circle, cradle of the kingdom of God, was for years his world. Even in his later life he departed but little beyond the familiar limits of his childhood. For yonder, northwards, a glimpse is caught, almost on the flank of Hermon, of Cæsarea-Philippi, his furthest point of advance into the Gentile world; and here, southwards, the more sombre aspect of these Samaritan hills foreshadows the dreariness of Judea beyond, parched as by a scorching wind of desolation and death.

If the world, remaining Christian, but attaining to a better idea of the esteem in which the origin of its religion should be held, should ever wish to replace by authentic holy places the mean and apocryphal sanctuaries to which the piety of dark ages attached itself, it is upon this height of Nazareth that it will rebuild its temple. There, at the birthplace of Christianity, and in the centre of the actions of its Founder, the great church ought to be raised in which all Christians may worship. There, also, on this spot where sleep Joseph the Carpenter and thousands of forgotten Nazarenes who never passed beyond the horizon of their valley, would be a better station than any in the world beside for the philosopher to contemplate the course of human affairs, to console himself for their uncertainty, and to reassure himself as to the Divine end which the world pursues through countless falterings, and in spite of the universal vanity.

CHAPTER III

EDUCATION OF JESUS

THIS aspect of nature, at once smiling and grand, was the whole education of Jesus. He learned to read and to write, doubtless, according to the Eastern method, which consisted in putting in the hands of the child a book, which he repeated in cadence with his little comrades, until he knew it by heart. It is doubtful, however, if he understood the Hebrew writings in their original tongue. His biographers make him quote them according to the translations in the Aramean tongue; his principles of exegesis, as far as we can judge of them by those of his disciples, much resembled those which were then in vogue, and which form the spirit of the *Targums* and the *Midrashim*.

The schoolmaster in the small Jewish towns was the *hazzan*, or reader in the synagogues. Jesus frequented little the higher schools of the scribes or *sopherim* (Nazareth had perhaps none of them), and he had none of those titles which confer, in the eyes of the vulgar, the privileges of knowledge. It would, nevertheless, be a great error to imagine that Jesus was what we call ignorant. Scholastic education among us draws a profound distinction, in respect of personal worth, between those who have received and those who have been deprived of it. It was not so in the East, nor, in general, in the good old times. The state of ignorance in which, among us, owing to our isolated and entirely individual life, those remain who have not passed through the schools, was unknown in those societies where moral culture, and especially the general spirit of the age, was transmitted by the perpetual intercourse of man with man. The Arab, who has never had a teacher, is often, nevertheless, a very superior man; for the tent is a kind of school always open, where, from the contact of well-educated men, there is produced a great intellectual and even literary movement. The refinement of manners and the acuteness of the intellect have, in the East, nothing in common with what we call education. It is the men from

the schools, on the contrary, who are considered badly
trained and pedantic. In this social state ignorance, which,
among us, condemns a man to an inferior rank, is the
condition of great things and of great originality.

It is not probable that Jesus knew Greek. This language
was very little spread in Judea beyond the classes who
participated in the Government and the towns inhabited
by pagans, like Cæsarea. The real mother tongue of Jesus
was the Syrian dialect mixed with Hebrew, which was then
spoken in Palestine. Still less probably had he any knowledge of Greek culture. This culture was proscribed by
the doctors of Palestine, who included in the same male-
diction " he who rears swine and he who teaches his son
Greek science." At all events, it had not penetrated into
little towns like Nazareth. Notwithstanding the anathema
of the doctors, some Jews, it is true, had already embraced
the Hellenic culture. Without speaking of the Jewish
school of Egypt, in which the attempts to amalgamate
Hellenism and Judaism had been in operation nearly two
hundred years, a Jew, Nicholas of Damascus, had become,
even at this time, one of the most distinguished men, one
of the best informed, and one of the most respected of his
age. Josephus was destined soon to furnish another
example of a Jew completely Grecianised. But Nicholas
was only a Jew in blood. Josephus declares that he himself
was an exception among his contemporaries; and the
whole schismatic school of Egypt was detached to such a
degree from Jerusalem that we do not find the least allusion
to it either in the Talmud or in Jewish tradition. Certain
it is that Greek was very little studied at Jerusalem, that
Greek studies were considered as dangerous, and even
servile, that they were regarded, at the best, as a mere
womanly accomplishment. The study of the Law was the
only one accounted liberal and worthy of a thoughtful
man. Questioned as to the time when it would be proper
to teach children " Greek wisdom," a learned Rabbi had
answered : " At the time when it is neither day nor night ;
since it is written of the Law, Thou shalt study it day and
night."

Neither directly nor indirectly, then, did any element of
Greek culture reach Jesus. He knew nothing beyond
Judaism; his mind preserved that free innocence which
an extended and varied culture always weakens. In the
very bosom of Judaism, he remained a stranger to many
efforts often parallel to his own. On the one hand, the
asceticism of the Essenes or the Therapeutæ ; on the other,

he fine efforts of religious philosophy put forth by the
ewish school of Alexandria, and of which Philo, his con-
emporary, was the ingenious interpreter, were unknown to
im. The frequent resemblances which we find between
im and Philo, those excellent maxims about the love of
God, charity, rest in God, which are like an echo between
he Gospel and the writings of the illustrious Alexandrian
hinker, proceed from the common tendencies which the
vants of the time inspired in all elevated minds.

Happily for him, he was also ignorant of the strange
cholasticism which was taught at Jerusalem, and which
vas soon to constitute the Talmud. If some Pharisees had
lready brought it into Galilee, he did not associate with
hem, and when, later, he encountered this silly casuistry,
t only inspired him with disgust. We may suppose, how-
ver, that the principles of Hillel were not unknown to him.
Hillel, fifty years before him, had given utterance to aphor-
sms very analogous to his own. By his poverty, so meekly
ndured, by the sweetness of his character, by his opposition
o priests and hypocrites, Hillel was the true master of
Jesus, if, indeed, it may be permitted to speak of a master
n connection with so high an originality as his.

The perusal of the books of the Old Testament made
nuch impression upon him. The canon of the holy books
vas composed of two principal parts : the Law—that is to
ay, the Pentateuch—and the Prophets, such as we now
ossess them. An extensive allegorical exegesis was applied
o all these books ; and it was sought to draw from them
omething that was not in them, but which responded to
he aspirations of the age. The Law, which represented
10t the ancient laws of the country, but Utopias, the
actitious laws and pious frauds of the time of the pietistic
kings, had become, since the nation had ceased to govern
tself, an inexhaustible theme of subtle interpretations.
As to the Prophets and the Psalms, the popular persuasion
vas that almost all the somewhat mysterious traits that were
n these books had reference to the Messiah, and it was
ought to find there the type of him who should realise the
1opes of the nation. Jesus participated in the taste which
veryone had for these allegorical interpretations. But
he true poetry of the Bible, which escaped the puerile
xegetists of Jerusalem, was fully revealed to his grand
genius. The Law does not appear to have had much charm
or him ; he thought that he could do something better.
But the religious lyrics of the Psalms were in marvellous
accordance with his poetic soul ; they were, all his life, his

food and sustenance. The prophets—Isaiah in particular, and his successor in the record of the time of the captivity —with their brilliant dreams of the future, their impetuous eloquence, and their invectives mingled with enchanting pictures, were his true teachers. He read also, no doubt, many apocryphal works—*i.e.* writings somewhat modern —the authors of which, for the sake of an authority only granted to very ancient writings, had clothed themselves with the names of prophets and patriarchs. One of these books especially struck him—namely, the book of Daniel. This book, composed by an enthusiastic Jew of the time of Antiochus Epiphanes, under the name of an ancient sage, was the *résumé* of the spirit of those later times. Its author, a true creator of the philosophy of history, had for the first time dared to see in the march of the world and the succession of empires only a purpose subordinate to the destinies of the Jewish people. Jesus was early penetrated by these high hopes. Perhaps, also, he had read the books of Enoch, then revered equally with the holy books, and the other writings of the same class, which kept up so much excitement in the popular imagination. The advent of the Messiah, with his glories and his terrors—the nations falling down one after another, the cataclysm of heaven and earth—were the familiar food of his imagination; and, as these revolutions were reputed near, and a great number of persons sought to calculate the time when they should happen, the supernatural state of things into which such visions transport us appeared to him from the first perfectly natural and simple.

That he had no knowledge of the general state of the world is apparent from each feature of his most authentic discourses. The earth appeared to him still divided into kingdoms warring with one another; he seemed to ignore the " Roman peace," and the new state of society which its age inaugurated. He had no precise idea of the Roman power; the name of " Cæsar " alone reached him. He saw building, in Galilee or its environs, Tiberias, Julias, Diocæsarea, Cæsarea, gorgeous works of the Herods, who sought, by these magnificent structures, to prove their admiration for Roman civilisation, and their devotion towards the members of the family of Augustus—structures whose names, by a caprice of fate, now serve, though strangely altered, to designate miserable hamlets or Bedouins. He also probably saw Sebaste, a work of Herod the Great, a showy city, whose ruins would lead to the belief that it had been carried there ready made, like a machine which had only to be put up in its place. This ostentatious piece of architecture arrived in Judea by cargoes; these hundreds of columns, all of the same diameter, the ornament of some insipid *Rue de Rivoli*—these were what he called " the kingdoms of the world and all their glory." But this luxury of power, this administrative and official art, displeased him. What he loved were his Galilean villages, confused mixtures of huts, of nests and holes cut in the rocks, of wells, of tombs, of fig-trees, and of olives. He always clung close to nature. The courts of kings appeared to him as places where men wear fine clothes. The charming impossibilities with which his parables abound, when he brings kings and the mighty ones on the stage, prove that he never conceived of aristocratic society but as a young villager who sees the world through the prism of his simplicity.

Still less was he acquainted with the new idea, created by Grecian science, which was the basis of all philosophy, and which modern science has greatly confirmed—to wit, the exclusion of capricious gods, to whom the simple belief of ancient ages attributed the government of the universe. Almost a century before him Lucretius had expressed, in an admirable manner, the unchangeableness of the general system of nature. The negation of miracle—the idea that everything in the world happens by laws in which the personal intervention of superior beings has no share—was universally admitted in the great schools of all the countries which had accepted Grecian science. Perhaps even Babylon and Persia were not strangers to it. Jesus knew nothing of this progress. Although born at a time when the principle of positive science was already proclaimed, he lived entirely in the supernatural. Never, perhaps, had the Jews been more possessed with the thirst for the marvellous. Philo, who lived in a great intellectual centre, and who had received a very complete education, possessed only a chimerical and inferior knowledge of science.

Jesus on this point differed in no respect from his companions. He believed in the devil, whom he regarded as a kind of evil genius, and he imagined, like all the world, that nervous maladies were produced by demons who possessed the patient and agitated him. The marvellous was not the exceptional for him; it was his normal state. The notion of the supernatural, with its impossibilities, is coincident with the birth of experimental science. The man who is strange to all ideas of physical laws, who believes that by praying he can change the path of the clouds, arrest

C

disease, and even death, finds nothing extraordinary i
miracle, inasmuch as the entire course of things is to hir
the result of the free will of the Divinity. This intellectua
state was constantly that of Jesus. But in his great sou
such a belief produced effects quite opposed to thos
produced on the vulgar. Among the latter the belief i
the special action of God led to a foolish credulity, and th
deceptions of charlatans. With him it led to a profoun
idea of the familiar relations of man with God, and a
exaggerated belief in the power of man—beautiful error
which were the secret of his power; for if they were th
means of one day showing his deficiencies in the eyes of th
physicist and the chemist, they gave him a power over h
own age of which no individual had been possessed befor
his time, or has been since.

His distinctive character very early revealed itsel
Legend delights to show him even from his infancy in revo
against paternal authority, and departing from the commo
way to fulfil his vocation. It is certain, at least, that h
cared little for the relations of kinship. His family do n
seem to have loved him, and at times he seems to hav
been hard towards them. Jesus, like all men exclusivel
preoccupied by an idea, came to think little of the ties o
blood. The bond of thought is the only one that natur
of this kind recognise. "Behold my mother and m
brethren," said he, in extending his hand towards his di
ciples; "he who does the will of my Father, he is m
brother and my sister." The simple people did not unde
stand the matter thus, and one day a woman passing nea
him cried out, "Blessed is the womb that bare thee, an
the paps which gave thee suck!" But he said, "Ye
rather blessed are they that hear the word of God, an
keep it." Soon, in his bold revolt against nature, he wer
still further, and we shall see him trampling under foo
everything that is human—blood, love, and country—an
only keeping soul and heart for the idea which presente
itself to him as the absolute form of goodness and truth

CHAPTER IV

THE ORDER OF THOUGHT WHICH SURROUNDED THE DEVELOPMENT OF JESUS

As the cooled earth no longer permits us to understand the phenomena of primitive creation, because the fire which penetrated it is extinct, so deliberate explanations have always appeared somewhat insufficient when applying our timid methods of induction to the revolutions of the creative epochs which have decided the fate of humanity. Jesus lived at one of those times when the game of public life is freely played, and when the stake of human activity is increased a hundredfold. Every great part, then, entails death; for such movements suppose liberty and an absence of preventive measures which could not exist without a terrible alternative. In these days man risks little and gains little. In heroic periods of human activity man risked all and gained all. The good and the wicked, or at least those who believed themselves and are believed to be such, form opposite armies. The apotheosis is reached by the scaffold; characters have distinctive features, which engrave them as eternal types in the memory of men. Except in the French Revolution, no historical centre was so suitable as that in which Jesus was formed to develop those hidden forces which humanity holds as in reserve, and which are not seen except in days of excitement and peril.

If the government of the world were a speculative problem, and the greatest philosopher were the man best fitted to tell his fellows what they ought to believe, it would be from calmness and reflection that those great moral and dogmatic truths called religion would proceed. But it is not so. If we except Çakya-Mouni, the great religious founders have not been metaphysicians. Buddhism itself, whose origin is in pure thought, has conquered one-half of Asia by motives wholly political and moral. As to the Semitic religions, they are as little philosophical as possible. Moses and Mohammed were not men of speculation : they were men of action. It was in proposing action to their fellow countrymen and to their contemporaries that they governed humanity. Jesus, in like manner, was not a theologian or a philosopher, having a more or less well-composed system. In order to be a disciple of Jesus, it was not necessary to sign any formulary, or to pronounce any confession of faith; one thing only was necessary—to be attached to him, to love him. He never disputed about God, for he felt him directly in himself. The rock of metaphysical subtleties, against which Christianity broke from the third century, was in no wise created by the founder. Jesus had neither dogma nor system, but a fixed personal resolution, which, exceeding in intensity every other created will, directs to this hour the destinies of humanity.

The Jewish people had the advantage, from the captivity of Babylon up to the Middle Ages, of being in a state of the greatest tension. This is why the interpreters of the spirit of the nation, during this long period, seemed to write under the action of an intense fever, which placed them constantly either above or below reason, rarely in its middle path. Never did man seize the problem of the future and of his destiny with a more desperate courage, more determined to go to extremes. Not separating the lot of humanity from that of their little race, the Jewish thinkers were the first who sought for a general theory of the progress of our species. Greece, always confined within itself, and solely attentive to petty quarrels, has had admirable historians; but before the Roman epoch it would be in vain to seek in her a general system of the philosophy of history embracing all humanity. The Jew, on the contrary, thanks to a kind of prophetic sense which renders the Semite at times marvellously apt to see the great lines of the future, has made history enter into religion. Perhaps he owes a little of this spirit to Persia. Persia, from an ancient period, conceived the history of the world as a series of evolutions, over each of which a prophet presided. Each prophet had his *hazar*, or reign of a thousand years (chiliasm), and from these successive ages, analogous to the Avatār of India, is composed the course of events which prepared the reign of Ormuzd. At the end of the time when the cycle of chiliasms shall be exhausted, the complete paradise will come. Men then will live happy; the earth will be as one plain; there will be only one language, one law, and one government for all. But this advent will be preceded by terrible calamities. Dahak (the Satan of

Persia) will break his chains and fall upon the world. Two prophets will come to console mankind, and to prepare the great advent. These ideas ran through the world, and penetrated even to Rome, where they inspired a cycle of prophetic poems, of which the fundamental ideas were the division of the history of humanity into periods, the succession of the gods corresponding to these periods—a complete renovation of the world, and the final advent of a golden age. The book of Daniel, the book of Enoch, and certain parts of the Sibylline books are the Jewish expression of the same theory. These thoughts were certainly far from being shared by all; they were only embraced at first by a few persons of lively imagination, who were inclined towards strange doctrines. The dry and narrow author of the book of Esther never thought of the rest of the world except to despise it, and to wish it evil. The disabused epicurean who wrote Ecclesiastes thought so little of the future that he considered it even useless to labour for his children; in the eyes of this egotistical celibate the highest stroke of wisdom was to use his fortune for his own enjoyment. But the great achievements of a people are generally wrought by the minority. Notwithstanding all their enormous defects—hard, egotistical, scoffing, cruel, narrow, subtle, and sophistical—the Jewish people are the authors of the finest movement of disinterested enthusiasm which history records. Opposition always makes the glory of a country. The greatest men of a nation are those whom it puts to death. Socrates was the glory of the Athenians, who would not suffer him to live among them. Spinoza was the greatest Jew of modern times, and the synagogue expelled him with ignominy. Jesus was the glory of the people of Israel, who crucified him.

A gigantic dream haunted for centuries the Jewish people, constantly renewing its youth in its decrepitude. A stranger to the theory of individual recompense, which Greece diffused under the name of the immortality of the soul, Judea concentrated all its power of love and desire upon the national future. She thought she possessed divine promises of a boundless future; and as a bitter reality, from the ninth century before our era, gave more and more the dominion of the world to physical force, and brutally crushed these aspirations, she took refuge in the union of the most impossible ideas, and attempted the strangest gyrations. Before the captivity, when all the earthly hopes of the nation had become weakened by the separation of the northern tribes, they dreamt of the restoration of the house of David, the reconciliation of the two divisions of the people, and the triumph of theocracy and the worship of Jehovah over idolatry. At the epoch of the captivity a poet, full of harmony, saw the splendour of a future Jerusalem, of which the peoples and the distant isles should be tributaries, under colours so charming that one might say a glimpse of the visions of Jesus had reached him at a distance of six centuries.

The victory of Cyrus seemed at one time to realise all that had been hoped. The grave disciples of the Avesta and the adorers of Jehovah believed themselves brothers. Persia had begun by banishing the multiple *dévas*, and by transforming them into demons (*divs*), to draw from the old Arian imaginations (essentially naturalistic) a species of Monotheism. The prophetic tone of many of the teachings of Iran had much analogy with certain compositions of Hosea and Isaiah. Israel reposed under the Achemenidae, and under Xerxes (Ahasuerus) made itself feared by the Iranians themselves. But the triumphal and often cruel entry of Greek and Roman civilisation into Asia threw it back upon its dreams. More than ever it invoked the Messiah as judge and avenger of the people. A complete renovation, a revolution which should shake the world to its very foundation, was necessary in order to satisfy the enormous thirst of vengeance excited in it by the sense of its superiority, and by the sight of its humiliation.

If Israel had possessed the spiritualistic doctrine which divides man in two parts—the body and the soul—and finds it quite natural that while the body decays the soul should survive, this paroxysm of rage and of energetic protestation would have had no existence. But such a doctrine, proceeding from the Grecian philosophy, was not in the traditions of the Jewish mind. The ancient Hebrew writings contain no trace of future rewards or punishments. While the idea of the solidarity of the tribe existed, it was natural that a strict retribution according to individual merits should not be thought of. So much the worse for the pious man who happened to live in an epoch of impiety; he suffered like the rest the public misfortunes consequent on the general irreligion. This doctrine, bequeathed by the sages of the patriarchal era, constantly produced unsustainable contradictions. Already at the time of Job it was much shaken; the old men of Teman who professed it were considered behind the age, and the young Elihu, who intervened in order to combat them, dared to utter as his first word this essentially revolutionary sentiment, " Great men are not always wise; neither do the aged understand judgment." With the complications which had taken place in the world since the time of Alexander, the old Yemanite and Mosaic principle became still more intolerable. Never had Israel been more faithful to the Law, and yet it was subjected to the atrocious persecution of Antiochus. Only a declaimer, accustomed to repeat old phrases denuded of meaning, would dare to assert that these evils proceeded from the unfaithfulness of the people. What! these victims who died for their faith, these heroic Maccabees, his mother with her seven sons—will Jehovah forget them eternally? Will he abandon them to the corruption of the grave? Worldly and incredulous Sadduceeism might possibly not recoil before such a consequence, and a consummate sage, like Antigonus of Soco, might indeed maintain that we must not practise virtue like a slave in expectation of a recompense, that we must be virtuous without hope. But the mass of the people could not be contented with that. Some, attaching themselves to the principle of philosophical immortality, imagined the righteous living in the memory of God, glorious for ever in the remembrance of men, and judging the wicked who had persecuted them. " They live in the sight of God; . . . they are known of God." That was their reward. Others, especially the Pharisees, had recourse to the doctrine of the resurrection. The righteous will live again in order to participate in the Messianic reign. They will live again in the flesh, and for a world of which they will be the kings and the judges; they will be present at the triumph of their ideas and at the humiliation of their enemies.

We find among the ancient people of Israel only very indecisive traces of this fundamental dogma. The Sadducee, who did not believe it, was in reality faithful to the old Jewish doctrine; it was the Pharisee, the believer in the resurrection, who was the innovator. But in religion it is always the zealous sect which innovates, which progresses, and which has influence. Besides this, the resurrection, an idea totally different from that of the immortality of the soul, proceeded very naturally from the anterior doctrines and from the position of the people. Perhaps Persia also furnished some of its elements. In any case, combining with the belief in the Messiah, and with the doctrine of a speedy renewal of all things, it formed those apocalyptic theories which, without being articles of faith (the orthodox Sanhedrim of Jerusalem does not seem to have adopted them), pervaded all imaginations, and produced an extreme fermentation from one end of the Jewish world to the other. The total absence of dogmatic rigour caused very contradictory notions to be admitted at one time, even upon so primary a point. Sometimes the righteous were to await the resurrection; sometimes they were to be received at the moment of death into Abraham's bosom; sometimes the resurrection was to be general; sometimes it was to be reserved only for the faithful; sometimes it supposed a renewed earth and a new Jerusalem; sometimes it applied a previous annihilation of the universe.

Jesus, as soon as he began to think, entered into the burning atmosphere which was created in Palestine by the ideas we have just stated. These ideas were taught in no school; but they were in the very air, and his soul was early penetrated by them. Our hesitations and our doubts never reached him. On this summit of the mountain of Nazareth, where no man can sit to-day without an uneasy, though it may be a frivolous, feeling about his destiny, Jesus sat often untroubled by a doubt. Free from selfishness—that source of our troubles which makes us seek with eagerness a reward for virtue beyond the tomb—he thought only of his work, of his race, and of humanity. Those mountains, that sea, that azure sky, those high plains in the horizon, were for him not the melancholy vision of a soul which interrogates Nature upon her fate, but the certain symbol, the transparent shadow, of an invisible world and of a new heaven.

He never attached much importance to the political events of his time, and he probably knew little about them. The court of the Herods formed a world so different to his that he doubtless knew it only by name. Herod the Great died about the year in which Jesus was born, leaving imperishable remembrances—monuments which must compel the most malevolent posterity to associate his name with that of Solomon; nevertheless, his work was incomplete, and could not be continued. Profanely ambitious, and lost in a maze of religious controversies, this astute Idumean had the advantage which coolness and judgment, stripped of morality, give over passionate fanatics. But his idea of a secular kingdom of Israel, even if it had not been an anachronism in the state of the world in which it was conceived, would inevitably have miscarried, like the similar project which Solomon formed, owing to the difficulties proceeding from the character of the nation. His three sons were only lieutenants of the Romans, analogous to the rajahs of India under the English dominion. Antipater, or Antipas, tetrarch of Galilee and of Peræa, of whom Jesus was a subject all his life, was an idle and useless prince, a favourite and flatterer of Tiberius, and too often misled by the bad influence of his second wife, Herodias. Philip, tetrarch of Gaulonitis and Batanea, into whose dominions Jesus made frequent journeys, was a much better sovereign. As to Archelaus, ethnarch of Jerusalem, Jesus could not know him, for he was about ten years old when this man, who was weak and without character, though sometimes violent, was deposed by Augustus. The last trace of self-government was thus lost to Jerusalem. United to Samaria and Idumea, Judea formed a kind of dependency of the province of Syria, in which the senator Publius Sulpicius Quirinus, well known as consul, was the imperial legate. A series of Roman procurators, subordinate in important matters to the imperial legate of Syria—Coponius, Marcus Ambivius, Annius Rufus, Valerius Gratus, and, lastly (in the twenty-sixth year of our era), Pontius Pilate—followed each other, and were constantly occupied in extinguishing the volcano which was seething beneath their feet.

Continual seditions, excited by the zealots of Mosaism, did not cease, in fact, to agitate Jerusalem during all this time. The death of the seditious was certain; but death, when the integrity of the Law was in question, was sought with avidity. To overturn the Roman eagle, to destroy the works of art raised by the Herods, in which the Mosaic regulations were not always respected—to rise up against the votive escutcheons put up by the procurators, the inscriptions of which appeared tainted with idolatry—were perpetual temptations to fanatics, who had reached that degree of exaltation which removes all care for life. Judas, son of Sariphea, Matthias, son of Margaloth, two very celebrated doctors of the law, formed against the established order a boldly aggressive party, which continued after their execution. The Samaritans were agitated by movements of a similar nature. The Law had never counted a greater number of impassioned disciples than at this time, when he already lived who, by the full authority of his genius and of his great soul, was about to abrogate it. The " Zelotes " (Kenaïm), or " Sicarii," pious assassins, who imposed on themselves the task of killing whoever in their estimation broke the Law, began to appear. Representatives of a totally different spirit, the Thaumaturges, considered as in some sort divine, obtained credence in consequence of the imperious want which the age experienced for the supernatural and the divine.

C 2

A movement which had much more influence upon Jesus was that of Judas the Gaulonite, or Galilean. Of all the exactions to which the country newly conquered by Rome was subjected, the census was the most unpopular. This measure, which always astonishes people unaccustomed to the requirements of great central administrations, was particularly odious to the Jews. We see that already, under David, a numbering of the people provoked violent recriminations and the menaces of the prophets. The census, in fact, was the basis of taxation; now taxation, to a pure theocracy, was almost an impiety. God being the sole Master whom man ought to recognise, to pay tithe to a secular sovereign was, in a manner, to put him in the place of God. Completely ignorant of the idea of the State, the Jewish theocracy only acted up to its logical induction—the negation of civil society and of all government. The money of the public treasury was accounted stolen money. The census ordered by Quirinus (in the year 6 of the Christian era) powerfully reawakened these ideas, and caused a great fermentation. An insurrection broke out in the northern provinces. One Judas, of the town of Gamala, upon the eastern shore of the Lake of Tiberias, and a Pharisee named Sadoc, by denying the lawfulness of the tax, created a numerous party, which soon broke out in open revolt. The fundamental maxims of this party were—that they ought to call no man " master," this title belonging to God alone; and that liberty was better than life. Judas had, doubtless, many other principles, which Josephus, always careful not to compromise his co-religionists, designedly suppresses; for it is impossible to understand how, for so simple an idea, the Jewish historian should give him a place among the philosophers of his nation, and should regard him as the founder of a fourth school, equal to those of the Pharisees, the Sadducees, and the Essenes. Judas was evidently the chief of a Galilean sect, deeply imbued with the Messianic idea, and which became a political movement. The procurator, Coponius, crushed the sedition of the Gaulonite; but the school remained and preserved its chiefs. Under the leadership of Menahem, son of the founder, and of a certain Eleazar, his relative, we find them again very active in the last contests of the Jews against the Romans. Perhaps Jesus saw this Judas, whose idea of the Jewish revolution was so different from his own; at all events, he knew his school, and it was probably to avoid his error that he pronounced the axiom upon the penny of Cæsar. Jesus, more wise, and far removed from all sedition, profited by the fault of his predecessor, and dreamed of another kingdom and another deliverance.

Galilee was thus an immense furnace wherein the most diverse elements were seething. An extraordinary contempt of life, or, more properly speaking, a kind of longing for death, was the consequence of these agitations. Experience counts for nothing in these great fanatical movements. Algeria, at the commencement of the French occupation, saw arise, each spring, inspired men, who declared themselves invulnerable, and sent by God to drive away the infidels; the following year their death was forgotten, and their successors found no less credence. The Roman power, very stern on the one hand, yet little disposed to meddle, permitted a good deal of liberty. Those great brutal despotisms, terrible in repression, were not so suspicious as powers which have a faith to defend. They allowed everything up to the point when they thought it necessary to be severe. It is not recorded that Jesus was even once interfered with by the civil power in his wandering career. Such freedom, and, above all, the happiness which Galilee enjoyed in being much less confined in the bonds of Pharisaic pedantry, gave to this district a real superiority over Jerusalem. The revolution, or, in other words, the belief in the Messiah, caused here a general fermentation. Men deemed themselves on the eve of the great renovation; the Scriptures, tortured into divers meanings, fostered the most colossal hopes. In each line of the simple writings of the Old Testament they saw the assurance, and in a manner the programme, of the future reign, which was to bring peace to the righteous, and to seal for ever the work of God.

From all time this division into two parties, opposed in interest and spirit, had been for the Hebrew nation a principle which contributed to their moral growth. Every nation called to high destinies ought to be a little world in itself, including opposite poles. Greece presented, at a few leagues' distance from each other, Sparta and Athens —to a superficial observer, the two antipodes; but, in reality, rival sisters, necessary to one another. It was the same with Judea. Less brilliant in one sense than the development of Jerusalem, that of the North was on the whole much more fertile; the greatest achievements of the Jewish people have always proceeded thence. A complete absence of the love of nature, bordering upon something dry, narrow, and ferocious, has stamped all the works purely Hierosolymite with a degree of grandeur, though sad, arid, and repulsive. With its solemn doctors, its insipid canonists, its hypocritical and atrabilious devotees, Jerusalem has not conquered humanity. The North has given to the world the simple Shunammite, the humble Canaanite, the impassioned Magdalene, the good foster-father Joseph, and the Virgin Mary. The North alone has made Christianity; Jerusalem, on the contrary, is the true home of that obstinate Judaism, which, founded by the Pharisees, and fixed by the Talmud, has traversed the Middle Ages, and come down to us.

A beautiful external nature tended to produce a much less austere spirit—a spirit less sharply monotheistic, if I may use the expression—which imprinted a charming and idyllic character on all the dreams of Galilee. The saddest country in the world is perhaps the region round about Jerusalem. Galilee, on the contrary, was a very green, shady, smiling district, the true home of the Song of Songs, and the songs of the well-beloved. During the two months of March and April the country forms a carpet of flowers of an incomparable variety of colours. The animals are small and extremely gentle—delicate and lively turtle-doves, blue-birds so light that they rest on a blade of grass without bending it, crested larks which venture almost under the feet of the traveller, little river tortoises with mild and lively eyes, storks with grave and modest mien, which, laying aside all timidity, allow man to come quite near them, and seem almost to invite his approach. In no country in the world do the mountains spread themselves out with more harmony or inspire higher thoughts. Jesus seems to have had a peculiar love for them. The most important acts of his divine career took place upon the mountains. It was there that he was the most inspired; it was there that he held secret communion with the ancient prophets; and it was there that his disciples witnessed his transfiguration.

This beautiful country has now become sad and gloomy through the ever-impoverishing influence of Islamism. But still everything which man cannot destroy breathes an air of freedom, mildness, and tenderness, and at the time of Jesus it overflowed with happiness and prosperity. The Galileans were considered energetic, brave, and laborious. If we except Tiberias, built by Antipas in honour of Tiberius (about the year 15), in the Roman style, Galilee had no large towns. The country was, never-theless, well peopled, covered with small towns and large villages, and cultivated in all parts with skill. From the ruins which remain of its ancient splendour we can trace an agricultural people, no way gifted in art, caring little for luxury, indifferent to the beauties of form, and exclusively idealistic. The country abounded in fresh streams and in fruits; the large farms were shaded with vines and fig-trees; the gardens were filled with trees bearing apples, walnuts, and pomegranates. The wine was excellent, if we may judge by that which the Jews still obtain at Safed, and they drank much of it. This contented and easily satisfied life was not like the gross materialism of our peasantry, the coarse pleasures of agricultural Normandy, or the heavy mirth of the Flemish. It spiritualised itself in ethereal dreams—in a kind of poetic mysticism, blending heaven and earth. Leave the austere Baptist in his desert of Judea to preach penitence, to inveigh without ceasing, and to live on locusts in the company of jackals. Why should the companions of the bridegroom fast while the bridegroom is with them? Joy will be a part of the kingdom of God. Is she not the daughter of the humble in heart, of the men of goodwill?

The whole history of infant Christianity has become in this manner a delightful pastoral. A Messiah at the marriage festival—the courtesan and the good Zaccheus called to his feasts—the founders of the kingdom of heaven like a bridal procession—that is what Galilee has boldly offered, and what the world has accepted. Greece has drawn pictures of human life by sculpture and by charming poetry, but always without backgrounds or distant receding perspectives. In Galilee were wanting the marble, the practised workmen, the exquisite and refined language. But Galilee has created the most sublime ideal for the popular imagination; for behind its idyl moves the fate of humanity, and the light which illumines its picture is the sun of the kingdom of God.

Jesus lived and grew amid these enchanting scenes. From his infancy he went almost annually to the feast at Jerusalem. The pilgrimage was a sweet solemnity for the provincial Jews. Entire series of psalms were consecrated to celebrate the happiness of thus journeying in family companionship during several days in the spring across the hills and valleys, each one having in prospect the splendours of Jerusalem, the solemnities of the sacred courts, and the joy of brethren dwelling together in unity. The route which Jesus ordinarily took in these journeys was that which is followed to this day through Ginæa and

Shechem. From Shechem to Jerusalem the journey is very toilsome. But the neighbourhood of the old sanctuaries of Shiloh and Bethel, near which the travellers pass, keep their interest alive. *Ain-el-Haramie*, the last halting-place, is a charming and melancholy spot, and few impressions equal that experienced on encamping there for the night. The valley is narrow and sombre, and a dark stream issues from the rocks, full of tombs, which form its banks. It is, I think, the " valley of tears," or of dropping waters, which is described as one of the stations on the way in the delightful eighty-fourth Psalm, and which became the emblem of life for the sad and sweet mysticism of the Middle Ages. Early the next day they would be at Jerusalem; such an expectation even now sustains the caravan, rendering the night short and slumber light.

These journeys, in which the assembled nation exchanged its ideas, and which were almost always centres of great agitation, placed Jesus in contact with the mind of his countrymen, and no doubt inspired him while still young with a lively antipathy for the defects of the official representatives of Judaism. It is supposed that very early the desert had great influence on his development, and that he made long stays there. But the God he found in the desert was not his God. It was rather the God of Job, severe and terrible, accountable to no one. Sometimes Satan came to tempt him. He returned, then, into his beloved Galilee, and found again his heavenly Father in the midst of the green hills and the clear fountains—and among the crowds of women and children, who, with joyous soul and the song of angels in their hearts, awaited the salvation of Israel.

CHAPTER V

THE FIRST SAYINGS OF JESUS—THE IDEAS OF A DIVINE
FATHER AND OF A PURER RELIGION—FIRST DISCIPLES

JOSEPH died before his son had taken any public part.
Mary remained, in a manner, the head of the family, and
this explains why her son, when it was wished to distinguish him from others of the same name, was most
frequently called the " son of Mary." It seems that having, by the death of her husband, been left friendless at
Nazareth, she withdrew to Cana, from which she may have
come originally. Cana was a little town at from two to
two and a half hours' journey from Nazareth, at the foot
of the mountains which bound the plain of Asochis on the
north. The prospect, less grand than at Nazareth, extends
over all the plain, and is bounded in the most picturesque
manner by the mountains of Nazareth and the hills of Sep-
phoris. Jesus appears to have resided some time in this
place. Here he probably passed a part of his youth, and
here his greatness first revealed itself.

He followed the trade of his father, which was that of a
carpenter. This was not in any degree humiliating or
grievous. The Jewish customs required that a man
devoted to intellectual work should learn a trade. The
most celebrated doctors did so; thus St. Paul, whose
education had been so carefully tended, was a tent-maker.
Jesus never married. All his power of love centred upon
that which he regarded as his celestial vocation. The
extremely delicate feeling towards women which we remark
in him was not separated from the exclusive devotion
which he had for his mission. Like Francis d'Assisi and
Francis de Sales, he treated as sisters the women who were
loved of the same work as himself; he had his St. Clare, his
Frances de Chantal. It is, however, probable that these
loved him more than the work; he was, no doubt, more
beloved than loving. Thus, as often happens in very
elevated natures, tenderness of the heart was transformed
in him into an infinite sweetness, a vague poetry, and a

universal charm. His relations, free and intimate, but of an entirely moral kind, with women of doubtful character, are also explained by the passion which attached him to the glory of his Father, and which made him jealously anxious for all beautiful creatures who could contribute to it.

What was the progress of the ideas of Jesus during this obscure period of his life? Through what meditations did he enter upon the prophetic career? We have no information on these points, his history having come to us in scattered narratives, without exact chronology. But the development of character is everywhere the same; and there is no doubt that the growth of so powerful an individuality as that of Jesus obeyed very rigorous laws. A high conception of the Divinity—which he did not owe to Judaism, and which seems to have been in all its parts the creation of his great mind—was in a manner the source of all his power. It is essential here that we put aside the ideas familiar to us, and the discussions in which little minds exhaust themselves. In order properly to understand the precise character of the piety of Jesus, we must forget all that is placed between the Gospel and ourselves. Deism and Pantheism have become the two poles of theology. The paltry discussions of scholasticism, the dryness of spirit of Descartes, the deep-rooted irreligion of the eighteenth century by lessening God, and by limiting him, in a manner, by the exclusion of everything which is not his very self, have stifled in the breast of modern rationalism all fertile ideas of the Divinity. If God, in fact, is a personal being outside of us, he who believes himself to have peculiar relations with God is a " visionary," and, as the physical and physiological sciences have shown us that all supernatural visions are illusions, the logical Deist finds it impossible to understand the great beliefs of the past. Pantheism, on the other hand, in suppressing the Divine personality, is as far as it can be from the living God of the ancient religions. Were the men who have best comprehended God—Çakya-Mouni, Plato, St. Paul, St. Francis d'Assisi, and St. Augustine (at some periods of his fluctuating life)—Deists or Pantheists? Such a question has no meaning. The physical and metaphysical proofs of the existence of God were quite indifferent to them. They felt the Divine within themselves. We must place Jesus in the first rank of this great family of the true sons of God. Jesus had no visions; God did not speak to him as to one outside of himself; God was in him; he felt himself with

God, and he drew from his heart all he said of his Father. He lived in the bosom of God by constant communication with him; he saw him not, but he understood him, without need of the thunder and the burning bush of Moses, of the revealing tempest of Job, of the oracle of the old Greek sages, of the familiar genius of Socrates, or of the angel Gabriel of Mohammed. The imagination and the hallucination of a St. Theresa, for example, are useless here. The intoxication of the Soufi proclaiming himself identical with God is also quite another thing. Jesus never once gave utterance to the sacrilegious idea that he was God. He believed himself to be in direct communion with God; he believed himself to be the Son of God. The highest consciousness of God which has existed in the bosom of humanity was that of Jesus.

We understand, on the other hand, how Jesus, starting with such a disposition of spirit, could never be a speculative philosopher like Çakya-Mouni. Nothing is further from scholastic theology than the Gospel. The speculations of the Greek fathers on the Divine essence proceed from an entirely different spirit. God, conceived simply as Father, was all the theology of Jesus. And this was not with him a theoretical principle, a doctrine more or less proved, which he sought to inculcate in others. He did not argue with his disciples; he demanded from them no effort of attention. He did not preach his opinions; he preached himself. Very great and very disinterested minds often present, associated with much elevation, that character of perpetual attention to themselves, and extreme personal susceptibility, which, in general, is peculiar to women. Their conviction that God is in them, and occupies himself perpetually with them, is so strong that they have no fear of obtruding themselves upon others : our reserve, and our respect for the opinion of others, which is a part of our weakness, could not belong to them. This exaltation of self is not egotism; for such men, possessed by their idea, give their lives freely, in order to seal their work : it is the identification of self with the object it has embraced, carried to its utmost limit. It is regarded as vain glory by those who see in the new teaching only the personal phantasy of the founder; but it is the finger of God to those who see the result. The fool stands side by side here with the inspired man; only the fool never succeeds. It has not yet been given to insanity to influence seriously the progress of humanity.

Doubtless, Jesus did not attain at first this high affirmation of himself. But it is probable that, from the first, he regarded his relationship with God as that of a son with his father. This was his great act of originality; in this he had nothing in common with his race. Neither the Jew nor the Mussulman has understood this delightful theology of love. The God of Jesus is not that tyrannical master who kills us, damns us, or saves us, according to his pleasure. The God of Jesus is our Father. We hear him in listening to the gentle inspiration which cries within us, " Abba, Father." The God of Jesus is not the partial despot who has chosen Israel for his people and specially protects them. He is the God of humanity. Jesus was not a patriot, like the Maccabees; or a theocrat, like Judas the Gaulonite. Boldly raising himself above the prejudices of his nation, he established the universal fatherhood of God. The Gaulonite maintained that we should die rather than give to another than God the name of " Master "; Jesus left this name to anyone who liked to take it, and reserved for God a dearer name. While he accorded to the powerful of the earth, who were to him representatives of force, a respect full of irony, he proclaimed the supreme consolation—the recourse to the Father which each one has in heaven—and the true kingdom of God, which each one bears in his heart.

This name of " kingdom of God," or " kingdom of heaven," was the favourite term of Jesus to express the revolution which he brought into the world. Like almost all the Messianic terms, it came from the book of Daniel. According to the author of this extraordinary book, the four profane empires, destined to fall, were to be succeeded by a fifth empire, that of the saints, which should last for ever. This reign of God upon earth naturally led to the most diverse interpretations. To Jewish theology the " kingdom of God " is most frequently only Judaism itself— the true religion, the monotheistic worship, piety. In the later periods of his life Jesus believed that this reign would be realised in a material form by a sudden renovation of the world. But doubtless this was not his first idea. The admirable moral which he draws from the idea of God as Father is not that of enthusiasts who believe the world is near its end, and who prepare themselves by asceticism for a chimerical catastrophe; it is that of men who have lived and still would live. " The kingdom of God is within you," said he to those who sought with subtilty for external signs. The realistic conception of the Divine advent was but a cloud, a transient error, which his death has made us forget. The Jesus who founded the true kingdom of God, the kingdom of the meek and the humble, was the Jesus of early life—of those chaste and pure days when the voice of his Father re-echoed within him in clearer tones. It was then for some months, perhaps a year, that God truly dwelt upon the earth. The voice of the young carpenter suddenly acquired an extraordinary sweetness. An infinite charm was exhaled from his person, and those who had seen him up to that time no longer recognised him. He had not yet any disciples, and the group which gathered around him was neither a sect nor a school; but a common spirit, a sweet and penetrating influence was felt. His amiable character, accompanied doubtless by one of those lovely faces which sometimes appear in the Jewish race, threw around him a fascination from which no one in the midst of these kindly and simple populations could escape.

Paradise would, in fact, have been brought to earth if the ideas of the young Master had not far transcended the level of ordinary goodness beyond which it has not been found possible to raise the human race. The brotherhood of men, as sons of God, and the moral consequences which result therefrom, were deduced with exquisite feeling. Like all the rabbis of the time, Jesus was little inclined towards consecutive reasonings, and clothed his doctrine in concise aphorisms, and in an expressive form, at times enigmatical and strange. Some of these maxims come from the books of the Old Testament. Others were the thoughts of more modern sages, especially those of Antigonus of Soco, Jesus, son of Sirach, and Hillel, which had reached him, not from learned study, but as oft-repeated proverbs. The synagogue was rich in very happily expressed sentences, which formed a kind of current proverbial literature. Jesus adopted almost all this oral teaching, but imbued it with a superior spirit. Exceeding the duties laid down by the Law and the elders, he demanded perfection. All the virtues of humility—forgiveness, charity, abnegation, and self-denial—virtues which with good reason have been called Christian, if we mean by that that they have been truly preached by Christ—were in this first teaching, though undeveloped. As to justice, he was content with repeating the well-known axiom—" Whatsoever ye would that men should do to you, do ye even so to them." But this old though somewhat selfish wisdom did not satisfy him. He went to excess and said—" Whosoever shall smite thee on thy right cheek, turn to him the other also.

And if any man will sue thee at the law, and take away thy coat, let him have thy cloak also." " If thy right eye offend thee, pluck it out, and cast it from thee." " Love your enemies, do good to them that hate you, pray for them that persecute you." " Judge not, that ye be not judged." " Forgive, and ye shall be forgiven." " Be ye therefore merciful as your Father also is merciful." " It is more blessed to give than to receive." " Whosoever shall exalt himself shall be abased; and he that shall humble himself shall be exalted."

Upon alms, pity, good works, kindness, peacefulness, and complete disinterestedness of heart, he had little to add to the doctrine of the synagogue. But he placed upon them an emphasis full of unction, which made the old maxims appear new. Morality is not composed of more or less well-expressed principles. The poetry which makes the precept loved is more than the precept itself, taken as an abstract truth. Now, it cannot be denied that these maxims borrowed by Jesus from his predecessors produce quite a different effect in the Gospel to that in the ancient Law, in the *Pirké Aboth*, or in the Talmud. It is neither the ancient Law nor the Talmud which has conquered and changed the world. Little original in itself—if we mean by that that one might recompose it almost entirely by the aid of older maxims—the morality of the Gospels remains, nevertheless, the highest creation of human conscience— the most beautiful code of perfect life that any moralist has traced.

Jesus did not speak against the Mosaic law, but it is clear that he saw its insufficiency, and allowed it to be seen that he did so. He repeated unceasingly that more must be done than the ancient sages had commanded. He forbade the least harsh word; he prohibited divorce and all swearing; he censured revenge; he condemned usury; he considered voluptuous desire as criminal as adultery; he insisted upon a universal forgiveness of injuries. The motive on which he rested these maxims of exalted charity was always the same. . . . " That ye may be the children of your Father which is in heaven : for he maketh his sun to rise on the evil and the good. For if ye love them which love you, what reward have ye ? do not even the publicans the same ? And if ye salute your brethren only, what do ye more than others ? do not even the publicans so ? Be ye therefore perfect, even as your Father which is in heaven is perfect."

A pure worship, a religion without priests and external

observances, resting entirely on the feelings of the heart, on the imitation of God, on the direct relation of the conscience with the heavenly Father, was the result of these principles. Jesus never shrank from this bold conclusion, which made him a thorough revolutionist in the very centre of Judaism. Why should there be mediators between man and his Father? As God only sees the heart, of what good are these purifications, these observances relating only to the body? Even tradition, a thing so sacred to the Jews, is nothing compared to sincerity. The hypocrisy of the Pharisees, who, in praying, turned their heads to see if they were observed, who gave their alms with ostentation, and put marks upon their garments, that they might be recognised as pious persons—all these grimaces of false devotion disgusted him. "They have their recompense," said he; "but thou, when thou doest thine alms, let not thy left hand know what thy right hand doeth, that thy alms may be in secret, and thy Father, which seeth in secret, himself shall reward thee openly." "And when thou prayest, thou shalt not be as the hypocrites are : for they love to pray standing in the synagogues, and in the corners of the streets, that they may be seen of men. Verily I say unto you, They have their reward. But thou, when thou prayest, enter into thy closet; and when thou hast shut thy door, pray to thy Father which is in secret; and thy Father, which seeth in secret, shall reward thee openly. But when ye pray, use not vain repetitions, as the heathen do : for they think that they shall be heard for their much speaking. Your Father knoweth what things ye have need of before ye ask him."

He did not affect any external signs of asceticism, contenting himself with praying, or rather meditating, upon the mountains and in the solitary places, where man has always sought God. This high idea of the relations of man with God, of which so few minds, even after him, have been capable, is summed up in a prayer which he taught to his disciples :—

"Our Father which art in heaven, hallowed be thy name; thy kingdom come; thy will be done on earth as it is in heaven. Give us this day our daily bread. Forgive us our trespasses, as we forgive those who trespass against us. Lead us not into temptation; deliver us from the evil one." He insisted particularly upon the idea that the heavenly Father knows better than we what we need, and that we almost sin against him in asking him for this or that particular thing.

Jesus in this only carried out the consequences of the great principles which Judaism had established, but which the official classes of the nation tended more and more to despise. The Greek and Roman prayers were almost always mere egotistical verbiage. Never had Pagan priest said to the faithful, " If thou bring thy offering to the altar, and there rememberest that thy brother hath aught against thee; leave there thy gift before the altar, and go thy way; first be reconciled with thy brother, and then come and offer thy gift." Alone in antiquity, the Jewish prophets, especially Isaiah, had, in their antipathy to the priesthood, caught a glimpse of the true nature of the worship man owes to God. " To what purpose is the multitude of your sacrifices unto me : I am full of the burnt-offerings of rams, and the fat of fed beasts; and I delight not in the blood of bullocks, or of lambs, or of he-goats. . . . Incense is an abomination unto me; for your hands are full of blood; cease to do evil, learn to do well, seek judgment, and then come." In later times, certain doctors, Simeon the just, Jesus, son of Sirach, Hillel, almost reached this point, and declared that the sum of the Law was righteousness. Philo, in the Judæo-Egyptian world, attained at the same time as Jesus ideas of a high moral sanctity, the consequences of which was the disregard of the observances of the Law. Shemaïa and Abtalion also more than once proved themselves to be very jealous casuists. Rabbi Johanan ere long placed works of mercy above even the study of the Law ! Jesus alone, however, proclaimed these principles in an effective manner. Never has any one been less a priest than Jesus, never a greater enemy of forms, which stifle religion under the pretext of protecting it. By this we are all his disciples and his successors; by this he has laid the eternal foundation-stone of true religion; and if religion is essential to humanity, he has by this deserved the Divine rank the world has accorded to him. An absolutely new idea, the idea of a worship founded on purity of heart, and on human brother-hood, through him entered into the world—an idea so elevated that the Christian Church ought to make it its distinguishing feature, but an idea which, in our days, only few minds are capable of embodying.

An exquisite sympathy with nature furnished him each moment with expressive images. Sometimes a remarkable ingenuity, which we call wit, adorned his aphorisms; at other times their liveliness consisted in the happy use of popular proverbs. " How wilt thou say to thy brother,

Let me pull out the mote out of thine eye; and, behold, a beam is in thine own eye? Thou hypocrite, first cast out the beam out of thine own eye, and then thou shalt see clearly to cast out the mote out of thy brother's eye."

These lessons, long hidden in the heart of the young Master, soon gathered around him a few disciples. The spirit of the time favoured small churches; it was the period of the Essenes or Therapeutæ. Rabbis, each having his distinctive teaching, Shemaïa, Abtalion, Hillel, Shammai, Judas the Gaulonite, Gamaliel, and many others whose maxims form the Talmud, appeared on all sides. They wrote very little; the Jewish doctors of this time did not write books; everything was done by conversations, and in public lessons, to which it was sought to give a form easily remembered. The proclamation by the young Carpenter of Nazareth of these maxims, for the most part already generally known, but which, thanks to him, were to regenerate the world, was therefore no striking event. It was only one Rabbi more (it is true, the most charming of all), and around him some young men, eager to hear him, and thirsting for knowledge. It requires time to command the attention of men. As yet there were no Christians; though true Christianity was founded, and, doubtless, it was never more perfect than at this first period. Jesus added to it nothing durable afterwards. Indeed, in one sense, he compromised it; for every movement, in order to triumph, must make sacrifices; we never come from the contest of life unscathed.

To conceive the good, in fact, is not sufficient; it must be made to succeed among men. To accomplish this less pure paths must be followed. Certainly, if the Gospel was confined to some chapters of Matthew and Luke, it would be more perfect, and would not now be open to so many objections; but would Jesus have converted the world without miracles? If he had died at the period of his career we have now reached, there would not have been in his life a single page to wound us; but, greater in the eyes of God, he would have remained unknown to men; he would have been lost in the crowd of great unknown spirits, himself the greatest of all; the truth would not have been promulgated, and the world would not have profited from the great moral superiority with which his Father had endowed him. Jesus, son of Sirach, and Hillel had uttered aphorisms almost as exalted as those of Jesus. Hillel, however, will never be accounted the true founder of Christianity. In morals, as in art, precept is nothing;

practice is everything. The idea which is hidden in a picture of Raphael is of little moment; it is the picture itself which is prized. So, too, in morals, truth is but little prized when it is a mere sentiment, and only attains its full value when realised in the world as fact. Men of indifferent morality have written very good maxims. Very virtuous men, on the other hand, have done nothing to perpetuate in the world the tradition of virtue. The palm is his who has been mighty both in words and in works, who has discerned the good, and at the price of his blood has caused its triumph. Jesus, from this double point of view, is without equal; his glory remains entire, and will ever be renewed.

CHAPTER VI

JOHN THE BAPTIST—VISIT OF JESUS TO JOHN, AND HIS
   ABODE IN THE DESERT OF JUDEA—ADOPTION OF THE
   BAPTISM OF JOHN

An extraordinary man, whose position, from the absence
of documentary evidence, remains to us in some degree
enigmatical, appeared about this time, and was unquestionably to some extent connected with Jesus. This connection tended rather to make the young Prophet of
Nazareth deviate from his path; but it suggested many
important accessories to his religious institution, and, at
all events, furnished a very strong authority to his disciples
in recommending their Master in the eyes of a certain class
of Jews.

About the year 28 of our era (the fifteenth year of the
reign of Tiberius) there spread throughout Palestine the
reputation of a certain Johanan, or John, a young ascetic
full of zeal and enthusiasm. John was of the priestly race,
and born, it seems, at Juttah, near Hebron, or at Hebron
itself. Hebron, the patriarchal city *par excellence*, situated
at a short distance from the desert of Judea, and within a
few hours' journey of the great desert of Arabia, was at
this period what it is to-day—one of the bulwarks of Semitic
ideas, in their most austere form. From his infancy John
was *Nazir*—that is to say, subjected by vow to certain
abstinences. The desert by which he was, so to speak,
surrounded early attracted him. He led there the life of
a Yogi of India, clothed with skins or stuffs of camels'
hair, having for food only locusts and wild honey. A certain number of disciples were grouped around him, sharing
his life and studying his severe doctrine. We might imagine
ourselves transported to the banks of the Ganges, if particular traits had not revealed in this recluse the last
descendant of the great prophets of Israel.

From the time that the Jewish nation had begun to
reflect upon its destiny with a kind of despair, the imagination of the people had reverted with much complacency to

69

the ancient prophets. Now, of all the personages of the past, the remembrance of whom came like the dreams of a troubled night to awaken and agitate the people, the greatest was Elias. This giant of the prophets, in his rough solitude of Carmel, sharing the life of savage beasts, dwelling in the hollows of the rocks, whence he came like a thunderbolt to make and unmake kings, had become, by successive transformations, a sort of superhuman being, sometimes visible, sometimes invisible, and as one who had not tasted death. It was generally believed that Elias would return and restore Israel. The austere life which he had led, the terrible remembrances he had left behind him—the impression of which is still powerful in the East—the sombre image which, even in our own time, causes trembling and death—all this mythology, full of vengeance and terror, vividly struck the mind of the people, and stamped as with a birth-mark all the creations of the popular mind. Whoever aspired to act powerfully upon the people must imitate Elias; and, as solitary life had been the essential characteristic of this prophet, they were accustomed to conceive "the man of God" as a hermit. They imagined that all the holy personages had had their days of penitence, of solitude, and of austerity. The retreat to the desert thus became the condition and the prelude of high destinies.

No doubt this thought of imitation had occupied John's mind. The anchorite life, so opposed to the spirit of the ancient Jewish people, and with which the vows, such as those of the Nazirs and the Rechabites, had no relation, pervaded all parts of Judea. The Essenes or Therapeutæ were grouped near the birthplace of John, on the eastern shores of the Dead Sea. It was imagined that the chiefs of sects ought to be recluses, having rules and institutions of their own, like the founders of religious orders. The teachers of the young were also at times species of anchorites, somewhat resembling the *gourous* of Brahminism. In fact, might there not in this be a remote influence of the *mounis* of India? Perhaps, some of those wandering Buddhist monks who overran the world, as the first Franciscans did in later times, preaching by their actions and converting people who knew not their language, might have turned their steps towards Judea, as they certainly did towards Syria and Babylon? On this point we have no certainty. Babylon had become for some time a true focus of Buddhism. Boudasp (Bodhisattva) was reputed a wise Chaldean, and the founder of Sabeism. *Sabeism* was, as its etymology indicates, *baptism*—that is to say, the religion of many baptisms—the origin of the sect still existing called "Christians of St. John," or Mendaites, which the Arabs call *el-Mogtasila*, "the Baptists." It is difficult to unravel these vague analogies. The sects floating between Judaism, Christianity, Baptism, and Sabeism, which we find in the region beyond the Jordan during the first centuries of our era, present to criticism the most singular problem, in consequence of the confused accounts of them which have come down to us. We may believe, at all events, that many of the external practices of John, of the Essenes, and of the Jewish spiritual teachers of this time, were derived from influences then but recently received from the far East. The fundamental practice which characterised the sect of John, and gave it its name, has always had its centre in lower Chaldea, and constitutes a religion which is perpetuated there to the present day.

This practice was baptism, or total immersion. Ablutions were already familiar to the Jews, as they were to all religions of the East. The Essenes had given them a peculiar extension. Baptism had become an ordinary ceremony on the introduction of proselytes into the bosom of the Jewish religion, a sort of initiatory rite. Never before John the Baptist, however, had either this importance or this form been given to immersion. John had fixed the scene of his activity in that part of the desert of Judea which is in the neighbourhood of the Dead Sea. At the periods when he administered baptism, he went to the banks of the Jordan, either to Bethany or Bethabara, upon the eastern shore, probably opposite to Jericho, or to a place called Ænon, or "the Fountains," near Salim, where there was much water. Considerable crowds, especially of the tribe of Judah, hastened to him to be baptised. In a few months he thus became one of the most influential men in Judea, and acquired much importance in the general estimation.

The people took him for a prophet, and many imagined that it was Elias who had risen again. The belief in these resurrections was widely spread : it was thought that God would raise from the tomb certain of the ancient prophets to guide Israel towards its final destiny. Others held John to be the Messiah himself, although he made no such pretension. The priests and the scribes, opposed to this revival of prophetism, and the constant enemies of enthusiasts, despised him. But the popularity of the Baptist awed them, and they dared not speak against him. It was a victory which the ideas of the multitude gained over the priestly aristocracy. When the chief priests were compelled to declare themselves explicitly on this point, they were considerably embarrassed.

Baptism with John was only a sign destined to make an impression, and to prepare the minds of the people for some great movement. No doubt he was possessed in the highest degree with the Messianic hope, and that his principal action was in accordance with it. "Repent," said he "for the kingdom of heaven is at hand." He announced a "great wrath"—that is to say, terrible calamities which should come to pass—and declared that the axe was already laid at the root of the tree, and that the tree would soon be cast into the fire. He represented the Messiah with a fan in his hand, collecting the good wheat and burning the chaff. Repentance (of which baptism was the type), the giving of alms, the reformation of habits, were, in John's view, the great means of preparation for the coming events, though we do not know exactly in what light he conceived them. It is, however, certain that he preached with much power against the same adversaries as Jesus, against rich priests, the Pharisees, the doctors—in one word, against official Judaism; and that, like Jesus, he was specially welcomed by the despised classes. He made no account of the title "son of Abraham," and said that God could raise up sons unto Abraham from the stones of the road. It does not seem that he possessed even the germ of the great idea which led to the triumph of Jesus—the idea of a pure religion; but he powerfully served this idea in substituting a private rite for the legal ceremonies which required priests, as the Flagellants of the Middle Ages were the precursors of the Reformation, by depriving the official clergy of the monopoly of the sacraments and of absolution. The general tone of his sermons was stern and severe. The expressions which he used against his adversaries appear to have been most violent. It was a harsh and continuous invective. It is probable that he did not remain quite a stranger to politics. Josephus, who, through his teacher Banou, was brought into almost direct connection with John, suggests as much by his ambiguous words, and the catastrophe which put an end to John's life seems to imply this. His disciples led a very austere life, fasted often, and affected a sad and anxious demeanour. We have at times glimpses of communism—the rich man being ordered to share all that he had with the poor; the poor man appeared as the one who would be specially benefited by the kingdom of God.

Although the centre of John's action was Judea, his fame quickly penetrated to Galilee and reached Jesus, who, by his first discourses, had already gathered around himself a small circle of hearers. Enjoying as yet little authority, and doubtless impelled by the desire to see a teacher whose instruction had so much in common with his own, Jesus quitted Galilee, and repaired with his small group of disciples to John. The newcomers were baptised like every one else. John welcomed this group of Galilean disciples, and did not object to their remaining distinct from his own. The two teachers were young; they had many ideas in common; they loved one another, and publicly vied with each other in exhibitions of kindly feeling. At the first glance, such a fact surprises us in John the Baptist, and we are tempted to call it in question. Humility has never been a feature of strong Jewish minds. It might have been expected that a character so stubborn, a sort of Lamennais always irritated, would be very passionate, and suffer neither rivalry nor half adhesion. But this manner of viewing things rests upon a false conception of the person of John. We imagine him an old man; he was, on the contrary, of the same age as Jesus, and very young according to the ideas of the time. In mental development, he was the brother rather than the father of Jesus. The two young enthusiasts, full of the same hopes and the same hatreds, were able to make common cause, and mutually to support each other. Certainly an aged teacher, seeing a man without celebrity approach him, and maintain towards him an aspect of independence, would have rebelled; we have scarcely an example of a leader of a school receiving with eagerness his future successor. But youth is capable of any sacrifice, and we may admit that John, having recognised in Jesus a spirit akin to his own, accepted him without any personal reservation. These good relations became afterwards the starting-point of a whole system developed by the evangelists, which consisted in giving the Divine mission of Jesus the primary basis of the attestation of John. Such was the degree of authority acquired by the Baptist that it was not thought possible to find in the world a better guarantee. But far from John abdicating in favour of Jesus, Jesus, during all the time that he passed with him, recognised him as his superior, and only developed his own genius with timidity.

It seems, in fact, that, notwithstanding his profound originality, Jesus, during some weeks at least, was the imitator of John. His way, as yet, was not clear before

him. At all times, moreover, Jesus yielded much to
opinion, and adopted many things which were not in exact
accordance with his own ideas, or for which he cared little,
merely because they were popular; but these accessories
never injured his principal idea, and were always subordinate to it. Baptism had been brought by John into
very great favour; Jesus thought himself obliged to do
like John; therefore he baptised, and his disciples baptised
also. No doubt he accompanied baptism with preaching,
similar to that of John. The Jordan was thus covered on
all sides with Baptists, whose discourses were more or less
successful. The pupil soon equalled the master, and his
baptism was much sought after. There was on this subject some jealousy among the disciples : the disciples of
John came to complain to him of the growing success of
the young Galilean, whose baptism would, they thought,
soon supplant his own. But the two teachers remained
superior to this meanness. The superiority of John was,
besides, too indisputable for Jesus, still little known, to
think of contesting it. Jesus only wished to increase under
John's protection; and thought himself obliged, in order
to gain the multitude, to employ the external means which
had given John such astonishing success. When he recom-
menced to preach after John's arrest, the first words put
into his mouth are but the repetition of one of the familiar
phrases of the Baptist. Many other of John's expressions
may be found repeated verbally in the discourses of Jesus.
The two schools appear to have lived long on good terms
with each other; and after the death of John, Jesus, as
his trusty friend, was one of the first to be informed of the
event.

John, in fact, was soon cut short in his prophetic career.
Like the ancient Jewish prophets, he was, in the highest
degree, a censurer of the established authorities. The
extreme vivacity with which he expressed himself at their
expense could not fail to bring him into trouble. In Judea,
John does not appear to have been disturbed by Pilate;
but in Perea, beyond the Jordan, he came into the territory
of Antipas. This tyrant was uneasy at the political leaven
which was so little concealed by John in his preaching.
The great assemblages of men gathered around the Baptist,
by religious and patriotic enthusiasm, gave rise to suspicion. An entirely personal grievance was also added to
these motives of State, and rendered the death of the
austere censor inevitable.

One of the most strongly marked characters of this

tragical family of the Herods was Herodias, grand-daughter of Herod the Great. Violent, ambitious, and passionate, she detested Judaism, and despised its laws. She had been married, probably against her will, to her uncle Herod, son of Mariamne, whom Herod the Great had disinherited, and who never played any public part. The inferior position of her husband in respect to the other persons of the family gave her no peace; she determined to be sovereign at whatever cost. Antipas was the instrument of whom she made use. This feeble man, having become desperately enamoured of her, promised to marry her, and to repudiate his first wife, daughter of Hareth, king of Petra, and emir of the neighbouring tribes of Perea. The Arabian princess, receiving a hint of this design, resolved to fly. Concealing her intention, she pretended that she wished to make a journey to Machero, in her father's territory, and caused herself to be conducted thither by the officers of Antipas.

Makaur, or Machero, was a colossal fortress built by Alexander Jannaeus, and rebuilt by Herod, in one of the most abrupt wâdys to the east of the Dead Sea. It was a wild and desolate country, filled with strange legends, and believed to be haunted by demons. The fortress was just on the boundary of the lands of Hareth and of Antipas. At that time it was in the possession of Hareth. The latter, having been warned, had prepared everything for the flight of his daughter, who was conducted from tribe to tribe to Petra.

The almost incestuous union of Antipas and Herodias then took place. The Jewish laws on marriage were a constant rock of offence between the irreligious family of the Herods and the strict Jews. The members of this numerous and rather isolated dynasty being obliged to marry among themselves, frequent violations of the limits prescribed by the Law necessarily took place. John, in energetically blaming Antipas, was the echo of the general feeling. This was more than sufficient to decide the latter to follow up his suspicions. He caused the Baptist to be arrested, and ordered him to be shut up in the fortress of Machero, which he had probably seized after the departure of the daughter of Hareth.

More timid than cruel, Antipas did not desire to put him to death. According to certain rumours, he feared a popular sedition. According to another version, he had taken pleasure in listening to the prisoner, and these conversations had thrown him into great perplexities. It is certain that the detention was prolonged, and that John, in his prison, preserved an extended influence. He corresponded with his disciples, and we find him again in connection with Jesus. His faith in the near approach of the Messiah only became firmer; he followed with attention the movements outside, and sought to discover in them the signs favourable to the accomplishment of the hopes which he cherished.

CHAPTER VII

͏EVELOPMENT OF THE IDEAS OF JESUS RESPECTING THE KINGDOM OF GOD

͏p to the arrest of John, which took place about the summer ͏ the year 29, Jesus did not quit the neighbourhood of the ͏ead Sea and of the Jordan. An abode in the desert of ͏dea was generally considered as the preparation for ͏eat things, as a sort of " retreat " before public acts. ͏sus followed in this respect the example of others, and ͏ssed forty days with no other companions than savage ͏easts, maintaining a rigorous fast. The disciples specu- ͏ted much concerning this sojourn. The desert was ͏pularly regarded as the residence of demons. There ͏ist in the world few regions more desolate, more abandoned ͏y God, more shut out from life, than the rocky declivity ͏hich forms the western shore of the Dead Sea. It was ͏elieved that during the time which Jesus passed in this ͏ightful country he had gone through terrible trials; that ͏atan had assailed him with his illusions or tempted him ͏ith seductive promises; that afterwards, in order to ͏compense him for his victory, the angels had come to ͏inister to him.

͏It was probably in coming from the desert that Jesus ͏arnt of the arrest of John the Baptist. He had no longer ͏ny reason to prolong his stay in a country which was ͏artly strange to him. Perhaps he feared also being involved ͏ the severities exercised towards John, and did not wish ͏o expose himself at a time in which, seeing the little celebrity ͏e had, his death could in no way serve the progress of his ͏eas. He regained Galilee, his true home, ripened by an ͏nportant experience, and having, through contact with ͏ great man very different from himself, acquired a ͏onsciousness of his own originality.

͏On the whole, the influence of John had been more hurtful ͏han useful to Jesus. It checked his development; for ͏verything leads us to believe that he had, when he ͏escended towards the Jordan, ideas superior to those of

D

John, and that it was by a sort of concession that he incline
for a time towards baptism. Perhaps if the Baptist, whos
authority it would have been difficult for him to escape
had remained free, Jesus would not have been able to throw
off the yoke of external rites and ceremonies, and woul
then, no doubt, have remained an unknown Jewish sectary
for the world would not have abandoned its old ceremonie
merely for others of a different kind. It has been by the powe
of a religion, free from all external forms, that Christianit
has attracted elevated minds. The Baptist once im-
prisoned, his school was soon diminished, and Jesus foun
himself left to his own impulses. The only things he owe
to John were lessons in preaching and in popular action
From this moment, in fact, he preached with greate
power, and spoke to the multitude with authority.

It seems also that his sojourn with John had, not so muc
by the influence of the Baptist as by the natural progres
of his own thought, considerably ripened his ideas on " th
kingdom of heaven." His watchword henceforth is th
" good tidings," the announcement that the kingdom of Go
is at hand. Jesus is no longer simply a delightful moralis
aspiring to express sublime lessons in short and livel
aphorisms; he is the transcendent revolutionary, wh
essays to renovate the world from its very basis, and t
establish upon earth the ideal which he had conceived
" To await the kingdom of God " is henceforth synonymou
with being a disciple of Jesus. This phrase, " kingdom c
God," or " kingdom of heaven," was, as we have said
already long familiar to the Jews. But Jesus gave it
moral sense, a social application, which even the author c
the book of Daniel, in his apocalyptic enthusiasm, ha
scarcely dared to imagine.

He declared that in the present world evil is the reignin
power. Satan is " the prince of this world," and every
thing obeys him. The kings kill the prophets. Th
priests and the doctors do not that which they comman
others to do; the righteous are persecuted, and the onl
portion of the good is weeping. The " world " is in th
manner the enemy of God and his saints; but God wi
awaken and avenge his saints. The day is at hand, for th
abomination is at its height. The reign of goodness wi
have its turn.

The advent of this reign of goodness will be a great an
sudden revolution. The world will seem to be turne
upside down : the actual state being bad, in order t
represent the future, it suffices to conceive nearly the revers

f that which exists. The first shall be last. A new order
hall govern humanity. Now the good and the bad are
nixed, like the tares and the good grain in a field. The
naster lets them grow together; but the hour of violent
eparation will arrive. The kingdom of God will be as the
asting of a great net, which gathers both good and bad fish;
he good are preserved, and the rest are thrown away.
The germ of this great revolution will not be recognisable
n its beginning. It will be like a grain of mustard-seed,
which is the smallest of seeds, but which, thrown into the
arth, becomes a tree under the foliage of which the birds
epose; or it will be like the leaven which, deposited in the
neal, makes the whole to ferment. A series of parables,
ften obscure, was designed to express the suddenness of
his advent, its apparent injustice, and its inevitable and
nal character.

Who was to establish this kingdom of God? Let us
emember that the first thought of Jesus, a thought so
eeply rooted in him that it had probably no beginning,
nd formed part of his very being, was that he was the Son
f God, the friend of his Father, the doer of his will. The
nswer of Jesus to such a question could not therefore be
oubtful. The persuasion that he was to establish the
ingdom of God took absolute possession of his mind. He
egarded himself as the universal reformer. The heavens,
he earth, the whole of nature, madness, disease, and death,
vere but his instruments. In his paroxysm of heroic will
e believed himself all-powerful. If the earth would not
ubmit to this supreme transformation, it would be broken
p, purified by fire, and by the breath of God. A new
eaven would be created, and the entire world would be
eopled with the angels of God.

A radical revolution, embracing even nature itself, was
he fundamental idea of Jesus. Henceforward, without
oubt, he renounced politics; the example of Judas, the
Gaulonite, had shown him the inutility of popular seditions.
He never thought of revolting against the Romans and
etrarchs. His was not the unbridled and anarchical
rinciple of the Gaulonite. His submission to the estab-
shed powers, though really derisive, was in appearance
omplete. He paid tribute to Cæsar, in order to avoid
isturbance. Liberty and right were not of this world,
vhy should he trouble his life with vain anxieties? Despis-
ng the earth, and convinced that the present world was
ot worth caring for, he took refuge in his ideal kingdom;
e established the great doctrine of transcendent disdain,

the true doctrine of liberty of souls, which alone can giv[e]
peace. But he had not yet said, " My kingdom is not o[f]
this world." Much darkness mixed itself with even h[is]
most correct views. Sometimes strange temptations crosse[d]
his mind. In the desert of Judea Satan had offered hi[m]
the kingdoms of the earth. Not knowing the power of th[e]
Roman empire, he might, with the enthusiasm there wa[s]
in the heart of Judea, and which ended soon after in s[o]
terrible an outbreak, hope to establish a kingdom by th[e]
number and the daring of his partisans. Many time[s]
perhaps, the supreme question presented itself—will th[e]
kingdom of God be realised by force or by gentleness, b[y]
revolt or by patience? One day, it is said, the simple me[n]
of Galilee wished to carry him away and make him king[,]
but Jesus fled into the mountain and remained there som[e]
time alone. His noble nature preserved him from th[e]
error which would have made him an agitator, or a chief o[f]
rebels, a Theudas or a Barkokeba.

The revolution he wished to effect was always a mora[l]
revolution; but he had not yet begun to trust to the angel[s]
and the last trumpet for its execution. It was upon me[n]
and by the aid of men themselves that he wished to act. [A]
visionary who had no other idea than the proximity of th[e]
last judgment would not have had this care for the ameliora[-]
tion of man, and would not have given utterance to th[e]
finest moral teaching that humanity has received. Muc[h]
vagueness no doubt tinged his ideas, and it was rather [a]
noble feeling than a fixed design that urged him to th[e]
sublime work which was realised by him, though in a ver[y]
different manner to what he imagined.

It was indeed the kingdom of God, or, in other words, th[e]
kingdom of the Spirit, which he founded; and if Jesus[,]
from the bosom of his Father, sees his work bear fruit i[n]
the world, he may indeed say with truth, " This is what [I]
have desired." That which Jesus founded, that which wil[l]
remain eternally his, allowing for the imperfections whic[h]
mix themselves with everything realised by humanity, i[s]
the doctrine of the liberty of the soul. Greece had alread[y]
had beautiful ideas on this subject. Various Stoics ha[d]
learnt how to be free even under a tyrant. But in genera[l]
the ancient world had regarded liberty as attached t[o]
certain political forms; freedom was personified in Har[-]
modius and Aristogiton, Brutus and Cassius. The tru[e]
Christian enjoys more real freedom; here below he is a[n]
exile. What matters it to him who is the transitory
governor of this earth, which is not his home? Liberty

or him is truth.   Jesus did not know history sufficiently
o understand that such a doctrine came most opportunely
t the moment when republican liberty ended, and when the
mall municipal constitutions of antiquity were absorbed in
he unity of the Roman empire.   But his admirable good
ense, and the truly prophetic instinct which he had of his
mission, guided him with marvellous certainty.   By the
entence, " Render unto Cæsar the things which are Cæsar's,
nd to God the things which are God's," he created some-
hing apart from politics, a refuge for souls in the midst of
he empire of brute force.   Assuredly such a doctrine had
ts dangers.   To establish as a principle that we must
ecognise the legitimacy of a power by the inscription on its
oins, to proclaim that the perfect man pays tribute with
orn and without question, was to destroy republicanism
n the ancient form, and to favour all tyranny.   Chris-
ianity, in this sense, has contributed much to weaken the
ense of duty of the citizen, and to deliver the world into the
bsolute power of existing circumstances.   But in constitut-
ng an immense free association, which during three hundred
years was able to dispense with politics, Christianity amply
ompensated for the wrong it had done to civic virtues.   The
power of the State was limited to the things of earth ; the
mind was freed, or at least the terrible rod of Roman
omnipotence was broken for ever.

The man who is especially preoccupied with the duties of
public life does not readily forgive those who attach little
importance to his party quarrels.   He especially blames
those who subordinate political to social questions, and
profess a sort of indifference for the former.   In one sense
he is right, for exclusive power is prejudicial to the good
government of human affairs.   But what progress have
" parties " been able to effect in the general morality of our
species ?   If Jesus, instead of founding his heavenly
kingdom, had gone to Rome, had expended his energies in
conspiring against Tiberius, or in regretting Germanicus,
what would have become of the world ?   As an austere
republican, or zealous patriot, he would not have arrested
the great current of the affairs of his age ; but, in declaring
that politics are insignificant, he has revealed to the world
this truth, that one's country is not everything, and that
the man is before, and higher than, the citizen.

Our principles of positive science are offended by the
dreams contained in the programme of Jesus.   We know
the history of the earth ; cosmical revolutions of the kind
which Jesus expected are only produced by geological or

astronomical causes, the connection of which with the spiritual things has never yet been demonstrated. But in order to be just to great originators, they must not be judged by the prejudices in which they have shared. Columbus discovered America, though starting from very erroneous ideas; Newton believed his foolish explanation of the Apocalypse to be as true as his system of the world. Shall we place an ordinary man of our time above a Francis d'Assisi, a St. Bernard, a Joan of Arc, or a Luther, because he is free from errors which these last have professed? Should we measure men by the correctness of their ideas of physics, and by the more or less exact knowledge which they possess of the true system of the world? Let us understand better the position of Jesus and that which made his power. The Deism of the eighteenth century, and a certain kind of Protestantism, have accustomed us to consider the founder of the Christian faith only as a great moralist, a benefactor of mankind. We see nothing more in the Gospel than good maxims; we throw a prudent veil over the strange intellectual state in which it was originated. There are even persons who regret that the French Revolution departed more than once from principles, and that it was not brought about by wise and moderate men. Let us not impose our petty and commonplace ideas on these extraordinary movements so far above our everyday life. Let us continue to admire the " morality of the Gospel "—let us suppress in our religious teachings the chimera which was its soul; but do not let us believe that with the simple ideas of happiness, or of individual morality, we stir the world. The idea of Jesus was much more profound; it was the most revolutionary idea ever formed in a human brain; it should be taken in its totality, and not with those timid suppressions which deprive it of precisely that which has rendered it efficacious for the regeneration of humanity.

The ideal is ever a Utopia. When we wish nowadays to represent the Christ of the modern conscience, the consoler, and the judge of the new times, what course do we take? That which Jesus himself did eighteen hundred and thirty years ago. We suppose the conditions of the real world quite other than what they are; we represent a moral liberator breaking without weapons the chains of the negro, ameliorating the condition of the poor, and giving liberty to oppressed nations. We forget that this implies the subversion of the world, the climate of Virginia and that of Congo modified, the blood and the race of millions of men changed, our social complications restored to a chimerical

implicity, and the political stratifications of Europe
.isplaced from their natural order.   The "restitution of all
hings" desired by Jesus was not more difficult.   This new
arth, this new heaven, this new Jerusalem which comes
rom above, this cry : "Behold I make all things new!"
re the common characteristics of reformers.   The contrast
f the ideal with the sad reality always produces in mankind
hose revolts against unimpassioned reason which inferior
ninds regard as folly, till the day arrives in which they
riumph, and in which those who have opposed them are
he first to recognise their reasonableness.

That there may have been a contradiction between the
belief in the approaching end of the world and the general
moral system of Jesus, conceived in prospect of a permanent state of humanity, nearly analogous to that which
now exists, no one will attempt to deny.   It was exactly
his contradiction that insured the success of his work.
The millenarian alone would have done nothing lasting; the
moralist alone would have done nothing powerful.   The
millenarianism gave the impulse; the moralist insured
the future.   Hence Christianity united the two conditions
of great success in this world—a revolutionary starting-
point and the possibility of continuous life.   Everything
which is intended to succeed ought to respond to these two
wants; for the world seeks both to change and to last.
Jesus, at the same time that he announced an unparalleled
subversion in human affairs, proclaimed the principles
upon which society has reposed for eighteen hundred years.

That which in fact distinguishes Jesus from the agitators
of his time, and from those of all ages, is his perfect idealism.
Jesus, in some respects, was an anarchist, for he had no idea
of civil government.   That government seems to him
purely and simply an abuse.   He spoke of it in vague
terms, and as a man of the people who had no idea of
politics.   Every magistrate appeared to him a natural
enemy of the people of God; he prepared his disciples for
contests with the civil powers, without thinking for a
moment that there was anything to be ashamed of.   But he
never shows any desire to put himself in the place of the
rich and the powerful.   He wishes to annihilate riches and
power, but not to appropriate them.   He predicts persecution and all kinds of punishment to his disciples; but never
once does the thought of armed resistance appear.   The
idea of being all-powerful by suffering and resignation, and
of triumphing over force by purity of heart, is indeed an
idea peculiar to Jesus.   Jesus is not a spiritualist, for to

him everything tended to a palpable realisation; he had no
the least notion of a soul separated from the body. But h
is a perfect idealist, matter being only to him the sign of th
idea, and the real, the living expression of that which doe
not appear.

To whom should we turn, to whom should we trust t
establish the kingdom of God? The mind of Jesus on thi
point never hesitated. That which is highly esteemed
among men is abomination in the sight of God. The
founders of the kingdom of God are the simple. Not the
rich, not the learned, not priests; but women, commor
people, the humble, and the young. The great characteristic
of the Messiah is that " the poor have the gospel preached
to them." The idyllic and gentle nature of Jesus here
resumed the superiority. A great social revolution, ir
which rank will be overturned, in which all authority in this
world will be humiliated, was his dream. The world wil
not believe him; the world will kill him. But his disciples
will not be of the world. They will be a little flock of the
humble and the simple, who will conquer by their very
humility. The idea which has made " Christian " the
antithesis of " worldly " has its full justification in the
thoughts of the master.

CHAPTER VIII

JESUS AT CAPERNAUM

BESET by an idea, gradually becoming more and more imperious and exclusive, Jesus proceeds henceforth with a kind of fatal impassibility in the path marked out by his astonishing genius and the extraordinary circumstances in which he lived. Hitherto he had only communicated his thoughts to a few persons secretly attracted to him; henceforward his teaching was sought after by the public. He was about thirty years of age. The little group of hearers who had accompanied him to John the Baptist had, doubtless, increased, and perhaps some disciples of John had attached themselves to him. It was with this first nucleus of a Church that he boldly announced, on his return into Galilee, the "good tidings of the kingdom of God." This kingdom was approaching, and it was he, Jesus, who was that "Son of Man" whom Daniel had beheld in his vision as the divine herald of the last and supreme revelation.

We must remember that, in the Jewish ideas, which were averse to art and mythology, the simple form of man had a superiority over that of *Cherubs*, and of the fantastic animals which the imagination of the people, since it had been subjected to the influence of Assyria, had ranged around the Divine Majesty. Already, in Ezekiel, the Being seated on the supreme throne, far above the monsters of the mysterious chariot, the great revealer of prophetic visions, had the figure of a man. In the book of Daniel, in the midst of the vision of the empires, represented by animals, at the moment when the great judgment commences, and when the books are opened, a Being "like unto a Son of Man" advances towards the Ancient of days, who confers on him the power to judge the world, and to govern it for eternity. *Son of Man*, in the Semitic languages, especially in the Aramean dialects, is a simple synonym of *man*. But this chief passage of Daniel struck the mind; the words, *Son of Man*, became, at least, in certain schools, one of the titles of the Messiah, regarded as judge of the world, and as king of the new era about to be inaugurated. The application which Jesus made of it to himself was therefore the proclamation of his Messiahship, and the affirmation of the coming catastrophe in which he was to figure as judge, clothed with the full powers which had been delegated to him by the Ancient of days.

The success of the teaching of the new prophet was this time decisive. A group of men and women, all characterised by the same spirit of juvenile frankness and simple innocence, adhered to him, and said, " Thou art the Messiah." As the Messiah was to be the son of David, they naturally conceded him this title, which was synonymous with the former. Jesus allowed it with pleasure to be given to him, although it might cause him some embarrassment, his birth being well known. The name which he preferred himself was that of " Son of Man," an apparently humble title, but one which connected itself directly with the Messianic hopes. This was the title by which he designated himself, and he used " The Son of Man " as synonymous with the pronoun " I," which he avoided. But he was never thus addressed, doubtless because the name in question would be fully applicable to him only on the day of his future appearance.

His centre of action, at this epoch of his life, was the little town of Capernaum, situated on the shore of the lake of Gennesareth. The name of Capernaum, containing the word *caphar*, " village," seems to designate a small town of the ancient character, in opposition to the great towns built according to the Roman method, like Tiberias. That name was so little known that Josephus, in one passage of his writings, takes it for the name of a fountain, the fountain having more celebrity than the village situated near it. Like Nazareth, Capernaum had no history, and had in no way participated in the profane movement favoured by the Herods. Jesus was much attached to this town, and made it a second home. Soon after his return he attempted to commence his work at Nazareth, but without success. He could not perform any miracle there, according to the simple remark of one of his biographers. The knowledge which existed there about his family, not an important one, injured his authority too much. People could not regard as the son of David one whose brother, sister, and brother-in-law they saw every day, and it is remarkable, besides, that his family were strongly opposed to him, and plainly refused to believe in his mission. The Nazarenes, much more violent, wished, it is said, to kill him by throwing him from a steep rock. Jesus aptly remarked that this treatment was the fate of all great men, and applied to himself the proverb, " No one is a prophet in his own country."

This check far from discouraged him. He returned to Capernaum, where he met with a much more favourable reception, and from thence he organised a series of missions among the small surrounding towns. The people of this beautiful and fertile country were scarcely ever assembled except on Saturday. This was the day which he chose for his teaching. At that time each town had its synagogue, or place of meeting. This was a rectangular room, rather small, with a portico, decorated in the Greek style. The Jews, not having any architecture of their own, never cared to give these edifices an original style. The remains of many ancient synagogues still exist in Galilee. They are all constructed of large and good materials; but their style is somewhat paltry, in consequence of the profusion of floral ornaments, foliage, and twisted work, which characterise the Jewish buildings. In the interior there were seats, a chair for public reading, and a closet to contain the sacred rolls. These edifices, which had nothing of the character of a temple, were the centre of the whole Jewish life. There the people assembled on the Sabbath for prayer and reading of the law and the prophets. As Judaism, except in Jerusalem, had, properly speaking, no clergy, the first comer stood up, gave the lessons of the day (*parasha* and *haphtara*), and added thereto a *midrash*, or entirely personal commentary, in which he expressed his own ideas. This was the origin of the " homily," the finished model of which we find in the small treatises of Philo. The audience had the right of making objections and putting questions to the reader; so that the meeting soon degenerated into a kind of free assembly. It had a president, " elders," a *hazzan*—*i.e.*, a recognised reader, or apparitor—deputies, who were secretaries or messengers, and conducted the correspondence between one synagogue and another, a *shammash*, or sacristan. The synagogues were thus really little independent republics, having an extensive jurisdiction. Like all municipal corporations, up to an advanced period of the Roman empire, they issued honorary decrees, voted resolutions, which had the force of law for the community, and ordained corporal punishments, of which the *hazzan* was the ordinary executor.

With the extreme activity of mind which has always characterised the Jews, such an institution, notwithstanding the arbitrary rigours it tolerated, could not fail to give rise to very animated discussions. Thanks to the synagogues,

Judaism has been able to sustain intact eighteen centuries of persecution. They were like so many little separate worlds, in which the national spirit was preserved, and which offered a ready field for intestine struggles. A large amount of passion was expended there. The quarrels for precedence were of constant occurrence. To have a seat of honour in the first rank was the reward of great piety, or the most envied privilege of wealth. On the other hand, the liberty, accorded to everyone, of instituting himself reader and commentator of the sacred text afforded marvellous facilities for the propagation of new ideas. This was one of the great instruments of power wielded by Jesus, and the most habitual means he employed to propound his doctrinal instruction. He entered the synagogue and stood up to read; the *hazzan* offered him the book, he unrolled it, and, reading the *parasha* or the *haphtara* of the day, he drew from his reading a lesson in conformity with his own ideas. As there were few Pharisees in Galilee, the discussion did not assume that degree of vivacity and that tone of acrimony against him which at Jerusalem would have arrested him at the outset. These good Galileans had never heard discourses so adapted to their cheerful imaginations. They admired him, they encouraged him, they found that he spoke well, and that his reasons were convincing. He answered the most difficult objections with confidence; the charm of his speech and his person captivated the people, whose simple minds had not yet been cramped by the pedantry of the doctors.

The authority of the young master thus continued increasing every day, and, naturally, the more people believed in him, the more he believed in himself. His sphere of action was very limited. It was confined to the valley in which the Lake of Tiberias is situated, and even in this valley there was one region which he preferred. The lake is five or six leagues long and three or four broad; although it presents the appearance of an almost perfect oval, it forms, commencing from Tiberias up to the entrance of the Jordan, a sort of gulf, the curve of which measures about three leagues. Such is the field in which the seed sown by Jesus found at last a well-prepared soil. Let us run over it step by step, and endeavour to raise the mantle of aridity and mourning with which it has been covered by the demon of Islamism.

On leaving Tiberias we find at first steep rocks, like a mountain which seems to roll into the sea. Then the mountains gradually recede; a plain (*El Ghoueir*) opens almost at the level of the lake. It is a delightful copse of rich verdure, furrowed by abundant streams, which proceed partly from a great round basin of ancient construction (*Ain-Medawara*). At the entrance of this plain, which is, properly speaking, the country of Gennesareth, there is the miserable village of *Medjdel*. At the other extremity of the plain (always following the sea) we come to the site of a town (*Khan-Minyeh*), with very beautiful streams (*Ain-et-Tin*), a pretty road, narrow and deep, cut out of the rock, which Jesus often traversed, and which serves as a passage between the plain of Gennesareth and the northern slopes of the lake. A quarter of an hour's journey from this place we cross a stream of salt water (*Ein-Tabiga*), issuing from the earth by several large springs at a little distance from the lake, and entering it in the midst of a dense mass of verdure. At last, after a journey of forty minutes further upon the arid declivity which extends from Ain-Tabiga to the mouth of the Jordan, we find a few huts and a collection of monumental ruins, called *Tell-Houm*.

Five small towns, the names of which mankind will remember as long as those of Rome and Athens, were, in the time of Jesus, scattered in the space which extends from the village of Medjdel to Tell-Houm. Of these five towns, Magdala, Dalmanutha, Capernaum, Bethsaida, and Chorazin, the first alone can be found at the present time with any certainty. The repulsive village of Medjdel has no doubt preserved the name and the place of the little town which gave to Jesus his most faithful female friend. Dalmanutha was probably near there. It is possible that Chorazin was a little more inland, on the northern side. As to Bethsaida and Capernaum, it is in truth almost at hazard that they have been placed at Tell-Houm, Ain-et-Tin, Khan-Minyeh, and Ain-Medawara. We might say that in topography, as well as in history, a profound design has wished to conceal the traces of the great founder. It is doubtful whether we shall ever be able, upon this extensively devastated soil, to ascertain the places where mankind would gladly come to kiss the imprint of his feet.

The lake, the horizon, the shrubs, the flowers, are all that remain of the little canton, three or four leagues in extent, where Jesus founded his Divine work. The trees have totally disappeared. In this country, in which the vegetation was formerly so brilliant that Josephus saw in it a kind of miracle—Nature, according to him, being pleased to bring hither, side by side the plants of cold countries, the productions of the torrid zone, and the trees of temperate climates, laden all the year with flowers and fruits—in this country travellers are obliged now to calculate a day beforehand the place where they will the next day find a shady resting-place. The lake has become deserted. A single boat in the most miserable condition now ploughs the waves once so rich in life and joy. But the waters are always clear and transparent. The shore, composed of rocks and pebbles, is that of a little sea, not that of a pond, like the shores of Lake Huleh. It is clean, neat, free from mud, and always beaten in the same place by the light movement of the waves. Small promontories, covered with rose laurels, tamarisks, and thorny caper bushes, are seen there; at two places, especially at the mouth of the Jordan, near Tarichea, and at the boundary of the plain of Gennesareth, there are enchanting parterres, where the waves ebb and flow over masses of turf and flowers. The rivulet of Ain-Tabiga makes a little estuary, full of pretty shells. Clouds of aquatic birds hover over the lake. The horizon is dazzling with light. The waters, of an empyrean blue, deeply imbedded amid burning rocks, seem, when viewed from the height of the mountains of Safed, to lie at the bottom of a cup of gold. On the north, the snowy ravines of Hermon are traced in white lines upon the sky; on the west, the high undulating plateaux of Gaulonitis and Perea, absolutely arid, and clothed by the sun with a sort of velvety atmosphere, form one compact mountain, or rather a long and very elevated terrace, which from Cæsarea Philippi runs indefinitely towards the south.

The heat on the shore is now very oppressive. The lake lies in a hollow six hundred and fifty feet below the level of the Mediterranean, and thus participates in the torrid conditions of the Dead Sea. An abundant vegetation formerly tempered these excessive heats; it would be difficult to understand that a furnace, such as the whole basin of the lake now is, commencing from the month of May, had ever been the scene of great activity. Josephus, moreover, considered the country very temperate. No doubt there has been here, as in the *campagna* of Rome, a change of climate introduced by historical causes. It is Islamism, and especially the Mussulman reaction against the Crusades, which has withered as with a blast of death the district preferred by Jesus. The beautiful country of Gennesareth never suspected that beneath the brow of this peaceful wayfarer its highest destinies lay hidden.

Dangerous countryman! Jesus has been fatal to the country which had the formidable honour of bearing him.

Having become a universal object of love or of hate, coveted by two rival fanaticisms, Galilee, as the price of its glory, has been changed to a desert. But who would say that Jesus would have been happier if he had lived obscure in his village to the full age of man? And who would think of these ungrateful Nazarenes, if one of them had not, at the risk of compromising the future of their town, recognised his Father, and proclaimed himself the Son of God?

Four or five large villages, situated at half an hour's journey from one another, formed the little world of Jesus at the time of which we speak. He appears never to have visited Tiberias, a city inhabited for most part by Pagans, and the habitual residence of Antipas. Sometimes, however, he wandered from his favourite region. He went by boat to the eastern shore, to Gergesa, for instance. Towards the north we see him at Paneas or Cæsarea Philippi, at the foot of Mount Hermon. Lastly, he journeyed once in the direction of Tyre and Sidon, a country which must have been marvellously flourishing at that time. In all these countries he was in the midst of Paganism. At Cæsarea he saw the celebrated grotto of *Panium*, thought to be the source of the Jordan, and with which the popular belief had associated strange legends; he could admire the marble temple which Herod had erected near there in honour of Augustus; he probably stopped before the numerous votive statues to Pan, to the Nymphs, to the Echo of the Grotto, which piety had already begun to accumulate in this beautiful place.

A rationalistic Jew, accustomed to take strange gods for deified men or for demons, would consider all these figurative representations as idols. The seductions of the naturalistic worships, which intoxicated the more sensitive nations, never affected him. He was doubtless ignorant of what the ancient sanctuary of Melkarth, at Tyre, might still contain of a primitive worship more or less analogous to that of the Jews. The Paganism which, in Phœnicia, had raised a temple and a sacred grove on every hill, all this aspect of great industry and profane riches, interested him but little. Monotheism takes away all aptitude for comprehending the Pagan religions; the Mussulman, thrown into polytheistic countries, seems to have no eyes. Jesus assuredly learnt nothing in these journeys. He returned always to his well-beloved shore of Gennesareth. There was the centre of his thoughts; there he found faith and love.

CHAPTER IX

THE DISCIPLES OF JESUS

In this terrestrial paradise, which the great revolutions of history had till then scarcely touched, there lived a population in perfect harmony with the country itself, active, honest, joyous, and tender-hearted. The Lake of Tiberias is one of the best supplied with fish of any in the world. Very productive fisheries were established, especially at Bethsaida and at Capernaum, and had produced a certain degree of wealth. These families of fishermen formed a gentle and peaceable society, extending by numerous ties of relationship through the whole district of the lake which we have described. Their comparatively easy life left entire freedom to their imagination. The ideas about the kingdom of God found in these small companies of worthy people more credence than anywhere else. Nothing of that which we call civilisation, in the Greek and worldly sense, had reached them. Neither was there any of our Germanic and Celtic earnestness; but, although goodness among them was often superficial and without depth, their habits were quiet, and they were in some degree intelligent and shrewd. We may imagine them as somewhat analogous to the better populations of the Lebanon, but with the gift—not possessed by the latter—of producing great men. Jesus met here his true family. He installed himself as one of them; Capernaum became " his own city "; in the centre of the little circle which adored him he forgot his sceptical brothers, ungrateful Nazareth and its mocking incredulity.

One house especially at Capernaum offered him an agreeable refuge and devoted disciples. It was that of two brothers, both sons of a certain Jonas, who probably was dead at the period when Jesus came to stay on the borders of the lake. These two brothers were Simon, surnamed *Cephas* or *Peter*, and Andrew. Born at Bethsaida, they were established at Capernaum when Jesus commenced his public life. Peter was married and had children; his mother-in-law lived with him. Jesus loved this house, and dwelt there habitually. Andrew appears to have been a disciple of John the Baptist, and Jesus had perhaps known him on the banks of the Jordan. The two brothers continued always, even at the period in which it seems they must have been most occupied with their master, to follow their business as fishermen. Jesus, who loved to play upon words, said at times that he would make them fishers of men. In fact, among all his disciples he had none more faithfully attached.

Another family, that of Zabdia or Zebedee, a well-to-do fisherman and owner of several boats, gave Jesus a welcome reception. Zebedee had two sons: James, who was the elder, and a younger son, John, who later was called to play so prominent a part in the history of infant Christianity. Both were zealous disciples. Salome, wife of Zebedee, was also much attached to Jesus, and accompanied him until his death.

Women, in fact, received him with eagerness. He manifested towards them those reserved manners which render a very sweet union of ideas possible between the two sexes. The separation of men from women, which has prevented all refined development among the Semitic peoples, was no doubt then, as in our days, much less rigorous in the rural districts and villages than in the large towns. Three or four devoted Galilean women always accompanied the young Master, and disputed the pleasure of listening to and of tending him in turn. They infused into the new sect an element of enthusiasm and of the marvellous, the importance of which had already begun to be understood. One of them, Mary of Magdala, who has rendered the name of this poor town so celebrated in the world, appears to have been of a very enthusiastic temperament. According to the language of the time, she had been possessed by seven demons. That is, she had been affected with nervous and apparently inexplicable maladies. Jesus, by his pure and sweet beauty, calmed this troubled nature. The Magdalene was faithful to him, even unto Golgotha, and on the day but one after his death played a prominent part; for, as we shall see later, she was the principal means by which faith in the resurrection was established. Joanna, wife of Chuza, one of the stewards of Antipas, Susanna, and others who have remained unknown, followed him constantly and ministered unto him. Some were rich, and by their fortune enabled the young prophet to live without following the trade which he had until then practised.

Many others followed him habitually, and recognised him as their Master: a certain Philip of Bethsaida;

Nathanael, son of Tolmai or Ptolemy, of Cana, perhaps a disciple of the first period; and Matthew, probably the one who was the Xenophon of the infant Christianity. The latter had been a publican, and, as such, doubtless handled the *Kalam* more easily than the others. Perhaps it was this that suggested to him the idea of writing the *Logia*, which are the basis of what we know of the teachings of Jesus. Among the disciples are also mentioned Thomas, or Didymus, who doubted sometimes, but who appears to have been a man of warm heart and of generous sympathies; one Lebbæus or Thaddeus; Simon Zelotes, perhaps a disciple of Judas the Gaulonite, belonging to the party of the *Kenaim*, which was formed about that time, and which was soon to play so great a part in the movements of the Jewish people. Lastly Judas, son of Simon, of the town of Kerioth, who was an exception in the faithful flock, and drew upon himself such a terrible notoriety. He was the only one who was not a Galilean. Kerioth was a town at the extreme south of the tribe of Judah, a day's journey beyond Hebron.

We have seen that in general the family of Jesus were little inclined towards him. James and Jude, however, his cousins by Mary Cleophas, henceforth became his disciples, and Mary Cleophas herself was one of the women who followed him to Calvary. At this period we do not see his mother beside him. It was only after the death of Jesus that Mary acquired great importance, and that the disciples sought to attach her to themselves. It was then also that the members of the family of the founder, under the title of " brothers of the Lord," formed an influential group, which was a long time at the head of the Church of Jerusalem, and which, after the sack of the city, took refuge in Batanea. The simple fact of having been familiar with him became a decisive advantage, in the same manner as after the death of Mahomet the wives and daughters of the prophet, who had no importance in his life, became great authorities.

In this friendly group Jesus had evidently his favourites, and, so to speak, an inner circle. The two sons of Zebedee, James and John, appear to have been in the first rank. They were full of fire and passion. Jesus had aptly surnamed them " sons of thunder," on account of their excessive zeal, which, if it could have controlled the thunder, would often have made use of it. John especially appears to have been on very familiar terms with Jesus. Perhaps the warm affection which the Master felt for this disciple has been exaggerated in his Gospel, in which the personal interests of the writer are not sufficiently concealed. The most significant fact is that, in the Synoptical Gospels, Simon Barjona, or Peter, James, son of Zebedee, and John, his brother, form a sort of intimate council, which Jesus calls at certain times when he suspects the faith and intelligence of the others. It seems, moreover, that they were all three associated in their fishing. The affection of Jesus for Peter was strong. The character of the latter—upright, sincere, impulsive—pleased Jesus, who at times permitted himself to smile at his resolute manners. Peter, little of a mystic, communicated to the Master his simple doubts, his repugnances, and his entirely human weaknesses with an honest frankness which recalls that of Joinville towards St. Louis. Jesus chided him, in a friendly manner, full of confidence and esteem. As to John, his youth, his exquisite tenderness of heart, and his lively imagination, must have had a great charm. The personality of this extraordinary man, who has exerted so peculiar an influence on infant Christianity, did not develop itself till afterwards. When old he wrote that strange Gospel, which contains such precious teachings, but in which, in our opinion, the character of Jesus is falsified upon many points. The nature of John was too powerful and too profound for him to bend himself to the impersonal tone of the first evangelists. He was the biographer of Jesus, as Plato was of Socrates. Accustomed to ponder over his recollections with the feverish restlessness of an excited mind, he transformed his Master in wishing to describe him, and sometimes he leaves it to be suspected (unless other hands have altered his work) that perfect good faith was not invariably his rule and law in the composition of this singular writing.

No hierarchy, properly speaking, existed in the new sect. They were to call each other " brothers," and Jesus absolutely proscribed titles of superiority, such as *rabbi*, " master," father—he alone being Master, and God alone being Father. The greatest was to become the servant of the others. Simon Barjona, however, was distinguished among his fellows by a peculiar degree of importance. Jesus lived with him, and taught in his boat; his house was the centre of the Gospel preaching. In public he was regarded as the chief of the flock; and it is to him that the overseers of the tolls address themselves to collect the taxes which were due from the community. He was the first who had recognised Jesus as the Messiah. In a moment of unpopularity, Jesus, asking of his disciples, " Will ye also go away ? " Simon answered, " Lord, to whom should we go ? Thou hast the words of eternal life." Jesus, at various times, gave him a certain priority in his church and gave him the Syrian surname of *Kepha* (stone), by which he wished to signify by that that he made him the corner stone of the edifice. At one time he seems even to promise him " the keys of the kingdom of heaven," and to grant him the right of pronouncing upon earth decisions which should always be ratified in eternity.

No doubt this priority of Peter excited a little jealousy. Jealousy was kindled especially in view of the future—and of this kingdom of God, in which all the disciples would be seated upon thrones, on the right and on the left of the Master, to judge the twelve tribes of Israel. They asked who would then be nearest to the Son of man, and act in a manner as his prime minister and assessor. The two sons of Zebedee aspired to this rank. Pre-occupied with such a thought, they prompted their mother Salome, who one day took Jesus aside, and asked him for the two places of honour for her sons. Jesus evaded the request by his habitual maxim that he who exalted himself should be humbled, and that the kingdom of heaven will be possessed by the lowly. This created some disturbance in the community; there was great discontent against James and John. The same rivalry appears to show itself in the Gospel of John, where the narrator unceasingly declares himself to be " the disciple whom Jesus loved," to whom the Master in dying confided his mother, and seeks systematically to place himself near Simon Peter, and at times to put himself before him, in important circumstances where the older evangelists had omitted mentioning him.

Among the preceding personages, all those of whom we know anything had begun by being fishermen. At all events, none of them belonged to a socially elevated class. Only Matthew or Levi, son of Alpheus, had been a publican. But those to whom they gave this name in Judea were not the farmers-general of taxes, men of elevated rank (always Roman patricians), who were called at Rome *publicani*. They were the agents of these contractors, employés of low rank, simply officers of the customs. The great route from Acre to Damascus, one of the most ancient routes of the world, which crossed Galilee, skirting the lake, made this class of employé very numerous there. Capernaum, which was perhaps on the road, possessed a numerous staff of them. This profession is never popular, but with the Jews it was considered quite criminal. Taxation, new to them, was the sign of their subjection; one school, that of Judas the Gaulonite, maintained that to pay it was an act of paganism. The customs officers, also, were abhorred by the zealots of the law. They were only named in company with assassins, highway robbers, and men of infamous life. The Jews who accepted such offices were excommunicated, and became incapable of making a will; their money was accursed, and the casuists forbade the changing of money with them. These poor men, placed under the ban of society, visited among themselves. Jesus accepted a dinner offered him by Levi, at which there were, according to the language of the time, " many publicans and sinners." This gave great offence. In these ill-reputed houses there was a risk of meeting bad society. We shall often see him thus, caring little to shock the prejudices of well-disposed persons, seeking to elevate the classes humiliated by the orthodox, and thus exposing himself to the liveliest reproaches of the zealots.

Jesus owed these numerous conquests to the infinite charm of his person and his speech. A penetrating word, a look falling upon a simple conscience, which only wanted awakening, gave him an ardent disciple. Sometimes Jesus employed an innocent artifice, which Joan of Arc also used : he affected to know something intimate respecting him whom he wished to gain, or he would perhaps recall to him some circumstance dear to his heart. It was thus that he attracted Nathanael, Peter, and the Samaritan woman. Concealing the true source of his strength—his superiority over all that surrounded him—he permitted people to believe (in order to satisfy the ideas of the time—ideas which, moreover, fully coincided with his own) that a revelation from on high revealed to him all secrets and laid bare all hearts. Every one thought that Jesus lived in a sphere superior to that of humanity. They said that he conversed on the mountains with Moses and Elias ; they believed that in his moments of solitude the angels came to render him homage, and established a supernatural intercourse between him and heaven.

CHAPTER X

THE PREACHINGS ON THE LAKE

Such was the group which, on the borders of the lake of Tiberias, gathered around Jesus. The aristocracy was represented there by a customs officer and by the wife of one of Herod's stewards. The rest were fishermen and common people. Their ignorance was extreme; their intelligence was feeble; they believed in apparitions and spirits. Not one element of Greek culture had penetrated this first assembly of the saints. They had very little Jewish instruction; but heart and goodwill overflowed. The beautiful climate of Galilee made the life of these honest fishermen a perpetual delight. They truly preluded the kingdom of God—simple, good, and happy—rocked gently on their delightful little sea, or at night sleeping on its shores. We do not realise to ourselves the intoxication of a life which thus glides away in the face of heaven—the sweet yet strong love which this perpetual contact with nature gives, and the dreams of these nights passed in the brightness of the stars, under an azure dome of infinite expanse. It was during such a night that Jacob, with his head resting upon a stone, saw in the stars the promise of an innumerable posterity, and the mysterious ladder by which the angels of God came and went from heaven to earth. At the time of Jesus the heavens were not closed, nor the earth grown cold. The cloud still opened above the Son of man; the angels ascended and descended upon his head; the visions of the kingdom of God were everywhere, for man carried them in his heart. The clear and mild eyes of these simple souls contemplated the universe in its ideal source. The world unveiled perhaps its secret to the divinely enlightened conscience of these happy children, whose purity of heart deserved one day to behold God.

Jesus lived with his disciples almost always in the open air. Sometimes he got into a boat, and instructed his hearers, who were crowded upon the shore. Sometimes he sat upon the mountains which bordered the lake, where the air is so pure and the horizon so luminous. The faithful band led thus a joyous and wandering life, gathering the inspirations of the Master in their first bloom. An innocent doubt was sometimes raised, a question slightly sceptical; but Jesus, with a smile or a look, silenced the objection. At each step—in the passing cloud, the germinating seed, the ripening corn—they saw the sign of the Kingdom drawing nigh, they believed themselves on the eve of seeing God, of being masters of the world; tears were turned into joy; it was the advent upon earth of universal consolation.

" Blessed," said the Master, " are the poor in spirit : for theirs is the kingdom of heaven.

" Blessed are they that mourn : for they shall be comforted.

" Blessed are the meek : for they shall inherit the earth.

" Blessed are they which do hunger and thirst after righteousness : for they shall be filled.

" Blessed are the merciful : for they shall obtain mercy.

" Blessed are the pure in heart : for they shall see God.

" Blessed are the peacemakers : for they shall be called the children of God.

" Blessed are they which are persecuted for righteousness' sake : for theirs is the kingdom of heaven."

His preaching was gentle and pleasing, breathing nature and the perfume of the fields. He loved the flowers, and took from them his most charming lessons. The birds of heaven, the sea, the mountains, and the games of children furnished in turn the subject of his instructions. His style had nothing of the Grecian in it, but approached much more to that of the Hebrew parabolists, and especially of sentences from the Jewish doctors, his contemporaries, such as we read them in the " Pirké Aboth." His teachings were not very extended, and formed a species of sorites in the style of the Koran, which, joined together, afterwards composed those long discourses which were written by Matthew. No transition united these diverse pieces; generally, however, the same inspiration penetrated them and made them one. It was, above all, in parable that the Master excelled. Nothing in Judaism had given him the model of this delightful style. He created it. It is true that we find in the Buddhist books parables of exactly the same tone and the same character as the Gospel parables; but it is difficult to admit that a Buddhist influence has been exercised in these. The spirit of gentleness and the depth of feeling which equally animate infant Christianity and Buddhism suffice perhaps to explain these analogies.

A total indifference to exterior life and the vain appanage of the "comfortable," which our drearier countries make necessary to us, was the consequence of the sweet and simple life lived in Galilee. Cold climates, by compelling man to a perpetual contest with external nature, cause too much value to be attached to researches after comfort and luxury. On the other hand, the countries which awaken few desires are the countries of idealism and of poesy. The accessories of life are there insignificant compared with the pleasure of living. The embellishment of the house is superfluous, for it is frequented as little as possible. The strong and regular food of less generous climates would be considered heavy and disagreeable. And as to the luxury of garments, what can rival that which God has given to the earth and the birds of heaven? Labour in climates of this kind appears useless: what it gives is not equal to what it costs. The animals of the field are better clothed than the most opulent man, and they do nothing. This contempt, which, when it is not caused by idleness, contributes greatly to the elevation of the soul, inspired Jesus with some charming apologues: "Lay not up for yourselves treasures upon earth," said he, "where moth and rust doth corrupt, and where thieves break through and steal, but lay up for yourselves treasures in heaven, where neither moth nor dust doth corrupt, and where thieves do not break through nor steal: for where your treasure is, there will your heart be also. No man can serve two masters: for either he will hate the one and love the other, or else he will hold to the one and despise the other. Ye cannot serve God and Mammon. Therefore I say unto you, take no thought for your life, what ye shall eat, or what ye shall drink; nor yet for your body what ye shall put on. Is not the life more than meat, and the body than raiment? Behold the fowls of the air: for they sow not, neither do they reap, nor gather into barns; yet your heavenly Father feedeth them. Are ye not much better than they? Which of you by taking thought can add one cubit unto his stature? And why take ye thought for raiment? Consider the lilies of the field, how they grow; they toil not, neither do they spin; and yet I say unto you, That even Solomon in all his glory was not arrayed like one of these. Wherefore, if God so clothe the grass of the field, which to-day is, and to-morrow is cast into the oven, shall he not much more clothe you, O ye of little faith? Therefore take no thought, saying, What shall we eat? or, What shall we drink? or, Wherewithal shall we be clothed? For after all these things do the Gentiles seek; for your heavenly Father knoweth that ye have need of all these things. But seek ye first the kingdom of God, and his righteousness; and all these things shall be added unto you. Take therefore no thought for the morrow : for the morrow shall take thought of the things of itself. Sufficient unto the day is the evil thereof."

This essentially Galilean sentiment had a decisive influence on the destiny of the infant sect. The happy flock, relying on the heavenly Father for the satisfaction of its wants, had for its first principle the regarding of the cares of life as an evil which choked the germ of all good in man. Each day they asked of God the bread for the morrow. Why lay up treasure ? The kingdom of God is at hand. " Sell that ye have and give alms," said the Master. " Provide yourselves bags which wax not old, a treasure in the heavens that faileth not." What more foolish than to heap up treasures for heirs whom thou wilt never behold ? As an example of human folly, Jesus loved to cite the case of a man who, after having enlarged his barns and amassed wealth for long years, died before having enjoyed it ! The brigandage which was deeply rooted in Galilee gave much force to these views. The poor, who did not suffer from it, would regard themselves as the favoured of God; while the rich, having a less sure possession, were the truly disinherited. In our societies, established upon a very rigorous idea of property, the position of the poor is horrible; they have literally no place under the sun. There are no flowers, no grass, no shade, except for him who possesses the earth. In the East these are gifts of God which belong to no one. The proprietor has but a slender privilege; nature is the patrimony of all.

The infant Christianity, moreover, in this only followed the footsteps of the Essenes, or Therapeutæ, and of the Jewish sects founded on the monastic life. A communistic element entered into all these sects, which were equally disliked by Pharisees and Sadducees. The Messianic doctrine, which was entirely political among the orthodox Jews, was entirely social among them. By means of a gentle, regulated, contemplative existence, leaving its share to the liberty of the individual, these little Churches thought to inaugurate the heavenly kingdom upon earth. Utopias of a blessed life, founded on the brotherhood of men and the worship of the true God, occupied elevated souls, and produced from all sides bold and sincere, but short-lived, attempts to realise these doctrines.

Jesus, whose relations with the Essenes are difficult to

determine (resemblances in history not always implying relations), was on this point certainly their brother. The community of goods was for some time the rule in the new society. Covetousness was the cardinal sin. Now, it must be remarked that the sin of covetousness, against which Christian morality has been so severe, was then the simple attachment to property. The first condition of becoming a disciple of Jesus was to sell one's property and to give the price of it to the poor. Those who recoiled from this extremity were not admitted into the community. Jesus often repeated that he who has found the kingdom of God ought to buy it at the price of all his goods, and that in so doing he makes an advantageous bargain. " The kingdom of heaven is like unto treasure hid in a field; the which when a man hath found, he hideth, and for joy thereof goeth and selleth all that he hath, and buyeth that field. Again the kingdom of heaven is like unto a merchantman seeking goodly pearls; who, when he had found one pearl of great price, went and sold all that he had and bought it." Alas! the inconveniences of this plan were not long in making themselves felt. A treasurer was wanted. They chose for that office Judas of Kerioth. Rightly or wrongly, they accused him of stealing from the common purse; it is certain that he came to a bad end.

Sometimes the Master, more versed in things of heaven than those of earth, taught a still more singular political economy. In a strange parable, a steward is praised for having made himself friends among the poor at the expense of his master, in order that the poor might in their turn introduce him into the kingdom of heaven. The poor, in fact, becoming the dispensers of this kingdom, will only receive those who have given to them. A prudent man, thinking of the future, ought therefore to seek to gain their favour. " And the Pharisees also," says the evangelist, " who were covetous, heard all these things : and they derided him." Did they also hear the formidable parable which follows ? " There was a certain rich man, which was clothed in purple and fine linen, and fared sumptuously every day : and there was a certain beggar named Lazarus, which was laid at his gate, full of sores, and desiring to be fed with the crumbs which fell from the rich man's table : moreover the dogs came and licked his sores. And it came to pass that the beggar died, and was carried by the angels into Abraham's bosom : the rich man also died, and was buried; and in hell he lifted up his eyes, being in torments, and seeth Abraham afar off, and Lazarus in his bosom.

And he cried and said, Father Abraham, have mercy on me, and send Lazarus that he may dip the tip of his finger in water, and cool my tongue; for I am tormented in this flame. But Abraham said, Son, remember that thou in thy lifetime receivedst thy good things; and likewise Lazarus evil things : but now he is comforted and thou art tormented." What more just ? Afterwards this parable was called that of the " wicked rich man." But it is purely and simply the parable of the " rich man." He is in hell because he is rich, because he does not give his wealth to the poor, because he dines well, while others at his door dine badly. Lastly, in a less extravagant moment, Jesus does not make it obligatory to sell one's goods, and give them to the poor except as a suggestion towards greater perfection. But he still makes this terrible declaration : " It is easier for a camel to go through the eye of a needle than for a rich man to enter into the kingdom of God."

An admirable idea governed Jesus in all this, as well as the band of joyous children who accompanied him and made him for eternity the true creator of the peace of the soul, the great consoler of life. In disengaging man from what he called " the cares of this world," Jesus might go to excess and injure the essential conditions of human society; but he founded that high spiritualism which for centuries has filled souls with joy in the midst of this vale of tears. He saw with perfect clearness that man's inattention, his want of philosophy and morality, come mostly from the distractions which he permits himself, the cares which besiege him, and which civilisation multiplies beyond measure. The Gospel, in this manner, has been the most efficient remedy for the weariness of ordinary life, a perpetual *sursum corda*, a powerful diversion from the miserable cares of earth, a gentle appeal like that of Jesus in the ear of Martha—" Martha, Martha, thou art careful and troubled about many things; but one thing is needful." Thanks to Jesus, the dullest existence, that most absorbed by sad or humiliating duties, has had its glimpse of heaven. In our busy civilisations the remembrance of the free life of Galilee has been like perfume from another world, like the " dew of Hermon," which has prevented drought and barrenness from entirely invading the field of God.

CHAPTER XI

THE KINGDOM OF GOD CONCEIVED AS THE INHERITANCE OF THE POOR

THESE maxims, good for a country where life is nourished by the air and the light, and this delicate communism of a band of children of God reposing in confidence on the bosom of their Father, might suit a simple sect constantly persuaded that its Utopia was about to be realised. But it is clear that they could not satisfy the whole of society. Jesus understood very soon, in fact, that the official world of his time would by no means adopt his kingdom. He took his resolution with extreme boldness. Leaving the world, with its hard heart and narrow prejudices on one side, he turned towards the simple. A vast substitution of classes would take place. The kingdom of God was made— 1st, For children, and those who resemble them; 2nd, For the outcasts of this world, victims of that social arrogance which repulses the good but humble man; 3rd, For heretics and schismatics, publicans, Samaritans, and Pagans of Tyre and Sidon. An energetic parable explained this appeal to the people, and justified it. A king has prepared a wedding feast, and sends his servants to seek those invited. Each one excuses himself; some ill-treat the messengers. The king, therefore, takes a decided step. The great people have not accepted his invitation. Be it so. His guests shall be the first comers; the people collected from the highways and byeways, the poor, the beggars, and the lame; it matters not who, the room must be filled. "For I say unto you," said he, "that none of those men which were bidden shall taste of my supper."

Pure *Ebionism*—that is, the doctrine that the poor (*ebionim*) alone shall be saved, that the reign of the poor is approaching—was, therefore, the doctrine of Jesus. "Woe unto you that are rich," said he, "for ye have received your consolation. Woe unto you that are full, for ye shall hunger. Woe unto you that laugh now, for ye shall mourn and weep." "Then said he also to him that bade him, When thou makest a dinner or a supper, call not thy friends, nor thy brethren, neither thy kinsmen, nor thy rich neighbours, lest they also bid thee again, and a recompense be made thee. But when thou makest a feast, call the poor, the maimed, the lame, the blind : and thou shalt be blessed; for they cannot recompense thee; for thou shalt be recompensed at the resurrection of the just." It is perhaps in an analogous sense that he often repeated, Be good bankers—that is to say, make good investments for the kingdom of God, in giving your wealth to the poor, conformably to the old proverb, "He that hath pity upon the poor, lendeth unto the Lord."

This, however, was not a new fact. The most exalted democratic movement of which humanity has preserved the remembrance (the only one, also, which has succeeded, for it alone has maintained itself in the domain of pure thought), had long disturbed the Jewish race. The thought that God is the avenger of the poor and the weak, against the rich and the powerful, is found in each page of the writings of the Old Testament. The history of Israel is of all histories that in which the popular spirit has most constantly predominated. The prophets, the true, and, in one sense, the boldest tribunes, had thundered incessantly against the great, and established a close relation, on the one hand, between the words " rich, impious, violent, wicked," and, on the other, between the words " poor, gentle, humble, pious." Under the Seleucidæ, the aristocrats having almost all apostatised and gone over to Hellenism, these associations of ideas only became stronger. The Book of Enoch contains still more violent maledictions than those of the Gospel against the world, the rich, and the powerful. Luxury is there depicted as a crime. The " Son of man," in this strange Apocalypse, enthrones kings, tears them from their voluptuous life, and precipitates them into hell. The initiation of Judea into secular life, the recent introduction of an entirely worldly element of luxury and comfort, provoked a furious reaction in favour of patriarchal simplicity. " Woe unto you who despise the humble dwelling and inheritance of your fathers ! Woe unto you who build your palaces with the sweat of others ! Each stone, each brick, of which it is built, is a sin." The name of " poor " (ebion) had become a synonym of " saint," of " friend of God." This was the name that Galilean disciples of Jesus loved to give themselves; it was for a long time the name of the Judaising Christians of Batanea and of the Hauran (Nazarenes, Hebrews) who remained faithful to the tongue, as well as to the primitive instructions of Jesus, and who boasted that they possessed among themselves the descendants of his family.   At the end of the second century, these good sectaries, having remained beyond the reach of the great current which had carried away all the other Churches, were treated as heretics (*Ebionites*), and a pretended heretical leader (*Ebion*) was invented to explain their name.

We may see, in fact, without difficulty, that this exaggerated taste for poverty could not be very lasting. It was one of those Utopian elements which always mingle in the origin of great movements, and which time rectifies. Thrown into the centre of human society, Christianity very easily consented to receive rich men into her bosom, just as Buddhism, exclusively monkish in its origin, soon began, as conversions multiplied, to admit the laity. But the mark of origin is ever preserved. Although it quickly passed away and became forgotten, *Ebionism* left a leaven in the whole history of Christian institutions which has not been lost. The collection of the *Logia*, or discourses of Jesus, was formed in the Ebionitish centre of Batanea. " Poverty " remained an ideal from which the true followers of Jesus were never after separated. To possess nothing was the truly evangelical state; mendicancy became a virtue, a holy condition. The great Umbrian movement of the thirteenth century, which, among all the attempts at religious construction, most resembles the Galilean movement, took place entirely in the name of poverty.   Francis d'Assisi, the man who, more than any other, by his exquisite goodness, by his delicate, pure, and tender intercourse with universal life, most resembled Jesus, was a poor man.   The mendicant orders, the innumerable communistic sects of the Middle Ages (*Pauvres de Lyon*, *Bégards*, *Bons-Hommes*, *Fratricelles*, *Humiliés*, *Pauvres évangéliques*, etc.) grouped under the banner of the " Everlasting Gospel," pretended to be, and in fact were, the true disciples of Jesus. But even in this case the most impracticable dreams of the new religion were fruitful in results. Pious mendicity, so impatiently born by our industrial and well-organised communities, was in its day, and in a suitable climate, full of charm. It offered to a multitude of mild and contemplative souls the only condition suited to them. To have made poverty an object of love and desire, to have raised the beggar to the altar, and to have sanctified the coat of the poor man, was a master-stroke which political

economy may not appreciate, but in the presence of which
the true moralist cannot remain indifferent. Humanity,
in order to bear its burden, needs to believe that it is not
paid entirely by wages. The greatest service which can
be rendered to it is to repeat often that it lives not by bread
alone.

Like all great men, Jesus loved the people and felt himself at home with them. The Gospel, in his idea, is made
for the poor; it is to them he brings the glad tidings of
salvation. All the despised ones of orthodox Judaism were
his favourites. Love of the people, and pity for its weakness (the sentiment of the democratic chief, who feels the
spirit of the multitude live in him, and recognise him as its
natural interpreter), shine forth at each moment in his acts
and discourses.

The chosen flock presented, in fact, a very mixed character,
and one likely to astonish rigorous moralists. It counted
in its fold men with whom a Jew respecting himself would
not have associated. Perhaps Jesus found in this society,
unrestrained by ordinary rules, more mind and heart than
in a pedantic and formal middle-class, proud of its apparent
morality. The Pharisees, exaggerating the Mosaic prescriptions, had come to believe themselves defiled by contact
with men less strict than themselves; in their meals they
almost rivalled the puerile distinctions of caste in India.
Despising these miserable aberrations of the religious
sentiment, Jesus loved to eat with those who suffered from
them; by his side at table were seen persons said to lead
wicked lives, perhaps only so called because they did not
share the follies of the false devotees. The Pharisees and
the doctors protested against the scandal. "See," said
they, "with what men he eats!" Jesus returned subtle
answers, which exasperated the hypocrites: "They that
be whole need not a physician." Or again: "What
man of you, having an hundred sheep, if he lose one of them,
doth not leave the ninety and nine in the wilderness, and
go after that which is lost until he find it? And when he
hath found it, he layeth it on his shoulder rejoicing." Or
again: "The Son of man is come to save that which was
lost." Or again: "I am not come to call the righteous,
but sinners." Lastly, that delightful parable of the
prodigal son, in which he who is fallen is represented as
having a kind of privilege of love above him who has always
been righteous. Weak or guilty women, surprised at so
much that was charming, and realising for the first time the
attractions of contact with virtue, approached him freely.

People were astonished that he did not repulse them.
" Now when the Pharisee which had bidden him saw it, he
spake within himself, saying, This man, if he were a prophet,
would have known who and what manner of woman this
is that toucheth him : for she is a sinner." Jesus replied
by the parable of a creditor who forgives his debtors'
unequal debts, and he did not hesitate to prefer the lot of
him to whom was remitted the greater debt. He appreciated conditions of soul only in proportion to the love
mingled therein. Women, with tearful hearts, and disposed through their sins to feelings of humility, were nearer
to his kingdom than ordinary natures, who often have little
merit in not having fallen. We may conceive, on the other
hand, that these tender souls, finding in their conversion
to the sect an easy means of restoration, would passionately
attach themselves to him.

Far from seeking to soothe the murmurs stirred up by his
disdain for the social susceptibilities of the time, he seemed
to take pleasure in exciting them. Never did anyone avow
more loftily this contempt for the " world," which is the
essential condition of great things and great originality.
He pardoned the rich man, but only when the rich man, in
consequence of some prejudice, was disliked by society.
He greatly preferred men of equivocal life and of small consideration in the eyes of the orthodox leaders. " The
publicans and the harlots go into the kingdom of God before
you. For John came unto you and ye believed him not :
but the publicans and the harlots believed him." We can
understand how galling the reproach of not having followed
the good example set by prostitutes must have been to men
making a profession of seriousness and rigid morality.

He had no external affectation or show of austerity. He
did not fly from pleasure ; he went willingly to marriage
feasts. One of his miracles was performed to enliven a
wedding at a small town. Weddings in the East take place
in the evening. Each one carries a lamp ; and the lights
coming and going produce a very agreeable effect. Jesus
liked this gay and animated aspect, and drew parables
from it. Such conduct, compared with that of John the
Baptist, gave offence. One day, when the disciples of John
and the Pharisees were observing the fast, it was asked,
" Why do the disciples of John and of the Pharisees fast,
but thy disciples fast not ? And Jesus said unto them, Can
the children of the bridechamber fast, while the bridegroom
is with them ? As long as they have the bridegroom with
them, they cannot fast. But the days will come when the

ridegroom shall be taken away from them, and then they hall fast in those days." His gentle gaiety found expression in lively ideas and amiable pleasantries. " But hereunto," said he, " shall I liken this generation? It is ke unto children sitting in the markets, and calling unto their fellows, and saying, We have piped unto you, and ye ave not danced; we have mourned unto you, and ye have ot lamented. For John came neither eating nor drinking, nd they say, He hath a devil. The Son of man came ating and drinking, and they say, Behold a man gluttonus, and a wine-bibber, a friend of publicans and sinners. But Wisdom is justified of her children."

He thus traversed Galilee in the midst of a continual east. He rode on a mule. In the East this is a good and afe mode of travelling; the large black eyes of the animal, haded by long eyelashes, give it an expression of gentleness. His disciples sometimes surrounded him with a kind of ustic pomp, at the expense of their garments, which they used as carpets. They placed them on the mule which arried him, or extended them on the earth in his path. His entering a house was considered a joy and a blessing. He stopped in the villages and the large farms, where he eceived an eager hospitality. In the East, the house into which a stranger enters becomes at once a public place. All the village assembles there, the children invade it, and, hough dispersed by the servants, always return. Jesus could not permit these simple auditors to be treated harshly; he caused them to be brought to him and embraced them. The mothers, encouraged by such a reception, brought him their children in order that he might touch them. Women came to pour oil upon his head and perfume on his feet. His disciples sometimes repulsed them as troublesome; but Jesus, who loved the ancient usages, and all that indicated simplicity of heart, repaired the ill done by his too zealous friends. He protected those who wished to honour him. Thus children and women adored him. The reproach of alienating from their families these gentle creatures, always easily misled, was one of the most frequent charges of his enemies.

The new religion was thus in many respects a movement of women and children. The latter were like a young guard around Jesus for the inauguration of his innocent royalty, and gave him little ovations which much pleased him, calling him " son of David," crying *Hosanna*, and bearing palms around him. Jesus, like Savonarola, perhaps made them serve as instruments for pious missions; he was

E

very glad to see these young apostles, who did not com
promise him, rush into the front and give him titles which
he dared not take himself. He let them speak, and, when
he was asked if he heard, he replied in an evasive manner
that the praise which comes from young lips is the most
agreeable to God.

He lost no opportunity of repeating that the little ones are
sacred beings, that the kingdom of God belongs to children
that we must become children to enter there, that we
ought to receive it as a child, that the heavenly Father
hides his secrets from the wise, and reveals them to the
little ones. The idea of disciples is, in his mind, almost
synonymous with that of children. On one occasion, when
they had one of those quarrels for precedence which were
not uncommon, Jesus took a little child, placed him in their
midst, and said unto them : " Whosoever therefore shall
humble himself as this little child, the same is greatest in
the kingdom of heaven."

It was infancy, in fact, in its divine spontaneity, in its
simple bewilderments of joy, which took possession of the
earth. Everyone believed at each moment that the kingdom so much desired was about to appear. Each one already
saw himself seated on a throne beside the Master. They
divided among themselves the positions of honour in the
new kingdom, and strove to reckon the precise date of its
advent. This new doctrine was called the " Good Tidings ";
it had no other name. An old word, " *paradise*," which
the Hebrew, like all the languages of the East, had borrowed
from the Persian, and which at first designated the parks
of the Achæmenidæ, summed up the general dream; a
delightful garden, where the charming life which was led
here below would be continued for ever. How long this
intoxication lasted we know not. No one, during the course
of this magical apparition, measured time any more than
we measure a dream. Duration was suspended; a week was
an age. But, whether it filled years or months, the dream
was so beautiful that humanity has lived upon it ever since,
and it is still our consolation to gather its weakened perfume. Never did so much joy fill the breast of man. For
a moment Humanity, in this the most vigorous effort she
ever made to rise above the world, forgot the leaden weight
which binds her to earth and the sorrows of the life below.
Happy he who has been able to behold this divine unfolding,
and to share, were it but for one day, this unexampled
illusion ! But still more happy, Jesus would say to us, is
he who, freed from all illusion, shall reproduce in himself

he celestial vision, and, with no millenarian dream, no himerical paradise, no signs in the heavens, but, by the .prightness of his will and the poetry of his soul, shall be ble to create anew in his heart the true kingdom of God !

CHAPTER XII

WHILE joyous Galilee was celebrating in feasts the comin[g]
of the well-beloved, the sorrowful John, in his prison o[f]
Machero, was pining away with expectation and desire[.]
The success of the young Master whom he had seen som[e]
months before as his auditor reached his ears. It was sai[d]
that the Messiah predicted by the prophets, he who was t[o]
re-establish the kingdom of Israel, was come, and wa[s]
proving his presence in Galilee by marvellous works. Joh[n]
wished to inquire into the truth of this rumour, and, as h[e]
communicated freely with his disciples, he chose two o[f]
them to go to Jesus in Galilee.

The two disciples found Jesus at the height of his fame[.]
The air of gladness which reigned around him surprise[d]
them. Accustomed to fasts, to persevering prayer, and t[o]
a life of aspiration, they were astonished to see themselve[s]
transported suddenly into the midst of the joys attendin[g]
the welcome of the Messiah. They told Jesus their message[.]
" Art thou he that should come? Or do we look fo[r]
another ? " Jesus, who from that time hesitated no longe[r]
respecting his peculiar character as Messiah, enumerate[d]
the works which ought to characterise the coming of th[e]
kingdom of God—such as the healing of the sick and th[e]
good tiding of a speedy salvation preached to the poor[.]
He did all these works. " And blessed is he," said Jesus[,]
" whosoever shall not be offended in me." We know no[t]
whether this answer found John the Baptist living or i[n]
what temper it put the austere ascetic. Did he die consoled and certain that he whom he had announced already
lived, or did he remain doubtful as to the mission of Jesus?
There is nothing to inform us. Seeing, however, that his
school continued to exist a considerable time parallel with
the Christian Churches, we are led to think that, notwithstanding his regard for Jesus, John did not look upon him
as the one who was to realise the divine promises. Death

ame, moreover, to end his perplexities. The untamable reedom of the ascetic was to crown his restless and stormy areer by the only end which was worthy of it.

The leniency which Antipas had at first shown towards ohn was not of long duration. In the conversations which, ccording to the Christian tradition, John had had with he tetrarch, he did not cease to declare to him that his narriage was unlawful, and that he ought to send away Ierodias. We can easily imagine the hatred which the rand-daughter of Herod the Great must have conceived owards this importunate counsellor. She only waited an pportunity to ruin him.

Her daughter, Salome, born of her first marriage, and, ike her, ambitious and dissolute, entered into her designs. That year (probably the year 30) Antipas was at Machero n the anniversary of his birthday. Herod the Great had onstructed in the interior of the fortress a magnificent palace, where the tetrarch frequently resided. He gave a great feast there, during which Salome executed one of those lances in character which were not considered in Syria as inbecoming a distinguished person. Antipas, being much pleased, asked the dancer what she most desired, and she eplied, at the instigation of her mother, " Give me here John Baptist's head in a charger." [1] Antipas was sorry, but he did not like to refuse. A guard took the dish, went and cut off the head of the prisoner, and brought it.

The disciples of the Baptist obtained his body and placed it in a tomb, but the people were much displeased. Six years after, Hareth having attacked Antipas, in order to recover Machero and avenge the dishonour of his daughter, Antipas was completely beaten; and his defeat was generally regarded as a punishment for the murder of John.

The news of John's death was brought to Jesus by the disciples of the Baptist. John's last act towards Jesus had effectually united the two schools in the most intimate bonds. Jesus, fearing an increase of ill-will on the part of Antipas, took precautions and retired to the desert, where many people followed him. By exercising an extreme frugality, the holy band was enabled to live there, and in this time there was naturally seen a miracle. From this time Jesus always spoke of John with redoubled admiration. He declared unhesitatingly that he was more than a prophet, that the Law and the ancient prophets had force

[1] A portable dish on which liquors and viands are served in the East.

only until he came, that he had abrogated them, but that
the kingdom of heaven would displace him in turn. In
fine, he attributed to him a special place in the economy of
the Christian mystery, which constituted him the link
of union between the Old Testament and the advent of
the new reign.

The prophet Malachi, whose opinion in this matter was
soon brought to bear, had announced with much energy
a precursor of the Messiah, who was to prepare men for the
final renovation, a messenger who should come to make
straight the paths before the elected one of God. This
messenger was no other than the prophet Elias, who
according to a widely-spread belief, was soon to descend
from heaven, whither he had been carried, in order to
prepare men by repentance for the great advent, and to
reconcile God with his people. Sometimes they associated
with Elias, either the patriarch Enoch, to whom for one
or two centuries they had attributed high sanctity; or
Jeremiah, whom they considered as a sort of protecting
genius of the people, constantly occupied in praying for
them before the throne of God. This idea, that two
ancient prophets should rise again in order to serve as precursors to the Messiah, is discovered in so striking a form
in the doctrine of the Parsees, that we feel much inclined
to believe that it comes from that source. However this
may be, it formed at the time of Jesus an integral portion
of the Jewish theories about the Messiah. It was admitted
that the appearance of " two faithful witnesses," clothed in
garments of repentance, would be the preamble of the
great drama about to be unfolded, to the astonishment of
the universe.

It will be seen that, with these ideas, Jesus and his
disciples could not hesitate about the mission of John the
Baptist. When the scribes raised the objection that the
Messiah could not have come because Elias had not yet
appeared, they replied that Elias was come, that John was
Elias raised from the dead. By his manner of life, by his
opposition to the established political authorities, John in
fact recalled that strange figure in the ancient history of
Israel. Jesus was not silent on the merits and excellencies
of his forerunner. He said that none greater were born
among the children of men. He energetically blamed the
Pharisees and the doctors for not having accepted his
baptism, and for not being converted at his voice.

The disciples of Jesus were faithful to these principles
of their Master. This respect for John continued during

the whole of the first Christian generation. He was supposed to be a relative of Jesus. In order to establish the mission of the latter upon testimony admitted by all, it was declared that John, at the first sight of Jesus, proclaimed him the Messiah; that he recognised himself his inferior, unworthy to unloose the latchets of his shoes; that he refused at first to baptise him, and maintained that it was he who ought to be baptised by Jesus. These were exaggerations, which are sufficiently refuted by the doubtful form of John's last message. But, in a more general sense, John remains in the Christian legend that which he was in reality—the austere forerunner, the gloomy preacher of repentance before the joy on the arrival of the bridegroom, the prophet who announces the kingdom of God and dies before beholding it. This giant in the early history of Christianity, this eater of locusts and wild honey, this rough redresser of wrongs, was the bitter which prepared the lip for the sweetness of the kingdom of God. His beheading by Herodias inaugurated the era of Christian martyrs; he was the first witness for the new faith. The worldly, who recognised in him their true enemy, could not permit him to live; his mutilated corpse, extended on the threshold of Christianity, traced the bloody path in which so many others were to follow.

The school of John did not die with its founder. It lived some time distinct from that of Jesus, and at first a good understanding existed between the two. Many years after the death of the two Masters people were baptised with the baptism of John. Certain persons belonged to the two schools at the same time—for example, the celebrated Apollos, the rival of St. Paul (towards the year 50), and a large number of the Christians of Ephesus. Josephus placed himself (year 53) in the school of an ascetic named Banou, who presents the greatest resemblance to John the Baptist, and who was perhaps of his school. This Banou lived in the desert, clothed with the leaves of trees; he supported himself only on wild plants and fruits, and baptised himself frequently, both day and night, in cold water, in order to purify himself. James, he who was called the "brother of the Lord" (there is here, perhaps, some confusion of homonyms), practised a similar asceticism. Afterwards, towards the year 80, Baptism was in strife with Christianity, especially in Asia Minor. John the Evangelist appears to combat it in an indirect manner. One of the Sibylline poems seems to proceed from this school. As to the sects of Hemero-baptists, Baptists, and

Elchasaïtes (*Sabiens Mogtasila* of the Arabian writers), who, in the second century, filled Syria, Palestine, and Babylonia, and whose representatives still exist in our days among the Mendaites, called " Christians of St. John," they have the same origin as the movement of John the Baptist, rather than an authentic descent from John. The true school of the latter, partly mixed with Christianity, became a small Christian heresy, and died out in obscurity. John had foreseen distinctly the destiny of the two schools. If he had yielded to a mean rivalry, he would to-day have been forgotten in the crowd of sectaries of his time. By his self-abnegation, he has attained a glorious and unique position in the religious pantheon of humanity.

---

[1] *Sabiens* is the Aramean equivalent of the word " Baptists." *Mogtasila* has the same meaning in Arabic.

CHAPTER XIII

FIRST ATTEMPTS ON JERUSALEM

JESUS, almost every year, went to Jerusalem for the feast of the passover. The details of these journeys are little known, for the Synoptics do not speak of them, and the notes of the fourth Gospel are very confused on this point. It was, it appears, in the year 31, and certainly after the death of John, that the most important of the visits of Jesus to Jerusalem took place. Many of the disciples followed him. Although Jesus attached from that time little value to the pilgrimage, he conformed himself to it in order not to wound Jewish opinion, with which he had not yet broken. These journeys, moreover, were essential to his design; for he felt already that, in order to play a leading part, he must go from Galilee, and attack Judaism in its stronghold, which was Jerusalem.

The little Galilean community were here far from being at home. Jerusalem was then nearly what it is to-day, a city of pedantry, acrimony, disputes, hatreds, and littleness of mind. Its fanaticism was extreme, and religious seditions very frequent. The Pharisees were dominant; the study of the Law, pushed to the most insignificant minutiæ, and reduced to questions of casuistry, was the only study. This exclusively theological and canonical culture contributed in no respect to define the intellect. It was something analogous to the barren doctrine of the Mussulman fakir, to that empty science discussed round about the mosques, and which is a great expenditure of time and useless argumentation, by no means calculated to advance the right discipline of the mind. The theological education of the modern clergy, although very dry, gives us no idea of this, for the Renaissance has introduced into all our teachings, even the most irregular, a share of *belles lettres* and of method, which has infused more or less of the *humanities* into scholasticism. The science of the Jewish doctor, of the *sofer* or scribe, was purely barbarous, unmitigatedly absurd, and denuded of all moral element.

To crown the evil, it filled with ridiculous pride those who had wearied themselves in acquiring it.   The Jewish scribe, proud of the pretended knowledge which had cost him so much trouble, had the same contempt for Greek culture which the learned Mussulman of our time has for European civilisation, and which the old Catholic theologian had for the knowledge of men of the world.   The tendency of this scholastic culture was to close the mind to all that was refined, to create esteem only for those difficult triflings on which they had wasted their lives, and which were regarded as the natural occupation of persons professing a degree of seriousness.

This odious society could not fail to weigh heavily on the tender and susceptible minds of the north.   The contempt of the Hierosolymites for the Galileans rendered the separation still more complete.   In the beautiful temple which was the object of all their desires they often only met with insult.   A verse of the pilgrim's psalm, " I had rather be a doorkeeper in the house of my God," seemed made expressly for them.   A contemptuous priesthood laughed at their simple devotion, as formerly in Italy the clergy, familiarised with the sanctuaries, witnessed coldly and almost jestingly the fervour of the pilgrim come from afar.   The Galileans spoke a rather corrupt dialect; their pronunciation was vicious; they confounded the different aspirations of letters, which led to mistakes which were much laughed at.   In religion they were considered as ignorant and somewhat heterodox; the expression, " foolish Galileans," had become proverbial.   It was believed (not without reason) that they were not of pure Jewish blood, and no one expected Galilee to produce a prophet.   Placed thus on the confines of Judaism, and almost outside of it, the poor Galileans had only one badly interpreted passage in Isaiah to build their hopes upon.   " Land of Zebulon, and land of Naphtali, way of the sea, Galilee of the nations ! The people that walked in darkness have seen a great light : they that dwell in the land of the shadow of death, upon them hath the light shined."   The reputation of the native city of Jesus was particularly bad.   It was a popular proverb, " Can there any good thing come out of Nazareth ? "

The parched appearance of nature in the neighbourhood of Jerusalem must have added to the dislike Jesus had for the place.   The valleys are without water;   the soil arid and stony.   Looking into the valley of the Dead Sea, the view is somewhat striking;   elsewhere it is monotonous. The hill of Mizpeh, around which cluster the most ancient historical remembrances of Israel, alone relieves the eye. The city presented, at the time of Jesus, nearly the same form that it does now. It had scarcely any ancient monuments, for, until the time of the Asmoneans, the Jews had remained strangers to all the arts. John Hyrcanus had begun to embellish it, and Herod the Great had made it one of the most magnificent cities of the East. The Herodian constructions, by their grand character, perfection of execution, and beauty of material, may dispute superiority with the most finished works of antiquity. A great number of superb tombs, of original taste, were raised at the same time in the neighbourhood of Jerusalem. The style of these monuments was Grecian, but appropriate to the customs of the Jews, and considerably modified in accordance with their principles. The ornamental sculptures of the human figure which the Herods had sanctioned, to the great discontent of the purists, were banished, and replaced by floral decorations. The taste of the ancient inhabitants of Phœnicia and Palestine for monoliths in solid stone seemed to be revived in these singular tombs cut in the rock, and in which Grecian orders are so strangely applied to an architecture of troglodytes. Jesus, who regarded works of art as a pompous display of vanity, viewed these monuments with displeasure. His absolute spiritualism, and his settled conviction that the form of the old world was about to pass away, left him no taste except for things of the heart.

The temple, at the time of Jesus, was quite new, and the exterior works of it were not completed. Herod had begun its reconstruction in the year 20 or 21 before the Christian era, in order to make it uniform with his other edifices. The body of the temple was finished in eighteen months; the porticoes took eight years; and the accessory portions were continued slowly, and were only finished a short time before the taking of Jerusalem. Jesus probably saw the work progressing, not without a degree of secret vexation. These hopes of a long future were like an insult to his approaching advent. Clearer-sighted than the unbelievers and the fanatics, he foresaw that these superb edifices were destined to endure but for a short time.

The temple formed a marvellously imposing whole, of which the present *haram*, notwithstanding its beauty, scarcely gives us any idea. The courts and the surrounding porticoes served as the daily rendezvous for a considerable number of persons—so much so that this great space was at once temple, forum, tribunal, and university. All the religious discussions of the Jewish schools, all the canonical instruction, even the legal processes and civil causes—in a word, all the activity of the nation was concentrated there. It was an arena where arguments were perpetually clashing, a battle-field of disputes, resounding with sophism and subtle questions. The temple had thus much analogy with a Mohammedan mosque. The Romans at this period treated all strange religions with respect when kept within proper limits, and carefully refrained from entering the sanctuary. Greek and Latin inscriptions marked the point up to which those who were not Jews were permitted to advance. But the tower of Antonia, the headquarters of the Roman forces, commanded the whole enclosure, and allowed all that passed therein to be seen. The guarding of the temple belonged to the Jews; the entire super-intendence was committed to a captain, who caused the gates to be opened and shut, and prevented any one from crossing the enclosure with a stick in his hand, or with dusty shoes, or when carrying parcels, or to shorten his path. They were especially scrupulous in watching that no one entered within the inner gates in a state of legal impurity. The women had an entirely separate court.

It was in the temple that Jesus passed his days while he remained at Jerusalem. The period of the feasts brought an extraordinary concourse of people into the city. Associated in parties of ten to twenty persons, the pilgrims invaded everywhere, and lived in that disordered state in which Orientals delight. Jesus was lost in the crowd, and his poor Galileans grouped around him were of small account. He probably felt that he was in a hostile world which would receive him only with disdain. Everything he saw set him against it. The temple, like much-frequented places of devotion in general, offered a not very edifying spectacle. The accessories of worship entailed a number of repulsive details, especially of mercantile operations, in consequence of which real shops were established within the sacred enclosure. There were sold beasts for the sacrifices; there were tables for the exchange of money; at times it seemed like a bazaar. The inferior officers of the temple fulfilled their functions doubtless with the irreligious vulgarity of the sacristans of all ages. This profane and heedless air in the handling of holy things wounded the religious sentiment of Jesus, which was at times carried even to a scrupulous excess. He said that they had made the house of prayer into a den of thieves. One day, it is even said, that, carried away by his anger,

he scourged the vendors with a " scourge of small cords,"
and overturned their tables.   In general, he had little love
for the temple.   The worship which he had conceived for
his Father had nothing in common with scenes of butchery.
All these old Jewish institutions displeased him, and he
suffered in being obliged to conform to them.   Except
among the Judaising Christians, neither the temple nor its
site inspired pious sentiments.   The true disciples of the
new faith held this ancient sanctuary in aversion.   Constantine and the first Christian emperors left the pagan
construction of Adrian existing there, and only the enemies
of Christianity, such as Julian, remembered the temple.
When Omar entered into Jerusalem, he found the site
designedly polluted in hatred of the Jews.   It was Islamism
—that is to say, a sort of resurrection of Judaism in its
exclusively Semitic form—which restored its glory.   The
place has always been anti-Christian.

The pride of the Jews completed the discontent of Jesus,
and rendered his stay in Jerusalem painful.   In the degree
that the great ideas of Israel ripened, the priesthood lost
its power.   The institution of synagogues had given to the
interpreter of the Law, to the doctor, a great superiority
over the priest.   There were no priests except at Jerusalem,
and even there, reduced to functions entirely ritual, almost,
like our parish priests, excluded from preaching, they were
surpassed by the orator of the synagogue, the casuist, and
the *sofer* or scribe, although the latter was only a layman.
The celebrated men of the Talmud were not priests; they
were learned men according to the ideas of the time.   The
high priesthood of Jerusalem held, it is true, a very elevated
rank in the nation; but it was by no means at the head of
the religious movement.   The sovereign pontiff, whose
dignity had already been degraded by Herod, became more
and more a Roman functionary, who was frequently
removed in order to divide the profits of the office.   Opposed to the Pharisees, who were very warm lay zealots,
the priests were almost all Sadducees—that is to say,
members of that unbelieving aristocracy which had been
formed around the temple, and which lived by the altar,
while they saw the vanity of it.   The sacerdotal caste was
separated to such a degree from the national sentiment,
and from the great religious movement which dragged the
people along, that the name of " Sadducee " (*sadoki*),
which at first simply designated a member of the sacerdotal
family of Sadok, had become synonymous with " Materialist '
and with " Epicurean."

A still worse element had begun, since the reign of Herod the Great, to corrupt the high-priesthood. Herod having fallen in love with Mariamne, daughter of a certain Simon, son of Boëthus of Alexandria, and having wished to marry her (about the year 28 B.C.), saw no other means of ennobling his father-in-law and raising him to his own rank than by making him high-priest. This intriguing family remained master, almost without interruption, of the sovereign pontificate for thirty-five years. Closely allied to the reigning family, it did not lose the office until after the deposition of Archelaus, and recovered it (the year 42 of our era) after Herod Agrippa had for some time re-enacted the work of Herod the Great. Under the name of *Boëthusim*, a new sacerdotal nobility was formed, very worldly and little devotional, and closely allied to the Sadokites. The *Boëthusim*, in the Talmud and the rabbinical writings, are depicted as a kind of unbelievers, and always reproached as Sadducees. From all this there resulted a miniature court of Rome around the temple, living on politics, little inclined to excesses of zeal, even rather fearing them, not wishing to hear of holy personages or of innovators, for it profited from the established routine. These epicurean priests had not the violence of the Pharisees; they only wished for quietness; it was their moral indifference, their cold irreligion, which revolted Jesus. Although very different, the priests and the Pharisees were thus confounded in his antipathies. But a stranger, and without influence, he was long compelled to restrain his discontent within himself, and only to communicate his sentiments to the intimate friends who accompanied him.

Before his last stay, which was by far the longest of all that he made at Jerusalem, and which was terminated by his death, Jesus endeavoured, however, to obtain a hearing. He preached; people spoke of him; and they conversed respecting certain deeds of his which were looked upon as miraculous. But from all that there resulted neither an established Church at Jerusalem nor a group of Hierosolymite disciples. The charming teacher who forgave everyone, provided they loved him, could not find much sympathy in this sanctuary of vain disputes and obsolete sacrifices. The only result was that he formed some valuable friendships, the advantage of which he reaped afterwards. He does not appear at that time to have made the acquaintance of the family of Bethany, which, amid the trials of the latter months of his life, brought him so much consolation. But very early he attracted the attention of a certain Nicodemus, a rich Pharisee, a member of the Sanhedrin, and a man occupying a high position in Jerusalem. This man, who appears to have been upright and sincere, felt himself attracted towards the young Galilean. Not wishing to compromise himself, he came to see Jesus by night, and had a long conversation with him. He doubtless preserved a favourable impression of him, for afterwards he defended Jesus against the prejudices of his colleagues, and, at the death of Jesus, we shall find him tending with pious care the corpse of the Master. Nicodemus did not become a Christian; he had too much regard for his position to take part in a revolutionary movement which as yet counted no men of note among its adherents. But he evidently felt great friendship for Jesus, and rendered him service, though unable to rescue him from a death which even at this period was all but decreed.

As to the celebrated doctors of the time, Jesus does not appear to have had any connection with them. Hillel and Shammai were dead; the greatest authority of the time was Gamaliel, grandson of Hillel. He was of a liberal spirit, and a man of the world, not opposed to secular studies, and inclined to tolerance by his intercourse with good society. Unlike the very strict Pharisees, who walked veiled or with closed eyes, he did not scruple to gaze even upon Pagan women. This, as well as his knowledge of Greek, was tolerated because he had access to the Court. After the death of Jesus, he expressed very moderate views respecting the new sect. St. Paul sat at his feet, but it is not probable that Jesus ever entered his school.

One idea, at least, which Jesus brought from Jerusalem, and which henceforth appears rooted in his mind, was that there was no possible union between him and the ancient Jewish religion. The abolition of the sacrifices which had caused him so much disgust, the suppression of an impious and haughty priesthood, and, in a general sense, the abrogation of the Law, appeared to him absolutely necessary. From this time he appears no more as a Jewish reformer, but as a destroyer of Judaism. Certain advocates of the Messianic ideas had already admitted that the Messiah would bring a new law, which should be common to all the earth. The Essenes, who were scarcely Jews, also appear to have been indifferent to the temple and to the Mosaic observances. But these were only isolated or unavowed instances of boldness. Jesus was the first who dared to say that from his time, or rather from that of

John, the Law was abolished. If sometimes he used more measured terms, it was in order not to offend existing prejudices too violently. When he was driven to extremities, he lifted the veil entirely, and declared that the Law had no longer any force. On this subject he used striking comparisons. " No man putteth a piece of new cloth into an old garment, neither do men put new wine into old bottles." This was really his chief characteristic as teacher and creator. The temple excluded all except Jews from its enclosure by scornful announcements. Jesus had no sympathy with this. The narrow, hard, and uncharitable Law was only made for the children of Abraham. Jesus maintained that every well-disposed man, every man who received and loved him, was a son of Abraham. The pride of blood appeared to him the great enemy which was to be combated. In other words, Jesus was no longer a Jew. He was in the highest degree revolutionary; he called all men to a worship founded solely on the fact of their being children of God. He proclaimed the rights of man, not the rights of the Jew; the religion of man, not the religion of the Jew; the deliverance of man, not the deliverance of the Jew. How far removed was this from a Gaulonite Judas or a Matthias Margaloth, preaching revolution in the name of the Law! The religion of humanity, established, not upon blood, but upon the heart, was founded. Moses was superseded, the temple was rendered useless, and was irrevocably condemned.

CHAPTER XIV

INTERCOURSE OF JESUS WITH THE PAGANS AND THE SAMARITANS

FOLLOWING out these principles, Jesus despised all religion which was not of the heart. The vain practices of the devotees, the exterior strictness which trusted to formality for salvation, had in him a mortal enemy. He cared little for fasting. He preferred forgiveness to sacrifice. The love of God, charity, and mutual forgiveness were his whole law. Nothing could be less priestly. The priest, by his office, ever advocates public sacrifice, of which he is the appointed minister; he discourages private prayer, which has a tendency to dispense with his office.

We should seek in vain in the Gospel for one religious rite recommended by Jesus. Baptism to him was only of secondary importance; and with respect to prayer he prescribes nothing, except that it should proceed from the heart. As is always the case, many thought to substitute mere goodwill for genuine love of goodness, and imagined they could win the kingdom of heaven by saying to him, " Rabbi, Rabbi." He rebuked them, and proclaimed that his religion consisted in doing good. He often quoted the passage in Isaiah which says : " This people honour me with their lips, but their heart is far from me."

The observance of the Sabbath was the principal point upon which was raised the whole edifice of Pharisaic scruples and subtleties. This ancient and excellent institution had become a pretext for the miserable disputes of casuists, and a source of superstitious beliefs. It was believed that nature observed it; all intermittent springs were accounted " Sabbatical." This was the point upon which Jesus loved best to defy his adversaries. He openly violated the Sabbath, and only replied by subtle raillery to the reproaches that were heaped upon him. He despised still more a multitude of modern observances, which tradition had added to the Law, and which were dearer than any other to the devotees on that very account. Ablutions, and the too subtle distinctions between pure and impure things, found in him a pitiless opponent. " There is nothing from without a man," said he, " that entering into him can defile him : but the things which come out of him, those are they that defile the man." The Pharisees, who were the propagators of these mummeries, were unceasingly denounced by him. He accused them of exceeding the Law, of inventing impossible precepts, in order to create occasions of sin. " Blind leaders of the blind," said he, " take care lest ye also fall into the ditch." " O generation of vipers, how can ye, being evil, speak good things ? for out of the abundance of the heart the mouth speaketh."

He did not know the Gentiles sufficiently to think of founding anything lasting upon their conversion. Galilee contained a great number of pagans, but, as it appears, no public and organised worship of false gods. Jesus could see this worship displayed in all its splendour in the country of Tyre and Sidon, at Cæsarea Philippi and in the Decapolis, but he paid little attention to it. We never find in him the wearisome pedantry of the Jews of his time, those declamations against idolatry, so familiar to his co-religionists from the time of Alexander, and which fill, for instance, the book of " Wisdom." That which struck him in the pagans was not their idolatry, but their servility. The young Jewish democrat, agreeing on this point with Judas the Gaulonite, and admitting no master but God, was hurt at the honours with which they surrounded the persons of sovereigns, and the frequently mendacious titles given to them. With this exception, in the greater number of instances in which he comes in contact with pagans, he shows great indulgence to them ; sometimes he professes to conceive more hope of them than of the Jews. The kingdom of God would be transferred to them. " When the lord, therefore, of the vineyard cometh, what will he do unto these husbandmen ? He will miserably destroy those wicked men, and will let out his vineyard unto other husbandmen, which shall render him the fruits in their seasons." Jesus adhered so much the more to this idea as the conversion of the Gentiles was, according to Jewish ideas, one of the surest signs of the advent of the Messiah. In his kingdom of God he represents as seated at a feast by the side of Abraham, Isaac, and Jacob, men come from the four winds of heaven, while the lawful heirs of the kingdom are rejected. Sometimes, it is true, there seems to be an entirely contrary tendency in the commands he gives to his disciples: he seems to recommend them only to preach salvation to the orthodox Jews; he speaks of pagans in a manner conformable to the prejudices of the Jews. But we must remember that the disciples, whose narrow minds did not share in this supreme indifference for the privileges of the sons of Abraham, may have given the instruction of their Master the bent of their own ideas. Besides, it is very possible that Jesus may have varied on this point, just as Mohammed speaks of the Jews in the Koran, sometimes in the most honourable manner, sometimes with extreme harshness, as he had hope of winning their favour or otherwise. Tradition, in fact, attributes to Jesus two entirely opposite rules of proselytism, which he may have practised in turn: " He that is not against us is on our part." " He that is not with me is against me." Impassioned conflict involves almost necessarily this kind of contradictions.

It is certain that he counted among his disciples many men whom the Jews called " Hellenes." This word had in Palestine divers meanings. Sometimes it designated the pagans; sometimes the Jews, speaking Greek, and dwelling among the pagans; sometimes men of pagan origin converted to Judaism. It was probably in the last-named category of Hellenes that Jesus found sympathy. The affiliation with Judaism had many degrees; but the proselytes always remained in a state of inferiority in regard to the Jew by birth. Those in question were called " proselytes of the gate," or " men fearing God," and were subject to the precepts of Noah, and not to those of Moses. This very inferiority was doubtless the cause which drew them to Jesus, and gained him his favour.

He treated the Samaritans in the same manner. Shut in, like a small island, between the two great provinces of Judaism (Judea and Galilee), Samaria formed in Palestine a kind of enclosure in which was preserved the ancient worship of Gerizim, closely resembling and rivalling that of Jerusalem. This poor sect, which had neither the genius nor the learned organisation of Judaism, properly so-called, was treated by the Hierosolymites with extreme harshness. They placed them in the same rank as pagans, but hated them more. Jesus, from a feeling of opposition, was well disposed towards Samaria, and often preferred the Samaritans to the orthodox Jews. If, at other times, he seems to forbid his disciples preaching to them, con-

fining his Gospel to the Israelites proper, this was no doubt
a precept arising from special circumstances, to which the
apostles have given too absolute a meaning. Sometimes,
in fact, the Samaritans received him badly, because they
thought him imbued with the prejudices of his co-religionists
—in the same manner as in our days the European free-
thinker is regarded as an enemy by the Mussulman, who
always believes him to be a fanatical Christian. Jesus
raised himself above these misunderstandings. He had
many disciples at Shechem, and he passed at least two
days there. On one occasion he meets with gratitude and
true piety from a Samaritan only. One of his most beautiful parables is that of the man wounded on the way to
Jericho. A priest passes by and sees him, but goes on his
way; a Levite also passes, but does not stop; a Samaritan
takes pity on him, approaches him, and pours oil into his
wounds, and bandages them. Jesus argues from this that
true brotherhood is established among men by charity,
and not by creeds. The " neighbour " who in Judaism
was specially the co-religionist, was in his estimation the
man who has pity on his kind without distinction of sect.
Human brotherhood in its widest sense overflows in all his
teaching.

These thoughts, which beset Jesus on his leaving Jerusalem, found their vivid expression in an anecdote which
has been preserved respecting his return. The road from
Jerusalem into Galilee passes at the distance of half-an-
hour's journey from Shechem, in front of the opening of
the valley commanded by mounts Ebal and Gerizim.
This route was in general avoided by the Jewish pilgrims,
who preferred making in their journeys the long detour
through Perea, rather than expose themselves to the insults
of the Samaritans, or ask anything of them. It was forbidden to eat and drink with them. It was an axiom of
certain casuists that " a piece of Samaritan bread is the
flesh of swine." When they followed this route, provisions
were always laid up beforehand; yet they rarely avoided
conflict and ill-treatment. Jesus shared neither these
scruples nor these fears. Having come to the point where
the valley of Shechem opens on the left, he felt fatigued,
and stopped near a well. The Samaritans were then as
now accustomed to give to all the localities of their valley
names drawn from patriarchal reminiscences. They regarded this well as having been given by Jacob to Joseph;
it was probably the same which is now called *Bir-Iakoub*.
The disciples entered the valley and went to the city to

buy provisions. Jesus seated himself at the side of the well, having Gerizim before him.

It was about noon. A woman of Shechem came to draw water. Jesus asked her to let him drink, which excited great astonishment in the woman, the Jews generally forbidding all intercourse with the Samaritans. Won by the conversation of Jesus, the woman recognised in him a prophet, and, expecting some reproaches about her worship, she anticipated him. " Sir," said she, " our fathers worshipped in this mountain, and ye say that in Jerusalem is the place where men ought to worship." Jesus saith unto her, " Woman, believe me, the hour cometh when ye shall neither in this mountain, nor yet at Jerusalem, worship the Father. But the hour cometh, and now is, when the true worshippers shall worship the Father in spirit and in truth."

The day on which he uttered this saying he was truly Son of God. He pronounced for the first time the sentence upon which will repose the edifice of eternal religion. He founded the pure worship of all ages, of all lands, that which all elevated souls will practise until the end of time. Not only was his religion on this day the best religion of humanity, it was the absolute religion; and if other planets have inhabitants gifted with reason and morality, their religion cannot be different from that which Jesus proclaimed near the well of Jacob. Man has not been able to maintain this position; for the ideal is realised but transitorily. This sentence of Jesus has been a brilliant light amid gross darkness; it has required eighteen hundred years for the eyes of mankind (what do I say ! for an infinitely small portion of mankind) to become accustomed to it. But the light will become the full day, and, after having run through all the cycles of error, mankind will return to this sentence as the immortal expression of its faith and its hope.

CHAPTER XV

COMMENCEMENT OF THE LEGENDS CONCERNING JESUS —HIS OWN IDEA OF HIS SUPERNATURAL CHARACTER

JESUS returned to Galilee, having completely lost his Jewish faith, and filled with revolutionary ardour. His ideas are now expressed with perfect clearness. The innocent aphorisms of the first part of his prophetic career, in part borrowed from the Jewish rabbis anterior to him and the beautiful moral precepts of his second period, are exchanged for a decided policy. The Law would be abolished; and it was to be abolished by him. The Messiah had come, and he was the Messiah. The kingdom of God was about to be revealed; and it was he who would reveal it. He knew well that he would be the victim of his boldness; but the kingdom of God could not be conquered without violence; it was by crises and commotions that it was to be established. The Son of man would reappear in glory, accompanied by legions of angels, and those who had rejected him would be confounded.

The boldness of such a conception ought not to surprise us. Long before this Jesus had regarded his relation to God as that of a son to his father. That which in others would be an insupportable pride ought not in him to be regarded as presumption.

The title of "Son of David" was the first which he accepted, probably without being concerned in the innocent frauds by which it was sought to secure it to him. The family of David had, as it seems, been long extinct; the Asmoneans, being of priestly origin, could not pretend to claim such a descent for themselves; neither Herod nor the Romans dreamt for a moment that any representative whatever of the ancient dynasty existed in their midst. But from the close of the Asmonean dynasty the dream of an unknown descendant of the ancient kings, who should avenge the nation of its enemies, filled every mind. The universal belief was that the Messiah would be son of David, and, like him, would be born at Bethleem. The first idea of Jesus was not precisely this. The remembrance of David, which was uppermost in the minds of the Jews, had nothing in common with his heavenly reign. He believed himself the Son of God, and not the son of David. His kingdom and the deliverance which he meditated were of quite another order. But public opinion on this point made him do violence to himself. The immediate consequence of the proposition, " Jesus is the Messiah," was this other proposition, " Jesus is the son of David." He allowed a title to be given him without which he could not hope for success. He ended, it seems, by taking pleasure therein, for he performed most willingly the miracles which were asked of him by those who used this title in addressing him. In this, as in many other circumstances of his life, Jesus yielded to the ideas which were current in his time, although they were not precisely his own. He associated with his doctrine of the " kingdom of God " all that could warm the heart and the imagination. It was thus that we have seen him adopt the baptism of John, although it could not have been of much importance to him.

One great difficulty presented itself, his birth at Nazareth, which was of public notoriety. We do not know whether Jesus strove against this objection. Perhaps it did not present itself in Galilee, where the idea that the son of David should be a Bethlehemite was less spread. To the Galilean idealist, moreover, the title of " son of David " was sufficiently justified if he to whom it was given revived the glory of his race and brought back the great days of Israel. Did Jesus authorise by his silence the fictitious genealogies which his partisans invented in order to prove his royal descent? Did he know anything of the legends invented to prove that he was born at Bethlehem;. and particularly of the attempt to connect his Bethlehemite origin with the census which had taken place by order of the Imperial legate, Quirinus? We know not. The in-exactitude and the contradictions of the genealogies lead to the belief that they were the result of popular ideas operating at various points, and that none of them were sanctioned by Jesus. Never does he designate himself as son of David. His disciples, much less enlightened than he, frequently magnified that which he said of himself; but, as a rule, he had no knowledge of these exaggerations. Let us add that during the first three centuries consider-able portions of Christianity absolutely denied the royal descent of Jesus and the authenticity of the genealogies.

The legends about him were thus the fruit of a great and entirely spontaneous conspiracy, and were developed around him during his lifetime. No great event in history has happened without having given rise to a cycle of fables; and Jesus could not have put a stop to these popular creations, even if he had wished to do so. Perhaps a sagacious observer would have recognised from this point the germ of the narratives which were to attribute to him a supernatural birth, and which arose, it may be, from the idea, very prevalent in antiquity, that the incomparable man could not be born of the ordinary relations of the two sexes; or, it may be, in order to respond to an imperfectly understood chapter of Isaiah, which was thought to foretell that the Messiah should be born of a virgin; or, lastly, it may be in consequence of the idea that the " breath of God," already regarded as a divine hypostasis, was a principle of fecundity. Already, perhaps, there was current more than one anecdote about his infancy, conceived with the intention of showing in his biography the accomplishment of the Messianic ideal; or, rather, of the prophecies which the allegorical exegesis of the time referred to the Messiah. At other times they connected him from his birth with celebrated men, such as John the Baptist, Herod the Great, Chaldean astrologers, who, it was said, visited Jerusalem about this time, and two aged persons, Simeon and Anna, who had left memories of great sanctity. A rather loose chronology characterised these combinations, which for the most part were founded upon real facts travestied. But a singular spirit of gentleness and goodness, a profoundly popular sentiment, permeated all these fables, and made them a supplement to his preaching. It was especially after the death of Jesus that such narratives became greatly developed; we may, however, believe that they circulated even during his life, exciting only a pious credulity and simple admiration.

That Jesus never dreamt of making himself pass for an incarnation of God is a matter about which there can be no doubt. Such an idea was entirely foreign to the Jewish mind; and there is no trace of it in the Synoptical Gospels : we only find it indicated in portions of the Gospel of John, which cannot be accepted as expressing the thoughts of Jesus. Sometimes Jesus even seems to take precautions to put down such a doctrine. The accusation that he made himself God, or the equal of God, is presented, even in the Gospel of John, as a calumny of the Jews. In this last Gospel he declares himself less than his Father. Elsewhere he avows that the Father has not revealed everything to him. He believes himself to be more than an ordinary man, but separated from God by an infinite distance. He is Son of God; but all men are, or may become so, in divers degrees. Everyone ought daily to call God his father; all who are raised again will be sons of God. The Divine son-ship was attributed in the Old Testament to beings whom it was by no means pretended were equal with God. The word " son " has the widest meanings in the Semitic language, and in that of the New Testament. Besides, the idea Jesus had of man was not that low idea which a cold Deism has introduced. In his poetic conception of nature one breath alone penetrates the universe : the breath of man is that of God ; God dwells in man and lives by man, the same as man dwells in God and lives by God. The transcendent idealism of Jesus never permitted him to have a very clear notion of his own personality. He is his Father ; his Father is he. He lives in his disciples ; he is everywhere with them ; his disciples are one, as he and his Father are one. The idea to him is everything ; the body, which makes the distinction of persons, is nothing.

The title " Son of God," or simply " Son," thus became for Jesus a title analogous to " Son of man," and, like that, synonymous with the " Messiah," with the sole difference that he called himself " Son of man," and does not seem to have made the same use of the phrase " Son of God." The title Son of man expressed his character as judge ; that of Son of God his power and his participation in the supreme designs. This power had no limits. His Father had given him all power. He had the power to alter even the Sabbath. No one could know the Father except through him. The Father had delegated to him exclusively the right of judging. Nature obeyed him but she obeys also all who believe and pray, for faith can do everything. We must remember that no idea of the laws of nature marked the limit of the impossible, either in his own mind or in that of his hearers. The witnesses of his miracles thanked God " for having given such power unto men." He pardoned sins ; he was superior to David, to Abraham, to Solomon, and to the prophets. We do not know in what form, nor to what extent, these affirmations of himself were made. Jesus ought not to be judged by the law of our petty conventionalities. The admiration of his disciples overwhelmed him and carried him away. It is evident that the title of *Rabbi*, with which he was at first contented, no longer sufficed him ; even the title of prophet or messenger of God responded no longer to his ideas. The position which he attributed to himself was that of a superhuman being, and he wished to be regarded as sustaining a higher relationship to God than other men. But it must be remarked that these words, " superhuman " and " supernatural," borrowed from our petty theology, had no meaning in the exalted religious consciousness of Jesus. To him nature and the development of humanity were not limited kingdoms apart from God—paltry realities subjected to the laws of a hopeless empiricism. There was no supernatural for him, because there was no nature. Intoxicated with infinite love, he forgot the heavy chain which holds the spirit captive; he cleared at one bound the abyss, impossible to most, which the weakness of the human faculties has created between God and man.

We cannot mistake in these affirmations of Jesus the germ of the doctrine which was afterwards to make of him a divine hypostasis, in identifying him with the Word, or " second God," or eldest Son of God, or *Angel Metathronos*,[1] which Jewish theology created apart from him. A kind of necessity caused this theology, in order to correct the extreme rigour of the old Monotheism, to place near God an assessor, to whom the eternal Father is supposed to delegate the government of the universe. The belief that certain men are incarnations of divine faculties or " powers " was widespread; the Samaritans possessed about the same time a thaumaturgus named Simon, whom they identified with the " great power of God." For nearly two centuries the speculative minds of Judaism had yielded to the tendency to personify the divine attributes, and certain expressions which were connected with the Divinity. Thus, the " breath of God," which is often referred to in the Old Testament, is considered as a separate being, the " Holy Spirit." In the same manner the " Wisdom of God " and the " Word of God " became distinct personages. This was the germ of the process which has engendered the *Sephiroth* of the Cabbala, the *Æons* of Gnosticism, the hypostasis of Christianity, and all that dry mythology, consisting of personified abstractions, to which Monotheism is obliged to resort when it wishes to pluralise the Deity.

Jesus appears to have remained a stranger to these refinements of theology, which were soon to fill the world with barren disputes. The metaphysical theory of the

---

[1] Μετάθρονος—that is, sharing the throne of God; a kind of divine secretary, keeping the register of merits and demerits.

Word, such as we find it in the writings of his contemporary Philo, in the Chaldean Targums, and even in the book of " Wisdom," is neither seen in the *Logia* of Matthew nor in general in the Synoptics, the most authentic interpreters of the words of Jesus. The doctrine of the Word, in fact, had nothing in common with Messianism. The " Word " of Philo, and of the Targums, is in no sense the Messiah. It was John the Evangelist, or his school, who afterwards endeavoured to prove that Jesus was the Word, and who created, in this sense, quite a new theology, very different from that of the " kingdom of God." The essential character of the Word was that of Creator and of Providence. Now, Jesus never pretended to have created the world, nor to govern it. His office was to judge it, to renovate it. The position of president at the final judgment of humanity was the essential attribute which Jesus attached to himself, and the character which all the first Christians attributed to him. Until the great day he will sit at the right hand of God, as his Metathronos, his first minister, and his future avenger. The superhuman Christ of the Byzantine apsides, seated as judge of the world, in the midst of the apostles in the same rank with him, and superior to the angels who only assist and serve, is the exact representation of that conception of the " Son of man " of which we find the first features so strongly indicated in the book of Daniel.

At all events, the strictness of a studied theology by no means existed in such a state of society. All the ideas we have just stated formed in the mind of the disciples a theological system so little settled that the Son of God, this species of divine duplicate, is made to act purely as man. He is tempted—he is ignorant of many things—he corrects himself—he is cast down, discouraged—he asks his Father to spare him trials—he is submissive to God as a son. He who is to judge the world does not know the day of judgment. He takes precautions for his safety. Soon after his birth he is obliged to be concealed to avoid powerful men who wish to kill him. In exorcisms the devil cheats him, and does not come out at the first command. In his miracles we are sensible of painful effort—an exhaustion as if something went out of him. All these are simply the acts of a messenger of God, of a man protected and favoured by God. We must not look here for either logic or sequence. The need Jesus had of obtaining credence, and the enthusiasm of his disciples, heaped up contradictory notions. To the Messianic believers of the millenarian school, and to the enthusiastic readers of the books of Daniel and of Enoch, he was the Son of man— to the Jews holding the ordinary faith, and to the readers of Isaiah and Micah, he was the Son of David—to the disciples he was the Son of God, or simply the Son. Others, without being blamed by the disciples, took him for John the Baptist risen from the dead, for Elias, for Jeremiah, conformable to the popular belief that the ancient prophets were about to reappear, in order to prepare the time of the Messiah.

An absolute conviction, or rather the enthusiasm, which freed him from even the possibility of doubt, shrouded all these boldnesses. We little understand, with our cold and scrupulous natures, how any one can be so entirely possessed by the idea of which he has made himself the apostle. To the deeply earnest races of the West, conviction means sincerity to one's self. But sincerity to one's self has not much meaning to Oriental peoples, little accustomed to the subtleties of a critical spirit. Honesty and imposture are words which, in our rigid consciences, are opposed as two irreconcilable terms. In the East they are connected by numberless subtle links and windings. The authors of the Apocryphal books (of " Daniel " and of " Enoch," for instance), men highly exalted, in order to aid their cause, committed, without a shadow of scruple, an act which we should term a fraud. The literal truth has little value to the Oriental; he sees everything through the medium of his ideas, his interests, and his passions.

History is impossible if we do not fully admit that there are many standards of sincerity. All great things are done through the people; now, we can only lead the people by adapting ourselves to its ideas. The philosopher who, knowing this, isolates and fortifies himself in his integrity is highly praiseworthy. But he who takes humanity with its illusions, and seeks to act with it and upon it, cannot be blamed. Cæsar knew well that he was not the son of Venus; France would not be what it is if it had not for a thousand years believed in the Holy Ampulla of Rheims. It is easy for us, who are so powerless, to call this falsehood, and, proud of our timid honesty, to treat with contempt the heroes who have accepted the battle of life under other conditions. When we have effected by our scruples what they accomplished by their false-hoods, we shall have the right to be severe upon them. At least, we must make a marked distinction between societies like our own, where everything takes place in the full light of reflection, and simple and credulous communities, in which the beliefs that have governed ages have been born. Nothing great has been established which does not rest on a legend. The only culprit in such cases is the humanity which is willing to be deceived.

CHAPTER XVI

MIRACLES

Two means of proof—miracles and the accomplishment of prophecies—could alone, in the opinion of the contemporaries of Jesus, establish a supernatural mission. Jesus, and especially his disciples, employed these two processes of demonstration in perfect good faith. For a long time Jesus had been convinced that the prophets had written only in reference to him. He recognised himself in their sacred oracles; he regarded himself as the mirror in which all the prophetic spirit of Israel had read the future. The Christian school, perhaps even in the lifetime of its founder, endeavoured to prove that Jesus responded perfectly to all that the prophets had predicted of the Messiah. In many cases these comparisons were quite superficial, and are scarcely appreciable by us. They were most frequently fortuitous or insignificant circumstances in the life of the Master which recalled to the disciples certain passages of the Psalms and the Prophets, in which, in consequence of their constant preoccupation, they saw images of him. The exegesis of the time consisted thus almost entirely in a play upon words, and in quotations made in an artificial and arbitrary manner. The synagogue had no officially settled list of the passages which related to the future reign. The Messianic references were very liberally created, and constituted artifices of style rather than serious reasoning.

As to miracles, they were regarded at this period as the indispensable mark of the divine, and as the sign of the prophetic vocation. The legends of Elijah and Elisha were full of them. It was commonly believed that the Messiah would perform many. In Samaria, a few leagues from where Jesus was, a magician, named Simon, acquired an almost divine character by his illusions. Afterwards, when it was sought to establish the reputation of Apollonius of Tyana, and to prove that his life had been the sojourn of a god upon the earth, it was not thought possible to

succeed therein except by inventing a vast cycle of miracles.
The Alexandrian philosophers themselves, Plotinus and
others, are reported to have performed several. Jesus was,
therefore, obliged to choose between these two alternatives—
either to renounce his mission or to become a thaumaturgus.
It must be remembered that all antiquity, with the exception
of the great scientific schools of Greece and their Roman
disciples, accepted miracles; and that Jesus not only
believed therein, but had not the least idea of an order of
nature regulated by fixed laws. His knowledge on this
point was in no way superior to that of his contemporaries.
Nay, more, one of his most deeply-rooted opinions was that
by faith and prayer man has entire power over nature.
The faculty of performing miracles was regarded as a
privilege frequently conferred by God upon men, and it
had nothing surprising in it.

The lapse of time has changed that which constituted the
power of the great founder of Christianity into something
offensive to our ideas, and if ever the worship of Jesus
loses its hold upon mankind, it will be precisely on account
of those acts which originally inspired belief in him. Criticism experiences no embarrassment in presence of this
kind of historical phenomenon. A thaumaturgus of our
days, unless of an extreme simplicity, like that manifested
by certain stigmatists of Germany, is odious, for he performs miracles without believing in them, and is a mere
charlatan. But, if we take a Francis d'Assisi, the question
becomes altogether different; the series of miracles attending the origin of the order of St. Francis, far from offending
us, affords us real pleasure. The founder of Christianity
lived in as complete a state of poetic ignorance as did St.
Clair and the *tres socii*. The disciples deemed it quite
necessary that their Master should have interviews with
Moses and Elias, that he should command the elements,
and that he should heal the sick. We must remember,
besides, that every idea loses something of its purity as
soon as it aspires to realise itself. Success is never attained
without some injury being done to the sensibility of the
soul. Such is the feebleness of the human mind that the
best causes are ofttimes gained only by bad arguments.
The demonstrations of the primitive apologists of Christianity
are supported by very poor reasonings. Moses, Christopher
Columbus, Mohammed, have only triumphed over obstacles
by constantly making allowance for the weakness of men,
and by not always giving the true reasons for the truth.
It is probable that the hearers of Jesus were more struck

by his miracles than by his eminently divine discourses.
Let us add that doubtless popular rumour, both before and
after the death of Jesus, exaggerated enormously the number
of occurrences of this kind. The types of the Gospel
miracles, in fact, do not present much variety : they are
repetitions of each other, and seem fashioned from a very
small number of models, accommodated to the taste of the
country.

It is impossible, among the miraculous narratives so
tediously enumerated in the Gospels, to distinguish the
miracles attributed to Jesus by public opinion from those
in which he consented to play an active part. It is especially
impossible to ascertain whether the offensive circumstances
attending them, the groanings, the strugglings, and other
features savouring of jugglery, are really historical, or
whether they are the fruit of the belief of the compilers,
strongly imbued with theurgy, and living, in this respect,
in a world analogous to that of the " spiritualists " of our
times. Almost all the miracles which Jesus thought he
performed appear to have been miracles of healing. Medicine
was at this period in Judea what it still is in the East—that
is to say, in no respect scientific, but absolutely surrendered
to individual inspiration. Scientific medicine, founded
by Greece five centuries before, was at the time of Jesus
unknown to the Jews of Palestine. In such a state of
knowledge, the presence of a superior man, treating the
diseased with gentleness, and giving him by some sensible
signs the assurance of his recovery, is often a decisive
remedy. Who would dare to say that in many cases
always excepting certain peculiar injuries, the touch of a
superior being is not equal to all the resources of pharmacy
The mere pleasure of seeing him cures. He gives only a
smile, or a hope, but these are not in vain.

Jesus had no more idea than his countrymen of a rational
medical science; he believed, like everyone else, that heal
ing was to be effected by religious practices, and such a
belief was perfectly consistent. From the moment that
disease was regarded as the punishment of sin, or as the act
of a demon, and by no means as the result of physical
causes, the best physician was the holy man who had power
in the supernatural world. Healing was considered a moral
act; Jesus, who felt his moral power, would believe himself
specially gifted to heal. Convinced that the touching of
his robe, the imposition of his hands, did good to the sick
he would have been unfeeling if he had refused to those who
suffered a solace which it was in his power to bestow. Th

ealing of the sick was considered as one of the signs of
he kingdom of God, and was always associated with the
mancipation of the poor. Both were the signs of the great
evolution which was to end in the redress of all infirmities.

One of the species of cure which Jesus most frequently
erformed was exorcism, or the expulsion of demons. A
trange disposition to believe in demons pervaded all minds.
t was a universal opinion, not only in Judea, but in the
vhole world, that demons seized hold of the bodies of certain
ersons and made them act contrary to their will. A Persian
iv, often named in the Avesta, *Aeschma-daëva*, the " div
f concupiscence," adopted by the Jews under the name of
Asmodeus, became the cause of all the hysterical afflictions
f women. Epilepsy, mental and nervous maladies, in
vhich the patient seems no longer to belong to himself,
nd infirmities the cause of which is not apparent, as
eafness, dumbness, were explained in the same manner.
he admirable treatise, *On Sacred Disease*, by Hippocrates,
vhich set forth the true principles of medicine on this subject
our centuries and a half before Jesus, had not banished
rom the world so great an error. It was supposed that
here were processes more or less efficacious for driving
way the demons; and the occupation of exorcist was a
egular profession, like that of physician. There is no
oubt that Jesus had in his lifetime the reputation of
ossessing the greatest secrets of this art. There were
t that time many lunatics in Judea, doubtless in conse-
uence of the great mental excitement. These mad persons,
vho were permitted to go at large, as they still are in the
ame districts, inhabited the abandoned sepulchral caves,
vhich were the ordinary retreat of vagrants. Jesus had
reat influence over these unfortunates. A thousand
ingular incidents were related in connection with his cures,
n which the credulity of the time gave itself full scope. But
till these difficulties must not be exaggerated. The dis-
rders, which were explained by " possessions," were often
ery slight. In our times, in Syria, they regard as mad or
ossessed by a demon (these two ideas were expressed by
he same word, *medjnoun* [1]) people who are only somewhat
ccentric. A gentle word often suffices in such cases to
rive away the demon. Such were doubtless the means

[1] The phrase, *Dæmonium habes* (Matt. xi. 18; Luke vii. 33; John
ii. 20, viii. 48, and following, x. 20, and following), should be translated
y " Thou art mad," as we should say in Arabic, *Medjnoun enté*. The
erb δαιμονᾷν has also, in all classical antiquity, the meaning of " to
e mad."

F

employed by Jesus. Who knows if his celebrity as exorcist was not spread almost without his own knowledge? Persons who reside in the East are occasionally surprised to find themselves, after some time, in possession of a great reputation, as doctors, sorcerers, or discoverers of treasures without being able to account to themselves for the facts which have given rise to these strange fancies.

Many circumstances, moreover, seem to indicate that Jesus only became a thaumaturgus late in life and against his inclination. He often performs his miracles only after he has been besought to do so, and with a degree of reluctance, reproaching those who asked them for the grossness of their minds. One singularity, apparently inexplicable, is the care he takes to perform his miracles in secret, and the request he addresses to those whom he heals to tell no one When the demons wish to proclaim him the Son of God he forbids them to open their mouths; but they recognise him in spite of himself. These traits are especially characteristic in Mark, who is pre-eminently the evangelist of miracles and exorcisms. It seems that the disciple, who has furnished the fundamental teachings of this Gospel importuned Jesus with his admiration of the wonderful, and that the Master, wearied of a reputation which weighed upon him, had often said to him, " See thou say nothing to any man." Once this discordance evoked a singular outburst, a fit of impatience, in which the annoyance these perpetual demands of weak minds caused Jesus breaks forth. One would say, at times, that the character of thaumaturgus was disagreeable to him, and that he sought to give as little publicity as possible to the marvels which, in a manner, grew under his feet. When his enemies asked a miracle of him, especially a celestial miracle, a " sign from heaven," he obstinately refused. We may therefore conclude that his reputation of thaumaturgus was imposed upon him, that he did not resist it much, but also that he did nothing to aid it, and that, at all events, he felt the vanity of popular opinion on this point.

We should neglect to recognise the first principles of history if we attached too much importance to our repugnances on this matter, and if, in order to avoid the objections which might be raised against the character of Jesus, we attempted to suppress facts which, in the eyes of his contemporaries, were considered of the greatest importance. It would be convenient to say that these are the additions of disciples much inferior to their Master who, not being able to conceive his true grandeur, have ought to magnify him by illusions unworthy of him. But the four narrators of the life of Jesus are unanimous in extolling his miracles : one of them, Mark, interpreter of the apostle Peter, insists so much on this point that, if we trace the character of Christ only according to this Gospel, we should represent him as an exorcist in possession of charms of rare efficacy, as a very potent sorcerer, who inspired fear, and whom the people wished to get rid of. We will admit, then, without hesitation, that acts which would now be considered as acts of illusion or folly held a large place in the life of Jesus. Must we sacrifice to these uninviting features the sublimer aspect of such a life ? God forbid. A mere sorcerer, after the manner of Simon the magician, would not have brought about a moral revolution like that effected by Jesus. If the thaumaturgus had effaced in Jesus the moralist and the religious reformer, there would have proceeded from him a school of theurgy, and not Christianity.

The problem, moreover, presents itself in the same manner with respect to all saints and religious founders. Things now considered morbid, such as epilepsy and seeing of visions, were formerly principles of power and greatness. Physicians can designate the disease which made the fortune of Mohammed. Almost in our own day the men who have done the most for their kind (the excellent Vincent de Paul himself !) were, whether they wished it or not, thaumaturgi. If we set out with the principle that every historical personage to whom acts have been attributed, which we in the nineteenth century hold to be irrational or savouring of quackery, was either a madman or a charlatan, all criticism is nullified. The school of Alexandria was a noble school, but, nevertheless, it gave itself up to the practices of an extravagant theurgy. Socrates and Pascal were not exempt from hallucinations. Facts ought to explain themselves by proportionate causes. The weaknesses of the human mind only engender weakness; great things have always great causes in the nature of man, although they are often developed amid a crowd of littlenesses which, to superficial minds, eclipse their grandeur.

In a general sense, it is therefore true to say that Jesus was only thaumaturgus and exorcist in spite of himself. Miracles are ordinarily the work of the public much more than of him to whom they are attributed. Jesus persistently shunned the performance of the wonders which the multitude would have created for him; the greatest miracle would have been his refusal to perform any; never

would the laws of history and popular psychology hav
suffered so great a derogation. The miracles of Jesus wer
a violence done to him by his age, a concession forced fron
him by a passing necessity. The exorcist and the thauma
turgus have alike passed away; but the religious reforme
will live eternally.

Even those who did not believe in him were struck witl
these acts, and sought to be witnesses of them. The pagans
and persons unacquainted with him, experienced a senti
ment of fear, and sought to remove him from their district
Many thought perhaps to abuse his name by connectin
it with seditious movements. But the purely moral an
in no respect political tendency of the character of Jesu
saved him from these entanglements. His kingdom wa
in the circle of disciples whom a like freshness of imaginatio
and the same foretaste of heaven had grouped and retaine
around him.

We suppose that this last phase of the activity of Jesus continued about eighteen months from the time of his return from the Passover of the year 31 until his journey to the feast of tabernacles of the year 32. During this time the mind of Jesus does not appear to have been enriched by the addition of any new element; but all his old ideas grew and developed with an ever-increasing degree of power and boldness.

The fundamental idea of Jesus from the beginning was the establishment of the kingdom of God. But this kingdom of God, as we have already said, appears to have been understood by Jesus in very different senses. At times we should take him for a democratic leader desiring only the triumph of the poor and the disinherited. At other times the kingdom of God is the literal accomplishment of the apocalyptic visions of Daniel and Enoch. Lastly, the kingdom of God is often a spiritual kingdom, and the approaching deliverance is a deliverance of the spirit. In this last sense the revolution desired by Jesus was the one which has really taken place—the establishment of a new worship, purer than that of Moses. All these thoughts appear to have existed at the same time in the mind of Jesus. The first one, however—that of a temporal revolution—does not appear to have impressed him much; he never regarded the earth or the riches of the earth, or material power, as worth caring for. He had no worldly ambition. Sometimes by a natural consequence, his great religious importance was in danger of being converted into mere social importance. Men came requesting him to judge and arbitrate on questions affecting their material interests. Jesus rejected these proposals with haughtiness, treating them as insults. Full of his heavenly ideal, he never abandoned his disdainful poverty. As to the other two conceptions of the kingdom of God, Jesus appears always to

have held them simultaneously. If he had been only a:
enthusiast, led away by the apocalypses on which the
popular imagination fed, he would have remained an
obscure sectary, inferior to those whose ideas he followed
If he had been only a puritan, a sort of Channing or " Savoy
ard vicar," he would undoubtedly have been unsuccessful
The two parts of his system, or, rather, his two conception
of the kingdom of God, rest one on the other, and this
mutual support has been the cause of his incomparable
success. The first Christians were dreamers, living in a
circle of ideas which we should term visionary; but, at the
same time, they were the heroes of that social war which
has resulted in the enfranchisement of the conscience
and in the establishment of a religion from which the
pure worship, proclaimed by the founder, will eventually
proceed.

The apocalyptic ideas of Jesus, in their most complete
form, may thus be summed up. The existing condition
of humanity is approaching its termination. This termina
tion will be an immense revolution, " an anguish " similar
to the pains of child-birth; a *palingenesis*, or, in the words
of Jesus himself, a " new birth," preceded by dark calamities
and heralded by strange phenomena. In the great day
there will appear in the heavens the sign of the Son of man
it will be a startling and luminous vision like that of Sinai
a great storm rending the clouds, a fiery meteor flashing
rapidly from east to west. The Messiah will appear in the
clouds, clothed in glory and majesty, to the sound of trum-
pets and surrounded by angels. His disciples will sit by
his side upon thrones. The dead will then arise, and the
Messiah will proceed to judgment.

At this judgment men will be divided into two classes
according to their deeds. The angels will be the executors
of the sentences. The elect will enter into delightful
mansions, which have been prepared for them from the
foundation of the world; there they will be seated, clothed
with light, at a feast presided over by Abraham, the
patriarchs and the prophets. They will be the smaller
number. The rest will depart into *Gehenna*. Gehenna
was the western valley of Jerusalem. There the worship
of fire had been practised at various times, and the place
had become a kind of sewer. Gehenna was, therefore, in
the mind of Jesus, a gloomy, filthy valley, full of fire. Those
excluded from the kingdom will there be burnt and eaten
by the never-dying worm, in company with Satan and his
rebel angels. There, there will be wailing and gnashing

of teeth. The kingdom of heaven will be as a closed room, lighted from within, in the midst of a world of darkness and torments.

This new order of things will be eternal. Paradise and Gehenna will have no end. An impassable abyss separates the one from the other. The Son of man, seated on the right hand of God, will preside over this final condition of the world and of humanity.

That all this was taken literally by the disciples and by the Master himself at certain moments appears clearly evident from the writings of the time. If the first Christian generation had one profound and constant belief, it was that the world was near its end, and that the great " revelation " of Christ was about to take place. The startling proclamation, " The time is at hand," which commences and closes the Apocalypse; the incessantly reiterated appeal, " He that hath ears to hear let him hear ! " were the cries of hope and encouragement for the whole Apostolic age. A Syrian expression, *Maran atha*, " Our Lord cometh ! " became a sort of password, which the believers used among themselves to strengthen their faith and their hope. The Apocalypse, written in the year 68 of our era, declares that the end will come in three years and a half. The " Ascension of Isaiah " adopts a calculation very similar to this.

Jesus never indulged in such precise details. When he was interrogated as to the time of his advent, he always refused to reply; once even he declared that the date of this great day was known only by the Father, who had revealed it neither to the angels nor to the Son. He said that the time when the kingdom of God was most anxiously expected was just that in which it would not appear. He constantly repeated that it would be a surprise, as in the times of Noah and of Lot; that we must be on our guard, always ready to depart; that each one must watch and keep his lamp trimmed as for a wedding procession, which arrives unforeseen; that the Son of man would come like a thief, at an hour when he would not be expected; that he would appear as a flash of lightning, running from one end of the heavens to the other. But his declarations on the nearness of the catastrophe leave no room for any equivocation. " This generation," said he, " shall not pass till all these things be fulfilled. There be some standing here which shall not taste of death till they see the Son of man coming in his kingdom." He reproaches those who do not believe in him for not being able to read the signs of the future kingdom. " When it is evening, ye say, It will be fair

weather, for the sky is red.   And in the morning, It will be
foul weather to-day, for the sky is red and lowering.   O ye
hypocrites, ye can discern the face of the sky, but can ye not
discern the signs of the times ? "   By an illusion common to
all great reformers, Jesus imagined the end to be much
nearer than it really was; he did not take into account
the slowness of the movements of humanity; he thought
to realise in one day that which, eighteen centuries later
has still to be accomplished.

These formal declarations preoccupied the Christian
family for nearly seventy years.   It was believed that some
of the disciples would see the day of the final revelation
before dying.   John, in particular, was considered as being
of this number; many believed that he would never die.
Perhaps this was a later opinion suggested towards the end
of the first century, by the advanced age which John seems
to have reached; this age having given rise to the belief
that God wished to prolong his life indefinitely until the great
day, in order to realise the words of Jesus.   However this
may be, at his death the faith of many was shaken, and his
disciples attached to the prediction of Christ a more sub-
dued meaning.

At the same time that Jesus fully admitted the
Apocalyptic beliefs, such as we find them in the apocryphal
Jewish books, he admitted the doctrine, which is the comple-
ment, or rather the condition, of them all—namely, the
resurrection of the dead.   This doctrine, as we have already
said, was still somewhat new in Israel: a number of people
either did not know it, or did not believe it.   It was the faith
of the Pharisees, and of the fervent adherents of the Messianic beliefs.   Jesus accepted it unreservedly, but always
in the most idealistic sense.   Many imagined that in
the resuscitated world they would eat, drink, and marry.
Jesus, indeed, admits into his kingdom a new passover, a
table, and a new wine; but he expressly excludes marriage
from it.   The Sadducees had on this subject an apparently
coarse argument, but one which was really in conformity
with the old theology.   It will be remembered that, according to the ancient sages, man survived only in his children.
The Mosaic code had consecrated this patriarchal theory by a
strange institution, the levirate law.   The Sadducees drew
from thence subtle deductions against the resurrection.
Jesus escaped them by formally declaring that in the life
eternal there would no longer exist differences of sex, and
that men would be like the angels.   Sometimes he seems
to promise resurrection only to the righteous, the punish-

ment of the wicked consisting in complete annihilation. Oftener, however, Jesus declares that the resurrection shall bring eternal confusion to the wicked.

It will be seen that nothing in all these theories was absolutely new. The Gospels and the writings of the Apostles scarcely contain anything as regards apocalyptic doctrines but what might be found already in " Daniel," " Enoch," and the " Sibylline Oracles," of Jewish origin. Jesus accepted the ideas, which were generally received among his contemporaries. He made them his basis of action, or rather one of his bases; for he had too profound an idea of his true work to establish it solely upon such fragile principles—principles so liable to be decisively refuted by facts.

It is evident, indeed, that such a doctrine, taken by itself in a literal manner, had no future. The world, in continuing to exist, caused it to crumble. One generation of man at the most was the limit of its endurance. The faith of the first Christian generation is intelligible, but the faith of the second generation is no longer so. After the death of John, or of the last survivor, whoever he might be, of the group which had seen the Master, the word of Jesus was convicted of falsehood. If the doctrine of Jesus had been simply belief in an approaching end of the world, it would certainly now be sleeping in oblivion. What is it, then, which has saved it? The great breadth of the Gospel conceptions, which has permitted doctrines suited to very different intellectual conditions to be found under the same creed. The world has not ended, as Jesus announced, and as his disciples believed. But it has been renewed, and in one sense renewed as Jesus desired. It is because his thought was two-sided that it has been fruitful. His chimera has not had the fate of so many others which have crossed the human mind, because it concealed a germ of life which, having been introduced, thanks to the covering of fable, into the bosom of humanity, has thus brought forth eternal fruits.

And let us not say that this is a benevolent interpretation, imagined in order to clear the honour of our great Master from the cruel contradiction inflicted on his dreams by reality. No, no; this true kingdom of God, this kingdom of the spirit, which makes each one king and priest; this kingdom which, like the grain of mustard seed, has become a tree which overshadows the world, and amid whose branches the birds have their nests, was understood, wished for, and founded by Jesus. By the side of the false, cold,

F 2

and impossible idea of an ostentatious advent, he conceived the real city of God, the true "palingenesis," the Sermon on the Mount, the apotheosis of the weak, the love of the people, regard for the poor, and the re-establishment of all that is humble, true, and simple. This re-establishment he has depicted as an incomparable artist, by features which will last eternally. Each of us owes that which is best in himself to him. Let us pardon him his hope of a vain apocalypse, and of a second coming in great triumph upon the clouds of heaven. Perhaps these were the errors of others rather than his own; and if it be true that he himself shared the general illusion, what matters it, since his dream rendered him strong against death, and sustained him in a struggle to which he might otherwise have been unequal?

We must, then, attach several meanings to the divine city conceived by Jesus. If his only thought had been that the end of time was near, and that we must prepare for it, he would not have surpassed John the Baptist. To renounce a world ready to crumble, to detach one's self little by little from the present life, and to aspire to the kingdom about to come, would have formed the gist of his preaching. The teaching of Jesus had always a much larger scope. He proposed to himself to create a new state of humanity, and not merely to prepare the end of that which was in existence. Elias or Jeremiah, reappearing in order to prepare men for the supreme crisis, would not have preached as he did. This is so true that this morality, attributed to the latter days, is found to be the eternal morality, that which has saved humanity. Jesus himself in many cases makes use of modes of speech which do not accord with the apocalyptic theory. He often declares that the kingdom of God has already commenced; that every man bears it within himself; and can, if he be worthy, partake of it; that each one silently creates this kingdom by the true conversion of the heart. The kingdom of God at such times is only the highest form of good. A better order of things than that which exists, the reign of justice, which the faithful, according to their ability, ought to help in establishing; or, again, the liberty of the soul, something analogous to the Buddhist "deliverance," the fruit of the soul's separation from matter and absorption in the divine essence. These truths, which are purely abstract to us, were living realities to Jesus. Everything in his mind was concrete and substantial. Jesus, of all men, believed most thoroughly in the reality of the ideal.

In accepting the Utopias of his time and his race, Jesus thus was able to make high truths of them, thanks to the fruitful misconceptions of their import. His kingdom of God was no doubt the approaching apocalypse, which was about to be unfolded in the heavens. But it was still, and probably above all the kingdom of the soul, founded on liberty and on the filial sentiment which the virtuous man feels when resting on the bosom of his Father. It was a pure religion, without forms, without temple, and without priest; it was the moral judgment of the world, delegated to the conscience of the just man, and to the arm of the people. This is what was designed to live; this is what has lived. When, at the end of a century of vain expectation, the materialistic hope of a near end of the world was exhausted, the true kingdom of God became apparent. Accommodating explanations throw a veil over the material kingdom, which was then seen to be incapable of realisation. The Apocalypse of John, the chief Canonical book of the New Testament, being too formally tied to the idea of an immediate catastrophe, became of secondary importance, was held to be unintelligible, tortured in a thousand ways, and almost rejected. At least, its accomplishment was adjourned to an indefinite future. Some poor benighted ones, who, in a fully enlightened age, still preserved the hopes of the first disciples, became heretics (Ebionites, Millenarians) lost in the shallows of Christianity. Mankind had passed to another kingdom of God. The degree of truth contained in the thought of Jesus had prevailed over the chimera which obscured it.

Let us not, however, despise this chimera, which has been the thick rind of the sacred fruit on which we live. This fantastic kingdom of heaven, this endless pursuit after a city of God, which has constantly preoccupied Christianity during its long career, has been the principle of that great instinct of futurity which has animated all reformers, persistent believers in the Apocalypse, from Joachim of Flora down to the Protestant sectary of our days. This impotent effort to establish a perfect society has been the source of the extraordinary tension which has always made the true Christian an athlete struggling against the existing order of things. The idea of the "kingdom of God," and the Apocalypse, which is the complete image of it, are thus, in a sense, the highest and most poetic expressions of human progress. But they have necessarily given rise to great errors. The end of the world, suspended as a perpetual menace over mankind, was, by the periodical panics which it caused during centuries, a great hindrance to all secular development. Society, being no longer certain of its existence, contracted therefrom a degree of trepidation, and those habits of servile humility, which rendered the Middle Ages so inferior to ancient and modern times. A profound change had also taken place in the mode of regarding the coming of Christ. When it was first announced to mankind that the end of the world was about to come, like the infant which receives death with a smile, it experienced the greatest access of joy that it has ever felt. But, in growing old, the world became attached to it. The day of grace, so long expected by the simple souls of Galilee, became to these iron ages a day of wrath : *Dies iræ, dies illa !* But, even in the midst of barbarism, the idea of the kingdom of God continued fruitful. In spite of the feudal church, of sects, and of religious orders, holy persons continued to protest, in the name of the Gospel, against the iniquity of the world. Even in our days, troubled days, in which Jesus has no more authentic followers than those who seem to deny him, the dreams of an ideal organisation of society, which have so much analogy with the aspirations of the primitive Christian sects, are only in one sense the blossoming of the same idea. They are one of the branches of that immense tree in which germinates all thought of a future, and of which the " kingdom of God " will be eternally the root and stem. All the social revolutions of humanity will be grafted on this phrase. But, tainted by a coarse materialism, and aspiring to the impossible—that is to say, to found universal happiness upon political and economical measures —the " socialist " attempts of our time will remain unfruitful, until they take as their rule the true spirit of Jesus, I mean absolute idealism—the principle that, in order to possess the world, we must renounce it.

The phrase, " kingdom of God," expresses also, very happily, the want which the soul experiences of a supplementary destiny, of a compensation for the present life. Those who do not accept the definition of man as a compound of two substances, and who regard the Deistical dogma of the immortality of the soul as in contradiction with physiology, love to fall back upon the hope of a final reparation, which, under an unknown form, shall satisfy the wants of the heart of man. Who knows if the highest term of progress after millions of ages may not evoke the absolute conscience of the universe, and in this conscience the awakening of all that has lived ? A sleep of a million of years is not longer than the sleep of an hour. St. Paul, on this hypothesis, was right in saying, *In ictu oculi !* It is certain that moral and virtuous humanity will have its reward, that one day the ideas of the poor but honest man will judge the world, and on that day the ideal figure of Jesus will be the confusion of the frivolous who have not believed in virtue, and of the selfish who have not been able to attain to it.   The favourite phrase of Jesus continues, therefore, full of an eternal beauty.   A kind of exalted divination seems to have maintained it in a vague sublimity, embracing at the same time various orders of truths.

CHAPTER XVIII

INSTITUTIONS OF JESUS

THAT Jesus was never entirely absorbed in his apocalyptic ideas is proved, moreover, by the fact that at the very time he was most preoccupied with them he laid with rare forethought the foundation of a Church destined to endure. It is scarcely possible to doubt that he himself chose from among his disciples those who were pre-eminently called the " Apostles," or the " Twelve," since on the day after his death we find them forming a distinct body, and filling up by election the vacancies that had arisen in their midst. They were the two sons of Jonas, the two sons of Zebedee; James, son of Cleophas; Philip; Nathaniel bar-Tolmai; Thomas; Levi, or Matthew, the son of Alphæus; Simon Zelotes; Thaddeus or Lebbæus; and Judas of Kerioth. It is probable that the idea of the twelve tribes of Israel had had some share in the choice of this number.

The " Twelve," at all events, formed a group of privileged disciples, among whom Peter maintained a fraternal priority, and to them Jesus confided the propagation of his work. There was nothing, however, which presented the appearance of a regularly organised sacerdotal school. The lists of the " Twelve," which have been preserved, contain many uncertainties and contradictions; two or three of those who figure in them have remained completely obscure. Two, at least, Peter and Philip, were married and had children.

Jesus evidently confided secrets to the Twelve, which he forbade them to communicate to the world. It seems as if his plan at times was to surround himself with a degree of mystery, to postpone the most important testimony respecting himself till after his death, and to reveal himself completely only to his disciples, confiding to them the care of demonstrating him afterwards to the world. " What I tell you in darkness, that speak ye in light; and what ye hear in the ear, that preach ye upon the housetops." This spared him the necessity of too precise declarations, and created a kind of medium between the public and himself. It is clear that there were certain teachings confined to the Apostles, and that he explained many parables to them, the meaning of which was ambiguous to the multitude. An enigmatical form and a degree of oddness in connecting ideas were customary in the teachings of the doctors, as may be seen in the sentences of the *Pirké Aboth*. Jesus explained to his intimate friends whatever was peculiar in his apothegms or in his apologues, and showed them his meaning stripped of the wealth of illustration which sometimes obscured it. Many of these explanations appear to have been carefully preserved.

During the lifetime of Jesus the Apostles preached, but without ever departing far from him. Their preaching, moreover, was limited to the announcement of the speedy coming of the kingdom of God. They went from town to town, receiving hospitality, or rather taking it themselves, according to the custom of the country. The guest in the East has much authority; he is superior to the master of the house, who has the greatest confidence in him. This fireside preaching is admirably adapted to the propagation of new doctrines. The hidden treasure is communicated, and payment is thus made for what is received; politeness and good feeling lend their aid; the household is touched and converted. Remove Oriental hospitality, and it would be impossible to explain the propagation of Christianity. Jesus, who adhered greatly to good old customs, encouraged his disciples to make no scruple of profiting by this ancient public right, probably already abolished in the great towns where there were hostelries. " The labourer," said he, " is worthy of his hire ! " Once installed in any house, they were to remain there, eating and drinking what was offered them as long as their mission lasted.

Jesus desired that, in imitation of his example, the messengers of the glad tidings should render their preaching agreeable by kindly and polished manners. He directed that, on entering into a house, they should give the salaam or greeting. Some hesitated; the salaam being then, as now, in the East, a sign of religious communion, which is not risked with persons of a doubtful faith. " Fear nothing," said Jesus; " if no one in the house is worthy of your salute, it will return unto you." Sometimes, in fact, the Apostles of the kingdom of God were badly received, and came to complain to Jesus, who generally sought to soothe them. Some of them, persuaded of the omnipotence of their Master, were hurt at this forbearance.

The sons of Zebedee wanted him to call down fire from heaven upon the inhospitable towns. Jesus received these outbursts with a subtle irony, and stopped them by saying: " The Son of man is not come to destroy men's lives, but to save them."

He sought in every way to establish as a principle that his Apostles were as himself. It was believed that he had communicated his marvellous virtues to them. They cast out demons, prophesied, and formed a school of renowned exorcists, although certain cases were beyond their power. They also wrought cures, either by the imposition of hands or by the anointing with oil, one of the fundamental processes of Oriental medicine. Lastly, like the Psylli, they could handle serpents and could drink deadly potions with impunity. The further we get from Jesus, the more offensive does this theurgy become. But there is no doubt that it was generally received by the primitive Church, and that it held an important place in the estimation of the world around. Charlatans, as generally happens, took advantage of this movement of popular credulity. Even in the lifetime of Jesus many, without being his disciples, cast out demons in his name. The true disciples were much displeased at this, and sought to prevent them. Jesus, who saw that this was really an homage paid to his renown, was not very severe towards them. It must be observed, moreover, that the exercise of these gifts had to some degree become a trade. Carrying the logic of absurdity to the extreme, certain men cast out demons by Beelzebub, the prince of demons. They imagined that this sovereign of the infernal regions must have entire authority over his subordinates, and that in acting through him they were certain to make the intruding spirit depart. Some even sought to buy from the disciples of Jesus the secret of the miraculous powers which had been conferred upon them. The germ of a Church from this time began to appear. This fertile idea of the power of men in association (*ecclesia*) was doubtless derived from Jesus. Full of the purely idealistic doctrine that it is the union of love which brings souls together, he declared that whenever men assembled in his name he would be in their midst. He confided to the Church the right to bind and to unbind (that is to say, to render certain things lawful or unlawful), to remit sins, to reprimand, to warn with authority, and to pray with the certainty of being heard favourably. It is possible that many of these words may have been attributed to the Master in order to give a warrant to the collective authority

which was afterwards sought to be substituted for that of
Jesus. At all events, it was only after his death that
particular Churches were established, and even this first
constitution was made purely and simply on the model of
the Synagogue. Many personages who had loved Jesus
much, and had founded great hopes upon him, as Joseph
of Arimathea, Lazarus, Mary Magdalen, and Nicodemus,
did not, it seems, join these Churches, but clung to the
tender or respectful memory which they had preserved of him.

Moreover, there is no trace, in the teaching of Jesus, of
an applied morality or of a canonical law, ever so slightly
defined. Once only, respecting marriage, he spoke decidedly,
and forbade divorce. Neither was there any theology or
creed. There were indefinite views respecting the Father,
the Son, and the Spirit, from which, afterwards, were drawn
the Trinity and the Incarnation, but they were then only
in a state of indeterminate imagery. The later books of
the Jewish canon recognised the Holy Spirit, a sort of
divine hypostasis, sometimes identified with Wisdom or the
Word. Jesus insisted upon this point, and announced to
his disciples a baptism by fire and by the spirit, as much
preferable to that of John, a baptism which they believed
they had received, after the death of Jesus, in the form of
a great wind and tongues of fire. The Holy Spirit thus sent
by the Father was to teach them all truth, and testify to
that which Jesus himself had promulgated. In order to
designate this Spirit, Jesus made use of the word *Peraklit*,
which the Syro-Chaldaic had borrowed from the Greek
(παράκλητος), and which appears to have had in his mind
the meaning of " advocate," " counsellor," and sometimes
that of " interpreter of celestial truths," and of " teacher
charged to reveal to men the hitherto hidden mysteries."
He regarded himself as a *Peraklit* to his disciples, and the
Spirit which was to come after his death would only take
his place. This was an application of the process which
the Jewish and Christian theologies would follow during
centuries, and which was to produce a whole series of
divine assessors, the *Metathronos*, the *Synadelphe* or *Sandal-
phon*, and all the personifications of the Cabbala. But in
Judaism these creations were to remain free and individual
speculations, while in Christianity, commencing with the
fourth century, they were to form the very essence of
orthodoxy and of the universal doctrine.

It is unnecessary to remark how remote from the thought
of Jesus was the idea of a religious book containing a code
and articles of faith. Not only did he not write, but it was

contrary to the spirit of the infant sect to produce sacred books. They believed themselves to be on the eve of the great final catastrophe. The Messiah came to put the seal upon the Law and the Prophets, not to promulgate new Scriptures. With the exception of the Apocalypse, which was in one sense the only revealed book of the infant Christianity, all the other writings of the Apostolic age were works evoked by existing circumstances, making no pretensions to furnish a completely dogmatic whole. The Gospels had at first an entirely personal character, and much less authority than tradition.

Had the sect, however, no sacrament, no rite, no sign of union? It had one which all tradition ascribes to Jesus. One of the favourite ideas of the Master was that he was the new bread—bread very superior to manna, and on which mankind was to live. This idea, the germ of the Eucharist, was at times expressed by him in singularly concrete forms. On one occasion especially, in the synagogue of Capernaum, he took a decided step, which cost him several of his disciples. " Verily, verily, I say unto you, Moses gave you not that bread from heaven; but my Father giveth you the true bread from heaven.'' And he added, " I am the bread of life : he that cometh to me shall never hunger, and he that believeth on me shall never thirst." These words excited much murmuring. " The Jews then murmured at him because he said, I am the bread which came down from heaven. And they said, Is not this Jesus the son of Joseph, whose father and mother we know? how is it then that he saith, I came down from heaven?" But Jesus insisting with still more force, said, " I am that bread of life; your fathers did eat manna in the wilderness and are dead. This is the bread which cometh down from heaven, that a man may eat thereof, and not die. I am the living bread which came down from heaven; if any man eat of this bread, he shall live for ever : and the bread that I will give is my flesh, which I will give for the life of the world." The offence was now at its height : " How can this man give us his flesh to eat?" Jesus going still further, said, " Verily, verily, I say unto you, Except ye eat the flesh of the Son of man, and drink his blood, ye have no life in you. Whoso eateth my flesh and drinketh my blood, hath eternal life, and I will raise him up at the last day. For my flesh is meat indeed, and my blood is drink indeed. He that eateth my flesh and drinketh my blood dwelleth in me, and I in him. As the living Father has sent me, and I live by the Father : so he that eateth me, even he shall live by me. This is that bread which came down from heaven : not as your fathers did eat manna, and are dead : he that eateth of this bread shall live for ever." Several of his disciples were offended at such obstinacy in paradox, and ceased to follow him. Jesus did not retract; he only added : " It is the spirit that quickeneth; the flesh profiteth nothing. The words that I speak unto you, they are spirit, and they are life." The Twelve remained faithful, notwithstanding this strange preaching. It gave to Cephas, in particular, an opportunity of showing his absolute devotion, and of proclaiming once more, " Thou art that Christ, the Son of the living God."

It is probable that from that time, in the common repasts of the sect, there was established some custom which was derived from the discourse so badly received by the men of Capernaum. But the Apostolic traditions on this subject are very diverse and probably intentionally incomplete. The Synoptical Gospels suppose that a unique sacramental act, served as basis to the mysterious rite, and declare this to have been " the last supper." John, who has preserved the incident at the synagogue of Capernaum, does not speak of such an act, although he describes the last supper at great length. Elsewhere we see Jesus recognised in the breaking of bread, as if this act had been to those who associated with him the most characteristic of his person. When he was dead, the form under which he appeared to the pious memory of his disciples was that of president of a mysterious banquet, taking the bread, blessing it, breaking and presenting it to those present. It is probable that this was one of his habits, and that at such times he was particularly loving and tender. One material circumstance, the presence of fish upon the table (a striking indication, which proves that the rite had its birth on the shore of Lake Tiberias) was itself almost sacramental, and became a necessary part of the conceptions of the sacred feast.

Their repasts were among the sweetest moments of the infant community. At these times they all assembled; the Master spoke to each one, and kept up a charming and lively conversation. Jesus loved these seasons, and was pleased to see his spiritual family thus grouped around him. The participation of the same bread was considered as a kind of communion, a reciprocal bond. The Master used, in this respect, extremely strong terms, which were afterwards taken in a very literal sense. Jesus was, at the same

time, very idealistic in his conceptions, and very materialistic in his expression of them. Wishing to express the
thought that the believer only lives by him, that altogether
(body, blood, and soul) he was the life of the truly faithful,
he said to his disciples, " I am your nourishment," a phrase
which, turned in figurative style, became, " My flesh is your
bread, my blood your drink." Added to this the modes of
speech employed by Jesus, always strongly subjective,
carried him still further. At table, pointing to the food,
he said, " I am here "—holding the bread—" this is my
body "; and of the wine, " This is my blood "—all
modes of speech which were equivalent to, " I am your
nourishment."

This mysterious rite obtained great importance in the
lifetime of Jesus. It was probably established some time
before the last journey to Jerusalem, and it was the result
of a general doctrine much more than a determinate act.
After the death of Jesus it became the great symbol of
Christian communion, and it is to the most solemn moment
of the life of the Saviour that its establishment is referred.
It was wished to see, in the consecration of bread and wine,
a farewell memorial which Jesus, at the moment of quitting
life, had left to his disciples. They recognised Jesus himself in this sacrament. The wholly spiritual idea of the
presence of souls, which was one of the most familiar to
the Master, which made him say, for instance, that he was
personally with his disciples when they were assembled in
his name, rendered this easily admissible. Jesus, we have
already said, never had a very defined notion of that which
constitutes individuality. In the degree of exaltation to
which he had attained, the ideal surpassed everything to
such an extent that the body counted for nothing. We
are one when we love one another, when we live in depend-
ence on each other; it was thus that he and his disciples
were one. His disciples adopted the same language. Those
who for years had lived with him had seen him constantly
take the bread and the cup " between his holy and vener-
able hands," and thus offer himself to them. It was he
whom they ate and drank; he became the true passover,
the former one having been abrogated by his blood. It is
impossible to translate into our essentially determined
idiom, in which a rigorous distinction between the material
and the metaphorical must always be observed, habits of
style the essential character of which is to attribute to
metaphor, or rather to the idea it represents, a complete
reality.

CHAPTER XIX

INCREASING PROGRESSION OF ENTHUSIASM AND OF EXALTATION

It is clear that such a religious society, founded solely on the expectation of the kingdom of God, must be in itself very incomplete. The first Christian generation lived almost entirely upon expectations and dreams. On the eve of seeing the world come to an end, they regarded as useless everything which only served to prolong it. Possession of property was interdicted. Everything which attaches man to earth, everything which draws him aside from heaven, was to be avoided. Although several of the disciples were married, there was to be no more marriage on becoming a member of the sect. The celibate was greatly preferred; even in marriage continence was recommended. At one time the Master seems to approve of those who should mutilate themselves in prospect of the kingdom of God. In this he was consistent with his principle : " If thy hand or thy foot offend thee, cut them off, and cast them from thee; it is better for thee to enter into life halt or maimed, rather than having two hands or two feet to be cast into everlasting fire. And if thine eye offend thee, pluck it out, and cast it from thee; it is better for thee to enter into life with one eye, rather than having two eyes to be cast into hell-fire." The cessation of generation was often considered as the sign and condition of the kingdom of God.

Never, we perceive, would this primitive Church have formed a lasting society but for the great variety of germs deposited by Jesus in his teaching. It required more than a century for the true Christian Church—that which has converted the world—to disengage itself from this little sect of " latter-day saints," and to become a framework applicable to the whole of human society. The same thing, indeed, took place in Buddhism, which at first was founded only for monks. The same thing would have happened in the order of St. Francis if that order had succeeded in its pretension of becoming the rule of the whole human society. Essentially Utopian in their origin, and succeeding by their very exaggeration, the great systems of which we have just spoken have only laid hold of the world by being profoundly modified, and by abandoning their excesses. Jesus did not advance beyond this first and entirely monachal period, in which it was believed that the impossible could be attempted with impunity. He made no concession to necessity. He boldly preached war against nature and total severance from ties of blood. " Verily I say unto you," said he, " there is no man that hath left house, or parents, or brethren, or wife, or children, for the kingdom of God's sake, who shall not receive manifold more in this present time, and in the world to come life everlasting."

The teachings which Jesus is reputed to have given to his disciples breathe the same exaltation. He who was so tolerant to the world outside, he who contented himself sometimes with half adhesions, exercised towards his own an extreme rigour. He would have no " all buts." We should call it an " order," constituted by the most austere rules. Faithful to his idea that the cares of life trouble man and draw him downwards, Jesus required from his associates a complete detachment from the earth, an absolute devotion to his work. They were not to carry with them either money or provisions for the way, not even a scrip, or change of raiment. They must practise absolute poverty, live on alms and hospitality. " Freely ye have received, freely give," said he, in his beautiful language. Arrested and arraigned before the judges, they were not to prepare their defence; the *Peraklit*, the heavenly advocate, would inspire them with what they ought to say. The Father would send them his Spirit from on high, which would become the principle of all their acts, the director of their thoughts, and their guide through the world. If driven from any town, they were to shake the dust from their shoes, declaring always the proximity of the kingdom of God, that none might plead ignorance. " Ye shall not have gone over the cities of Israel," added he, " till the Son of man be come."

A strange ardour animates all these discourses, which may in part be the creation of the enthusiasm of his disciples, but which even in that case came indirectly from Jesus, for it was he who had inspired the enthusiasm. He predicted for his followers severe persecutions and the hatred of mankind. He sent them forth as lambs in the midst of wolves. They would be scourged in the synagogues and dragged to prison. Brother should deliver up brother to death, and the father his son. When they were prosecuted in one country, they were to flee to another. "The disciple," said he, "is not above his Master, nor the servant above his lord. Fear not them which kill the body, but are not able to kill the soul. Are not two sparrows sold for a farthing? and one of them shall not fall to the ground without your Father. But the very hairs of your head are all numbered. Fear ye not, therefore, ye are of more value than many sparrows." "Whosoever, therefore," continued he, "shall confess to me before men, him will I confess also before my Father which is in heaven. But whosoever shall deny me before men, him will I also deny before my Father which is in heaven."

In these fits of severity he went so far as to abolish all natural ties. His requirements had no longer any bounds. Despising the healthy limits of man's nature, he demanded that he should exist only for him, that he should love him alone. "If any man come to me," he said, "and hate not his father, and mother, and wife, and children, and brethren, and sisters, and his own life also, he cannot be my disciple." "So, likewise, whosoever he be of you that forsaketh not all that he hath, he cannot be my disciple." There was, at such times, something strange and more than human in his words; they were like a fire utterly consuming life and reducing everything to a frightful wilderness. The harsh and gloomy feeling of distaste for the world, and of excessive self-abnegation, which characterises Christian perfection, was originated, not by the refined and cheerful moralist of earlier days, but by the sombre giant whom a kind of grand presentiment was withdrawing, more and more, out of the pale of humanity. We should almost say that, in these moments of conflict with the most legitimate cravings of the heart, Jesus had forgotten the pleasure of living, of loving, of seeing, and of feeling. Employing still more unmeasured language, he even said, "If any man will come after me, let him deny himself and follow me. He that loveth father or mother more than me is not worthy of me, and he that loveth son or daughter more than me is not worthy of me. He that findeth his life shall lose it, and he that loseth his life for my sake and the Gospel's shall find it. What is a man profited if he shall gain the whole world and lose his own soul?" Two anecdotes of the kind we cannot accept as historical, but which, although they were exaggerations, were intended to represent a characteristic feature, clearly illustrate this defiance of

nature. He said to one man, " Follow me ! " But he said,
" Lord, suffer me first to go and bury my father." Jesus
answered, " Let the dead bury their dead : but go thou
and preach the kingdom of God." Another said to him,
" Lord, I will follow thee; but let me first go bid them
farewell which are at home at my house." Jesus replied,
" No man, having put his hand to the plough, and looking
back, is fit for the kingdom of God." An extraordinary
confidence, and at times accents of singular sweetness,
reversing all our ideas of him, caused these exaggerations
to be easily received. " Come unto me," cried he, " all ye
that labour and are heavy-laden, and I will give you rest.
Take my yoke upon you, and learn of me : for I am meek
and lowly in heart : and ye shall find rest unto your souls.
For my yoke is easy, and my burden is light."

A great danger threatened the future of this exalted
morality, thus expressed in hyperbolical language and with
a terrible energy. By detaching man from earth the ties
of life were severed. The Christian would be praised for
being a bad son or a bad patriot if it was for Christ that he
resisted his father and fought against his country. The
ancient city, the parent republic, the state, or the law
common to all, were thus placed in hostility with the
kingdom of God. A fatal germ of theocracy was introduced
into the world.

From this point another consequence may be perceived.
This morality, created for a temporary crisis, when introduced into a peaceful country, and in the midst of a society
assured of its own duration, must seem impossible. The
Gospel was thus destined to become a Utopia for Christians
which few would care to realise. These terrible maxims
would, for the greater number, remain in profound oblivion
—an oblivion encouraged by the clergy itself; the Gospel
man would prove a dangerous man. The most selfish,
proud, hard, and worldly of all human beings, a Louis XIV.,
for instance, would find priests to persuade him, in spite of
the Gospel, that he was a Christian. But, on the other
hand, there would always be found holy men who would
take the sublime paradoxes of Jesus literally. Perfection
being placed beyond the ordinary conditions of society, and
a complete Gospel life being only possible away from the
world, the principle of asceticism and of monasticism was
established. Christian societies would have two moral
rules; the one moderately heroic for common men, the
other exalted in the extreme for the perfect man; and the
perfect man would be the monk, subjected to rules which

professed to realise the Gospel ideal. It is certain that this ideal, if only on account of the celibacy and poverty it imposed, could not become the common law. The monk would be thus, in one sense, the only true Christian. Common sense revolts at these excesses; and if we are guided by it, to demand the impossible, is a mark of weakness and error. But common sense is a bad judge where great matters are in question. To obtain little from humanity, we must ask much. The immense moral progress which we owe to the Gospel is the result of its exaggerations. It is thus that it has been, like stoicism, but with infinitely greater fullness, a living argument for the divine powers in man, an exalted monument of the potency of the will.

We may easily imagine that to Jesus, at this period of his life, everything which was not the kingdom of God had absolutely disappeared. He was, if we may say so, totally outside nature; family, friendship, country, had no longer any meaning for him. No doubt, from this moment he had already sacrificed his life. Sometimes we are tempted to believe that, seeing in his own death a means of founding his kingdom, he deliberately determined to allow himself to be killed. At other times, although such a thought only afterwards became a doctrine, death presented itself to him as a sacrifice, destined to appease his Father and to save mankind. A singular taste for persecution and torments possessed him. His blood appeared to him as the water of a second baptism with which he ought to be baptised, and he seemed possessed by a strange haste to anticipate this baptism which alone could quench his thirst.

The grandeur of his views upon the future was at times surprising. He did not conceal from himself the terrible storm he was about to cause in the world. " Think not," said he, with much boldness and beauty, " that I am come to send peace on earth : I came not to send peace, but a sword. There shall be five in one house divided, three against two, and two against three. I am come to set a man at variance against his father, and the daughter against her mother, and the daughter-in-law against her mother-in-law. And a man's foes shall be they of his own household." " I am come to send fire on the earth; and what will I, if it be already kindled ? " " They shall put you out of the synagogues," he continued; " yea, the time cometh, that whosoever killeth you, will think that he doeth God service." " If the world hate you, ye know that it hated me before it hated you. Remember the word that I said unto you : The servant is not greater than his lord. If they have persecuted me, they will also persecute you.''

Carried away by this fearful progression of enthusiasm, and governed by the necessities of a preaching becoming daily more exalted, Jesus was no longer free; he belonged to his mission, and, in one sense, to mankind. Sometimes one would have said that his reason was disturbed. He suffered great mental anguish and agitation. The great vision of the kingdom of God glistening before his eyes bewildered him. His disciples at times thought him mad. His enemies declared him to be possessed. His excessively impassioned temperament carried him incessantly beyond the bounds of human nature. He laughed at all human systems, and his work, not being a work of the reason, that which he most imperiously required was '' faith.'' This was the word most frequently repeated in the little guest-chamber. It is the watchword of all popular movements. It is clear that none of these movements would take place if it were necessary that their author should gain his disciples one by one by force of logic. Reflection leads only to doubt. If the authors of the French Revolution, for instance, had had to be previously convinced by lengthened meditations, they would all have become old without accomplishing anything; Jesus, in like manner, aimed less at convincing his hearers than at exciting their enthusiasm. Urgent and imperative, he suffered no opposition; men must be converted, nothing less would satisfy him. His natural gentleness seemed to have abandoned him; he was sometimes harsh and capricious. His disciples at times did not understand him, and experienced in his presence a feeling akin to fear. Sometimes his displeasure at the slightest opposition led him to commit inexplicable and apparently absurd acts.

It was not that his virtue deteriorated; but his struggle for the ideal against the reality became insupportable. Contact with the world pained and revolted him. Obstacles irritated him. His idea of the Son of God became disturbed and exaggerated. The fatal law which condemns an idea to decay as soon as it seeks to convert men applied to him. Contact with men degraded him to their level. The tone he had adopted could not be sustained more than a few months; it was time that death came to liberate him from an endurance strained to the utmost, to remove him from the impossibilities of an interminable path, and, by delivering him from a trial in danger of being too prolonged, introduce him henceforth sinless into celestial peace.

CHAPTER XX

OPPOSITION TO JESUS

DURING the first period of his career it does not appear that Jesus met with any serious opposition. His preaching, thanks to the extreme liberty which was enjoyed in Galilee, and to the number of teachers who arose on all hands, made no noise beyond a restricted circle. But when Jesus entered upon a path brilliant with wonders and public successes, the storm began to gather. More than once he was obliged to conceal himself and fly. Antipas, however, did not interfere with him, although Jesus expressed himself sometimes very severely respecting him. At Tiberias, his usual residence, the Tetrarch was only one or two leagues distant from the district chosen by Jesus for the centre of his activity; he heard speak of his miracles, which he doubtless took to be clever tricks, and desired to see them. The incredulous were at that time very curious about this class of illusions. With his ordinary tact, Jesus refused to gratify him. He took care not to prejudice his position by mingling with an irreligious world, which wished to draw from him an idle amusement; he aspired only to gain the people; he reserved for the simple means suitable to them alone.

On one occasion the report was spread that Jesus was no other than John the Baptist risen from the dead. Antipas became anxious and uneasy, and employed artifice to rid his dominions of the new prophet. Certain Pharisees, under the pretence of regard for Jesus, came to tell him that Antipas was seeking to kill him. Jesus, notwithstanding his great simplicity, saw the snare, and did not depart. His peaceful manners, and his remoteness from popular agitation, ultimately reassured the Tetrarch and dissipated the danger.

The new doctrine was by no means received with equal favour in all the towns of Galilee. Not only did incredulous Nazareth continue to reject him who was to become her glory; not only did his brothers persist in not believing in him, but the cities of the lake themselves, in general well-disposed, were not all converted. Jesus often complained of the incredulity and hardness of heart which he encountered, and although it is natural that in such reproaches we make allowance for the exaggeration of the preacher, although we are sensible of that kind of *convicium seculi* which Jesus affected in imitation of John the Baptist, it is clear that the country was far from yielding itself entirely a second time to the kingdom of God. " Woe unto thee, Chorazin! woe unto thee, Bethsaida! " cried he; " or if the mighty works which were done in you had been done in Tyre and Sidon they would have repented long ago in sackcloth and ashes. But I say unto you, It shall be more tolerable for Tyre and Sidon at the day of judgment than for you. And thou, Capernaum, which art exalted unto heaven, shalt be brought down to hell; for if the mighty works which have been done in thee had been done in Sodom it would have remained until this day. But I say unto you, That it shall be more tolerable for the land of Sodom in the day of judgment than for thee." " The queen of the south," added he, " shall rise up in the judgment of this generation, and shall condemn it: for she came from the uttermost parts of the earth to hear the wisdom of Solomon; and behold, a greater than Solomon is here. The men of Nineveh shall rise in judgment with this generation, and shall condemn it; because they repented at the preaching of Jonas; and behold, a greater than Jonas is here." His wandering life, at first so full of charm, now began to weigh upon him. " The foxes," he said, " have holes, and the birds of the air have nests; but the Son of man hath not where to lay his head." Bitterness and reproach took more and more hold upon him. He accused unbelievers of not yielding to evidence, and said that, even at the moment in which the Son of man should appear in his celestial glory, there would still be men who would not believe in him.

Jesus, in fact, was not able to receive opposition with the coolness of the philosopher, who, understanding the reason of the various opinions which divide the world, finds it quite natural that all should not agree with him. One of the principal defects of the Jewish race is its harshness in controversy and the abusive tone which it almost always infuses into it. There never were in the world such bitter quarrels as those of the Jews among themselves. It is the faculty of nice discernment which makes the polished and moderate man. Now, the lack of this faculty is one of the most constant features of the Semitic mind. Subtle and refined works, the dialogues of Plato, for example, are altogether unknown to these nations. Jesus, who was exempt from almost all the defects of his race, and whose leading quality was precisely an infinite delicacy, was led, in spite of himself, to make use of the general style in polemics. Like John the Baptist, he employed very harsh terms against his adversaries. Of an exquisite gentleness with the simple, he was irritated at incredulity, however little aggressive. He was no longer the mild teacher who delivered the " Sermon on the Mount," who had met with neither resistance nor difficulty. The passion that underlay his character led him to make use of the keenest invectives. This singular mixture ought not to surprise us. M. de Lamennais, a man of our own times, has strikingly presented the same contrast. In his beautiful book, *The Words of a Believer*, the most immoderate anger and the sweetest relentings alternate, as in a mirage. This man, who was extremely kind in the intercourse of life, became madly intractable towards those who did not agree with him. Jesus, in like manner, applied to himself, not without reason, the passage from Isaiah : " He shall not strive nor cry; neither shall any man hear his voice in the streets. A bruised reed shall he not break, and smoking flax shall he not quench." And yet many of the recommendations which he addressed to his disciples contain the germs of a true fanaticism—germs which the Middle Ages were to develop in a cruel manner. Must we reproach him for this ? No revolution is effected without some harshness. If Luther, or the actors in the French Revolution, had been compelled to observe the rules of politeness, neither the Reformation nor the Revolution would have taken place. Let us congratulate ourselves in like manner that Jesus encountered no law which punished the invectives he uttered against one class of citizens. Had such a law existed, the Pharisees would have been inviolate. All the great things of humanity have been accomplished in the name of absolute principles. A critical philosopher would have said to his disciples : Respect the opinion of others, and believe that no one is so completely right that his adversary is completely wrong. But the action of Jesus has nothing in common with the disinterested speculation of the philosopher. To know that we have touched the ideal for a moment, and have been deterred by the wickedness of a few, is a thought insupportable to an ardent soul. What must it have been for the founder of a new world ?

The invincible obstacle to the ideas of Jesus came especially from orthodox Judaism, represented by the Pharisees. Jesus became more and more alienated from the ancient Law. Now, the Pharisees were the true Jews—the nerve and sinew of Judaism. Although this party had its centre at Jerusalem, it had adherents either established in Galilee or who often came there. They were, in general, men of a narrow mind, caring much for externals; their devoutness was haughty, formal, and self-satisfied. Their manners were ridiculous, and excited the smiles of even those who respected them. The epithets which the people gave them, and which savour of caricature, prove this. There was the " bandy-legged Pharisee " (*Nikfi*), who walked in the streets dragging his feet and knocking them against the stones; the " bloody-browed Pharisee " (*Kizai*), who went with his eyes shut in order not to see the women, and dashed his head so much against the walls that it was always bloody; the " pestle Pharisee " (*Medinkia*), who kept himself bent double like the handle of a pestle; the " Pharisee of strong shoulders " (*Shikmi*), who walked with his back bent as if he carried on his shoulders the whole burden of the Law; the " *What-is-there-to-do ?-I-do-it Pharisee*," always on the search for a precept to fulfil; and, lastly, the " dyed Pharisee," whose externals of devotion were but a varnish of hypocrisy. This strictness was, in fact, often only apparent, and concealed in reality great moral laxity. The people, nevertheless, were duped by it. The people, whose instinct is always right, even when it is most astray respecting individuals, is very easily deceived by false devotees. That which it loves in them is good and worthy of being loved; but it has not sufficient penetration to distinguish the appearance from the reality.

It is easy to understand the antipathy which, in such an impassioned state of society, must necessarily break out between Jesus and persons of this character. Jesus recognised only the religion of the heart, while that of the Pharisees consisted almost exclusively in observances. Jesus sought the humble and outcasts of all kinds, and the Pharisees saw in this an insult to their religion of respectability. The Pharisee was an infallible and faultless man, a pedant always right in his own conceit, taking the first place in the synagogue, praying in the street, giving alms to the sound of a trumpet, and caring greatly for salutations. Jesus maintained that each one ought to await the kingdom of God with fear and trembling. The bad religious tendency represented by Pharisaism did not reign without opposition. Many men before or during the time of Jesus, such as Jesus, son of Sirach (one of the true ancestors of Jesus of Nazareth), Gamaliel, Antigonus of Soco, and especially the gentle and noble Hillel, had taught much more elevated, and almost Gospel, doctrines. But these good seeds had been choked. The beautiful maxims of Hillel, summing up the whole Law as equity, those of Jesus, son of Sirach, making worship consist in doing good, were forgotten or anathematised. Shammai, with his narrow and exclusive spirit, had prevailed. An enormous mass of " traditions " had stifled the Law, under pretext of protecting and interpreting it. Doubtless these conservative measures had their share of usefulness; it is well that the Jewish people loved its Law even to excess, since it is this frantic love which, in saving Mosaism under Antiochus Epiphanes and under Herod, has preserved the leaven from which Christianity was to emanate. But, taken in themselves, all these old precautions were only puerile. The synagogue, which was the depository of them, was no more than a parent of error. Its reign was ended; and yet to require its abdication was to require the impossible, that which an established power has never done or been able to do.

The conflicts of Jesus with official hypocrisy were continual. The ordinary tactics of the reformers who appeared in the religious state which we have just described, and which might be called " traditional formalism," were to oppose the " text " of the sacred books to " traditions." Religious zeal is always an innovator, even when it pretends to be in the highest degree conservative. Just as the neo-Catholics of our days become more and more remote from the Gospel, so the Pharisees left the Bible at each step more and more. This is why the Puritan reformer is generally essentially " biblical," taking the unchangeable text for his basis in criticising the current theology, which has changed with each generation. Thus acted later the Karaites and the Protestants. Jesus applied the axe to the root of the tree much more energetically. We see him sometimes, it is true, invoke the text against the false *Masores* or traditions of the Pharisees. But in general he dwelt little on exegesis —it was the conscience to which he appealed. With one stroke he cut through both text and commentaries. He showed indeed to the Pharisees that they seriously perverted Mosaism by their traditions, but he by no means pretended himself to return to Mosaism. His mission was concerned with the future, not with the past. Jesus was more than the reformer of an obsolete religion; he was the creator of the eternal religion of humanity.

Disputes broke out especially respecting a number of external practices introduced by tradition, which neither Jesus nor his disciples observed. The Pharisees reproached him sharply for this. When he dined with them, he scandalised them much by not observing the customary ablutions. "Give alms," said he, "of such things as ye have; and behold, all things are clean unto you." That which in the highest degree hurt his refined feeling was the air of assurance which the Pharisees carried into religious matters; their paltry worship, which ended in a vain seeking after precedents and titles, to the utter neglect of the improvement of their hearts. An admirable parable rendered this thought with infinite charm and justice. "Two men," said he, "went up into the temple to pray; the one a Pharisee, and the other a publican. The Pharisee stood and prayed thus with himself: God, I thank thee that I am not as other men are, extortioners, unjust, adulterers, or even as this publican. I fast twice in the week, I give tithes of all that I possess. And the publican, standing afar off, would not lift up so much as his eyes unto heaven, but smote upon his breast, saying, God be merciful to me a sinner. I tell you this man went down to his house justified rather than the other."

A hate which death alone could satisfy was the consequence of these struggles. John the Baptist had already provoked enmities of the same kind. But the aristocrats of Jerusalem, who despised him, had allowed simple men to take him for a prophet. In the case of Jesus, however, the war was to the death. A new spirit had appeared in the world, causing all that preceded to pale before it. John the Baptist was completely a Jew; Jesus was scarcely one at all. Jesus always appealed to the delicacy of the moral sentiment. He was only a disputant when he argued against the Pharisees, his opponents forcing him, as generally happens, to adopt their tone. His exquisite irony, his arch and provoking remarks, always struck home. They were everlasting stigmas, and have remained festering in the wound. This Nessus-shirt of ridicule which the Jew, son of the Pharisees, has dragged in tatters after him during eighteen centuries, was woven by Jesus with a divine skill. Masterpieces of fine raillery, their features are written in lines of fire upon the flesh of the hypocrite and the false devotee. Incomparable traits, worthy of a son of God! A god alone knows how to kill after this ashion. Socrates and Molière only touched the skin. He carried fire and rage to the very marrow.

But it was also just that this great master of irony should pay for his triumph with his life. Even in Galilee the Pharisees sought to ruin him, and employed against him the manœuvre which ultimately succeeded at Jerusalem. They endeavoured to interest in their quarrel the partisans of the new political faction which was established. The facilities Jesus found for escape in Galilee, and the weakness of the government of Antipas, baffled these attempts. He ran into danger of his own free will. He saw clearly that his action, if he remained confined to Galilee, was necessarily limited. Judea drew him as by a charm; he wished to try a last effort to gain the rebellious city; and seemed anxious to fulfil the proverb—that a prophet must not die outside Jerusalem.

G

CHAPTER XXI

LAST JOURNEY OF JESUS TO JERUSALEM

JESUS had for a long time been sensible of the dangers that surrounded him. During a period of time which we may estimate at eighteen months, he avoided going on a pilgrimage to Jerusalem. At the feast of Tabernacles of the year 32 (according to the hypothesis we have adopted) his relations, always malevolent and incredulous, pressed him to go there. The evangelist John seems to insinuate that there was some hidden project to ruin him in this invitation. " Depart hence, and go into Judea, that thy disciples also may see the works that thou doest. For there is no man that doeth anything in secret, and he himself seeketh to be known openly. If thou do these things, show thyself to the world." Jesus, suspecting some treachery, at first refused; but when the caravan of pilgrims had set out, he started on the journey, unknown to everyone, and almost alone. It was the last farewell which he bade to Galilee. The feast of Tabernacles fell at the autumnal equinox. Six months still had to elapse before the fatal denouement. But during this interval Jesus saw no more his beloved provinces of the north. The pleasant days had passed away; he must now traverse, step by step, the painful path that will terminate only in the anguish of death.

His disciples, and the pious women who tended him, met him again in Judea. But how much everything was changed for him there ! Jesus was a stranger at Jerusalem. He felt that there was a wall of resistance he could not penetrate. Surrounded by snares and difficulties, he was unceasingly pursued by the ill-will of the Pharisees. Instead of that illimitable faculty of belief, happy gift of youthful natures, which he found in Galilee—instead of those good and gentle people, among whom objections (always the fruit of some degree of ill-will and indocility) had no existence, he met there at each step an obstinate incredulity, upon which the means of action that had so well succeeded in the north had little effect. His disciples were despised as being Galileans. Nicodemus, who, on one of his former journeys, had had a conversation with him by night, almost compromised himself with the Sanhedrim by having wished to defend him. " Art thou also of Galilee ? " they said to him. " Search and look : for out of Galilee ariseth no prophet."

The city, as we have already said, displeased Jesus. Until then he had always avoided great centres, preferring for his action the country and the towns of small importance. Many of the precepts which he gave to his Apostles were absolutely inapplicable, except in a simple society of humble men. Having no idea of the world, and accustomed to the kindly communism of Galilee, remarks continually escaped him whose simplicity would at Jerusalem appear very singular. His imagination and his love of nature found themselves constrained within these walls. True religion does not proceed from the tumult of towns, but from the tranquil serenity of the fields.

The arrogance of the priests rendered the courts of the temple disagreeable to him. One day some of his disciples, who knew Jerusalem better than he, wished him to notice the beauty of the buildings of the temple, the admirable choice of materials, and the richness of the votive offerings that covered the walls. " Seest thou these buildings ? " said he ; " there shall not be left one stone upon another." He refused to admire anything, except it was a poor widow who passed at that moment and threw a small coin into the box. " She has cast in more than they all," said he ; " for all these have of their abundance cast unto the offerings of God : but she of her penury hath cast in all the living that she had." This manner of criticising all he observed at Jerusalem, of praising the poor who gave little, of slighting the rich who gave much, and of blaming the opulent priesthood who did nothing for the good of the people, naturally exasperated the sacerdotal caste. As the seat of a conservative aristocracy, the temple, like the Mussulman Haram which succeeded it, was the last place in the world where revolution could prosper. Imagine an innovator going in our days to preach the overthrow of Islamism round the mosque of Omar ! There, however, was the centre of the Jewish life, the point where it was necessary to conquer or die. On this Calvary, where certainly Jesus suffered more than at Golgotha, his days passed away in disputation and bitterness, in the midst of tedious controversies respecting canonical law and exegesis, for which his great moral elevation, instead of giving him the advantage, positively unfitted him.

In the midst of this troubled life, the sensitive and kindly heart of Jesus found a refuge, where he enjoyed moments of sweetness. After having passed the day disputing in the temple, towards evening Jesus descended into the valley of Kedron, and rested a while in the orchard of a farming establishment (probably for the making of oil) named Gethsemane, which served as a pleasure garden to the inhabitants. Thence he proceeded to pass the night upon the Mount of Olives, which limits the horizon of the city on the east. This side is the only one in the environs of Jerusalem which offers an aspect in any degree pleasing and verdant. The plantations of olives, figs, and palms were numerous there, and gave their names to the villages farms, or enclosures of Bethphage, Gethsemane, and Bethany. There were upon the Mount of Olives two great cedars, the memory of which was long preserved among the dispersed Jews; their branches served as an asylum to clouds of doves, and under their shade were established small bazaars. All this precinct was in a manner the abode of Jesus and his disciples; they knew it field by field and house by house.

The village of Bethany, in particular, situated at the summit of the hill, upon the incline which commands the Dead Sea and the Jordan, at a journey of an hour and a half from Jerusalem, was the place especially beloved by Jesus. He there made the acquaintance of a family composed of three persons, two sisters and a brother, whose friendship had a great charm for him. Of the two sisters the one named Martha was an obliging, kind, and assiduous person; the other, named Mary, on the contrary, pleased Jesus by a sort of languor and by her strongly-developed speculative instincts. Seated at the feet of Jesus, she often forgot, in listening to him, the duties of real life. He sister, upon whom fell all the duty at such times, gently complained. "Martha, Martha," said Jesus to her, "thou art troubled, and carest about many things; now, one thing only is needful. Mary has chosen the better part which will not be taken away." Her brother, Eleazar or Lazarus, was also much beloved by Jesus. Lastly, a certain Simon, the leper, who was the owner of the house formed, it appears, part of the family. It was there, in the enjoyment of a pious friendship, that Jesus forgot the vexations of public life. In this tranquil home he consoled himself for the bickerings with which the scribes and the Pharisees unceasingly surrounded him. He often sat on the Mount of Olives, facing Mount Moriah, having beneath his view the splendid perspective of the terraces of the temple, and its roofs covered with glittering plates of metal. This view struck strangers with admiration; at the rising of the sun, especially, the sacred mountain dazzled the eyes, and appeared like a mass of snow and of gold. But a profound feeling of sadness poisoned for Jesus the spectacle that filled all other Israelites with joy and pride. He cried out, in his moments of bitterness, " O Jerusalem, Jerusalem, thou that killest the prophets, and stonest them which are sent unto thee, how often would I have gathered thy children together, even as a hen gathereth her chickens under her wings, and ye would not."

It was not that many good people here, as in Galilee, were not touched; but such was the power of the dominant orthodoxy that very few dared to confess it. They feared to discredit themselves in the eyes of the Hierosolymites by placing themselves in the school of a Galilean. They would have risked being driven from the synagogue, which, in a mean and bigoted society, was the greatest degradation. Excommunication, besides, carried with it the confiscation of all possessions. By ceasing to be a Jew, a man did not become a Roman; but remained without protection, in the power of a theocratic legislation of the most atrocious severity. One day the inferior officers of the temple, who had been present at one of the discourses of Jesus, and had been enchanted with it, came to confide their doubts to the priests : " Have any of the rulers or of the Pharisees believed on him ? " was the reply to them; " but this people who knoweth not the Law are cursed." Jesus remained thus at Jerusalem, a provincial admired by provincials like himself, but rejected by all the aristocracy of the nation. The chiefs of schools and of sects were too numerous for anyone to be stirred by seeing one more appear. His voice made little noise in Jerusalem. The prejudices of race and of sect, the direct enemies of the spirit of the Gospel, were too deeply rooted there.

His teaching in this new world necessarily became much modified. His beautiful discourses, the effect of which was always observable upon youthful imaginations and consciences morally pure, here fell upon stone. He who was so much at his ease on the shores of his charming little lake felt constrained and not at home in the company of pedants. His perpetual self-assertion appeared somewhat fastidious. He was obliged to become controversialist, jurist, exegetist, and theologian. His conversations, generally so full of charm, became a rolling fire of disputes, an interminable train of scholastic battles. His harmonious genius was wasted in insipid argumentations upon the Law and the prophets, in which we should have preferred not seeing him sometimes play the part of aggressor. He lent himself, with a condescension we cannot but regret, to the captious criticisms to which the merciless cavillers subjected him. In general, he extricated himself from difficulties with much skill. His reasonings, it is true, were often subtle (simplicity of mind and subtlety touch each other; when simplicity reasons, it is often a little sophistical); we find that sometimes he courted misconceptions, and prolonged them intentionally; his reasoning, judged according to the rules of Aristotelian logic, was very weak. But when the unequalled charm of his mind could be displayed, he was triumphant. One day it was intended to embarrass him by presenting to him an adulteress and asking him what was to be done to her. We know the admirable answer of Jesus. The fine raillery of a man of the world, tempered by a divine goodness, could not be expressed in a more exquisite manner. But the wit which is allied to moral grandeur is that which fools forgive the least. In pronouncing this sentence of so just and pure a taste, " He that is without sin among you, let him first cast a stone at her," Jesus pierced hypocrisy to the heart, and with the same stroke sealed his own death-warrant.

It is probable, in fact, that but for the exasperation caused by so many bitter shafts, Jesus might long have remained unnoticed, and have been lost in the dreadful storm which was soon about to overwhelm the whole Jewish nation. The high priesthood and the Sadducees had rather disdained than hated him. The great sacerdotal families the *Boëthusim*, the family of Hanan, were only fanatical in their conservatism. The Sadducees, like Jesus, rejected the " traditions " of the Pharisees. By a very strange singularity, it was these unbelievers who, denying the resurrection, the oral Law, and the existence of angels, were the true Jews. Or rather, as the old Law in its simplicity no longer satisfied the religious wants of the time, those who strictly adhered to it, and rejected modern inventions, were regarded by the devotees as impious, just as an evangelical Protestant of the present day is regarded as an unbeliever in Catholic countries. At all events, from such a party no very strong reaction against Jesus could proceed. The official priesthood, with its attention turned towards political power, and intimately connected with it, did no comprehend these enthusiastic movements. It was the middle-class Pharisees, the innumerable *soferim*, or scribes, living on the science of " traditions," who took the alarm, and whose prejudices and interests were in reality threatened by the doctrine of the new teacher.

One of the most constant efforts of the Pharisees was to involve Jesus in the discussion of political questions, and to compromise him as connected with the party of Judas the Gaulonite. These tactics were clever; for it required all the deep wisdom of Jesus to avoid collision with the Roman authority while proclaiming the kingdom of God. They wanted to break through this ambiguity, and compel him to explain himself. One day a group of Pharisees and of those politicians named " Herodians " (probably some of the *Boëthusim*), approached him, and, under pretence of pious zeal, said unto him, " Master, we know that thou art true, and teachest the way of God in truth, neither carest thou for any man. Tell us, therefore, what thinkest thou ? Is it lawful to give tribute unto Cæsar or not ? " They hoped for an answer which would give them a pretext for delivering him up to Pilate. The reply of Jesus was admirable. He made them show him the image on the coin : " Render," said he, " unto Cæsar the things which are Cæsar's ; and unto God the things that are God's." Profound words, which have decided the future of Christianity ! Words of a perfected spiritualism, and of marvellous justness, which have established the separation between the spiritual and the temporal, and laid the basis of true liberalism and civilisation !

His gentle and penetrating genius inspired him when alone with his disciples with accents full of tenderness : ' Verily, verily, I say unto you, he that entereth not by the door into the sheepfold, but climbeth up some other way, the same is a thief and a robber. But he that entereth in by the door is the shepherd of the sheep. The sheep hear his voice : and he calleth his own sheep by name, and leadeth them out. He goeth before them, and the sheep follow him ; for they know his voice. The thief cometh not but for to steal, and to kill, and to destroy. But he that is an hireling, and not the shepherd, whose own the sheep are not, seeth the wolf coming, and leaveth the sheep, and fleeth. I am the good shepherd, and know my sheep, and am known of mine ; and I lay down my life for the sheep." The idea that the crisis of humanity was close at hand frequently recurred to him. " Now," said he, " learn a parable of the fig-tree : When his branch is yet tender, and putteth forth leaves, ye know that summer is nigh. Lift up your eyes and look on the fields; for they are white already to harvest."

His powerful eloquence always burst forth when contending with hypocrisy. "The scribes and Pharisees sit in Moses' seat. All, therefore, whatsoever they bid you observe, that observe and do; but do not ye after their works: for they say and do not. For they bind heavy burdens and grievous to be borne, and lay them on men's shoulders; but they themselves will not move them with one of their fingers.

"But all their works they do to be seen of men; they make broad their phylacteries, enlarge the borders of their garments, and love the uppermost rooms at feasts, and the chief seats in the synagogues, and greetings in the markets, and to be called of men Rabbi, Rabbi. Woe unto them! . . .

"Woe unto you, scribes and Pharisees, hypocrites! for you have taken away the key of knowledge, shut up the kingdom of heaven against men! for ye neither go in yourselves, neither suffer ye them that are entering to go in. Woe unto you, for ye devour widows' houses, and, for a pretence, make long prayers: therefore ye shall receive the greater damnation. Woe unto you, for ye compass sea and land to make one proselyte; and when he is made, ye make him twofold more the child of hell than yourselves! Woe unto you, for ye are as graves which appear not; and the men that walk over them are not aware of them.

"Ye fools, and blind! for ye pay tithe of mint and anise and cummin, and have omitted the weightier matters of the law, judgment, mercy, and faith: these ought ye to have done, and not to leave the other undone. Ye blind guides, which strain at a gnat and swallow a camel. Woe unto you!

"Woe unto you, scribes and Pharisees, hypocrites! for ye make clean the outside of the cup and of the platter; but within they are full of extortion and excess. Thou blind Pharisee, cleanse first that which is within the cup and platter, that the outside of them may be clean also.

"Woe unto you, scribes and Pharisees, hypocrites! for ye are like unto whited sepulchres, which indeed appear beautiful outward, but are within full of dead men's bones and of all uncleanness. Even so ye also outwardly appear righteous unto them, but within ye are full of hypocrisy and iniquity.

"Woe unto you, scribes and Pharisees, hypocrites! because ye build the tombs of the prophets, and garnish the sepulchres of the righteous, and say, ' If we had been in the days of our fathers, we would not have been partakers with them in the blood of the prophets.' Wherefore, ye be witnesses unto yourselves, that ye are the children of them which killed the prophets. Fill ye up then the measure of your fathers. ' Therefore, also,' said the Wisdom of God, ' I will send unto you prophets and wise men and scribes ; and some of them ye shall kill and crucify ; and some of them shall ye scourge in your synagogues, and persecute them from city to city. That upon you may come all the righteous blood shed upon the earth, from the blood of righteous Abel unto the blood of Zacharias, son of Barachias, whom ye slew between the temple and the altar.' Verily, I say unto you, all these things shall come upon this generation."

His terrible doctrine of the substitution of the Gentiles— the idea that the kingdom of God was about to be transferred to others, because those for whom it was destined would not receive it—is used as a fearful menace against the aristocracy. The title " Son of God," which he openly assumed in striking parables, wherein his enemies appeared as murderers of the heavenly messengers, was as an open defiance to the Judaism of the Law. The bold appeal he addressed to the poor was still more seditious. He declared that he had " come that they which see not might see, and that they which see might be made blind." One day his dislike of the temple forced from him an imprudent speech : " I will destroy this temple that is made with hands, and within three days I will build another made without hands." His disciples found strained allegories in this sentence ; but we do not know what meaning Jesus attached to it. But as only a pretext was wanted, this sentence was quickly laid hold of. It reappeared in the preamble of his death warrant, and rang in his ears amid the last agonies of Golgotha. These irritating discussions always ended in tumult. The Pharisees threw stones at him ; in doing which they only fulfilled an article of the Law, which commanded every prophet, even a thaumaturgus, who should turn the people from the ancient worship, to be stoned without a hearing. At other times they called him mad, possessed, Samaritan, and even sought to kill him. These words were taken note of in order to invoke against him the laws of an intolerant theocracy, which the Roman Government had not yet abrogated.

CHAPTER XXII

MACHINATIONS OF THE ENEMIES OF JESUS

JESUS passed the autumn and a part of the winter at Jerusalem. This season is there rather cold. The portico of Solomon, with its covered aisles, was the place where he habitually walked. This portico consisted of two galleries, formed by three rows of columns, and covered by a ceiling of carved wood. It commanded the valley of Kedron, which was doubtless less covered with debris than it is at the present time. The depth of the ravine could not be measured from the height of the portico; and it seemed, in consequence of the angle of the slopes, as if an abyss opened immediately beneath the wall. The other side of the valley even at that time was adorned with sumptuous tombs. Some of the monuments, which may be seen at the present day, were perhaps those cenotaphs in honour of ancient prophets which Jesus pointed out, when, seated under the portico, he denounced the official classes, who covered their hypocrisy or their vanity by these colossal piles.

At the end of the month of December he celebrated at Jerusalem the feast established by Judas Maccabeus in memory of the purification of the temple after the sacrileges of Antiochus Epiphanes. It was also called the "Feast of Lights," because, during the eight days of the feast, lamps were kept lighted in the houses. Jesus undertook soon after a journey into Perea and to the banks of the Jordan—that is to say, into the very country he had visited some years previously, when he followed the school of John, and in which he had himself administered baptism. He seems to have reaped consolation from this journey, specially at Jericho. This city, as the terminus of several important routes, or, it may be, on account of its gardens of spices and its rich cultivation, was a customs station of importance. The chief receiver, Zaccheus, a rich man, desired to see Jesus. As he was of small stature, he climbed a sycamore tree near the road which the procession had to pass. Jesus was touched with this simplicity in a person of consideration, and, at the risk of giving offence, he determined to stay with Zaccheus. There was much dissatisfaction at his honouring the house of a sinner by this visit. In parting, Jesus declared his host to be a good son of Abraham; and, as if to add to the vexation of the orthodox, Zaccheus became a Christian; he gave, it is said, the half of his goods to the poor, and restored fourfold to those whom he might have wronged. But this was not the only pleasure which Jesus experienced there. On leaving the town, the beggar Bartimeus pleased him much by persisting in calling him " son of David," although he was told to be silent. The cycle of Galilean miracles appeared for a time to recommence in this country, which was in many respects similar to the provinces of the north. The delightful oasis of Jericho, at that time well watered, must have been one of the most beautiful places in Syria. Josephus speaks of it with the same admiration as of Galilee, and calls it, like the latter province, a " divine country."

After Jesus had completed this kind of pilgrimage to the scenes of his earliest prophetic activity, he returned to his beloved abode in Bethany, where a singular event occurred, which seems to have had a powerful influence on the remaining days of his life. Tired of the cold reception which the kingdom of God found in the capital, the friends of Jesus wished for a great miracle which should strike powerfully the incredulity of the Hierosolymites. The resurrection of a man known at Jerusalem appeared to them most likely to carry conviction. We must bear in mind that the essential condition of true criticism is to understand the diversity of times, and to rid ourselves of the instinctive repugnances which are the fruit of a purely rational education. We must also remember that in this lull and impure city of Jerusalem Jesus was no longer himself. Not by any fault of his own, but by that of others, his conscience had lost something of its original purity. Desperate, and driven to extremity, he was no longer his own master. His mission overwhelmed him, and he yielded to the torrent. As always happens in the lives of great and inspired men, he suffered the miracles opinion demanded of him rather than performed them. At this distance of time, and with only a single text, bearing evident traces of artifices of composition, it is impossible to decide whether in this instance the whole is fiction, or whether a real fact which happened at Bethany has served as basis to the rumours which were spread about it. It

must be acknowledged, however, that the way John
narrates the incident differs widely from those description
of miracles, the offspring of the popular imagination, which
fill the Synoptics. Let us add that John is the only
evangelist who has a precise knowledge of the relations of
Jesus with the family of Bethany, and that it is impossible
to believe that a mere creation of the popular mind could
exist in a collection of remembrances so entirely personal
It is, then, probable that the miracle in question was not
one of those purely legendary ones for which no one is
responsible. In other words, we think that something
really happened at Bethany which was looked upon as a
resurrection.

Fame already attributed to Jesus two or three works of
this kind. The family of Bethany might be led, almost
without suspecting it, into taking part in the important
act which was desired. Jesus was adored by them. It
seems that Lazarus was sick, and that in consequence of
receiving a message from the anxious sisters Jesus left
Perea. They thought that the joy Lazarus would feel
at his arrival might restore him to life. Perhaps, also, the
ardent desire of silencing those who violently denied the
divine mission of Jesus carried his enthusiastic friends
beyond all bounds. It may be that Lazarus, still pallid
with disease, caused himself to be wrapped in bandages as
if dead, and shut up in the tomb of his family. These tombs
were large vaults cut in the rock, and were entered by a
square opening, closed by an enormous stone. Martha and
Mary went to meet Jesus, and, without allowing him to
enter Bethany, conducted him to the cave. The emotion
which Jesus experienced at the tomb of his friend, whom he
believed to be dead, might be taken by those present for
the agitation and trembling which accompanied miracles
Popular opinion required that the divine virtue should
manifest itself in man as an epileptic and convulsive prin
ciple. Jesus (if we follow the above hypothesis) desired to
see once more him whom he had loved; and, the stone
being removed, Lazarus came forth in his bandages, his
head covered with a winding-sheet. This reappearance
would naturally be regarded by everyone as a resurrection
Faith knows no other law than the interest of that which it
believes to be true. Regarding the object which it pursues
as absolutely holy, it makes no scruple of invoking bad
arguments in support of its thesis when good ones do not
succeed. If such and such a proof be not sound, many
others are! If such and such a wonder be not real, many

others have been ! Being intimately persuaded that Jesus was a thaumaturgus, Lazarus and his two sisters may have aided in the execution of one of his miracles, just as many pious men who, convinced of the truth of their religion, have sought to triumph over the obstinacy of their opponents by means of whose weakness they are well aware. The state of their conscience was that of the stigmatists, of the convulsionists, of the possessed ones in convents, drawn, by the influence of the world in which they live, and by their own belief, into feigned acts. As to Jesus, he was no more able than St. Bernard or St. Francis d'Assisi to moderate the avidity for the marvellous displayed by the multitude, and even by his own disciples. Death, moreover, in a few days would restore him his divine liberty, and release him from the fatal necessities of a position which each day became more exacting and more difficult to sustain.

Everything, in fact, seems to lead us to believe that the miracle of Bethany contributed sensibly to hasten the death of Jesus. The persons who had been witnesses of it were dispersed throughout the city, and spoke much about it. The disciples related the fact, with details as to its performance, prepared in expectation of controversy. The other miracles of Jesus were transitory acts, spontaneously accepted by faith, exaggerated by popular fame, and were not again referred to after they had once taken place. This was a real event, held to be publicly notorious, and one by which it was hoped to silence the Pharisees. The enemies of Jesus were much irritated at all this fame. They endeavoured, it is said, to kill Lazarus. It is certain that from that time a council of the chief priests was assembled, and that in this council the question was clearly put : " Can Jesus and Judaism exist together ? " To raise the question was to resolve it ; and, without being a prophet, as thought by the evangelist, the high priest could easily pronounce his cruel axiom : " It is expedient that one man should die for the people."

" The high priest of that same year," to use an expression of the fourth Gospel, which well expresses the state of abasement to which the sovereign pontificate was reduced, was Joseph Kaïapha, appointed by Valerius Gratus, and entirely devoted to the Romans. From the time that Jerusalem had been under the government of procurators the office of high priest had been a temporary one ; changes in it took place nearly every year. Kaïapha, however, held it longer than anyone else. He had assumed his office in the year 25, and he did not lose it till the year 36. His character is unknown to us, and many circumstances lead to the belief that his power was only nominal. In fact another personage is always seen in conjunction with, and even superior to, him, who, at the decisive moment we have now reached, seems to have exercised a preponderating power.

This personage was Hanan or Annas,[1] son of Seth, and father-in-law of Kaïapha. He was formerly the high priest, and had in reality preserved amid the numerous changes of the pontificate all the authority of the office. He had received the high priesthood from the legate Quirinius in the year 7 of our era. He lost his office in the year 14, on the accession of Tiberius; but he remained much respected. He was still called " high priest," although he was out of office, and he was consulted upon all important matters. During fifty years the pontificate continued in his family almost uninterruptedly; five of his sons successively sustained this dignity, besides Kaïapha, who was his son-in-law. His was called the " priestly family," as if the priesthood had become hereditary in it. The chief offices of the temple were almost all filled by them. Another family, that of Boëthus, alternated, it is true, with that of Hanan's in the pontificate. But the *Böethusim*, whose fortunes were of not very honourable origin, were much less esteemed by the pious middle class. Hanan was then in reality the chief of the priestly party. Kaïapha did nothing without him; it was customary to associate their names, and that of Hanan was always put first. It will be understood, in fact, that under this *régime* of an annual pontificate, changed according to the caprice of the procurators, an old high priest, who had preserved the secret of the traditions, who had seen many younger than himself succeed each other, and who had retained sufficient influence to get the office delegated to persons who were subordinate to him in family rank, must have been a very important personage. Like all the aristocracy of the temple, he was a Sadducee, " a sect," says Josephus, " particularly severe in its judgments." All his sons also were violent persecutors. One of them, named, like his father, Hanan, caused James, the brother of the Lord, to be stoned under circumstances not unlike those which surrounded the death of Jesus. The spirit of the family was haughty, bold, and cruel; it had that particular kind of proud and sullen

---

[1] The *Ananus* of Josephus. It is thus that the Hebrew name *Johanan* became in Greek *Joannes*, or *Joannas*.

wickedness which characterises Jewish politicians. Therefore, upon this Hanan and his family must rest the responsibility of all the acts which followed. It was Hanan (or
the party he represented) who killed Jesus. Hanan was
the principal actor in the terrible drama, and far more
than Kaïapha, far more than Pilate, ought to bear the
weight of the maledictions of mankind.

It is in the mouth of Kaïapha that the evangelist places
the decisive words which led to the death of Jesus. It
was supposed that the high priest possessed a certain gift
of prophecy; his declaration thus became an oracle full of
profound meaning to the Christian community. But such
an expression, whoever he might be that pronounced it, was
the feeling of the whole sacerdotal party. This party was
much opposed to popular seditions. It sought to put
down religious enthusiasts, rightly foreseeing that by their
excited preachings they would lead to the total ruin of the
nation. Although the excitement created by Jesus was in
nowise temporal, the priests saw, as an ultimate consequence
of this agitation, an aggravation of the Roman yoke and
the overturning of the temple, the source of their riches
and honours. Certainly the causes which, thirty-seven
years after, were to effect the ruin of Jerusalem did not
arise from infant Christianity. They arose in Jerusalem
itself, and not in Galilee. We cannot, however, say that
the motive alleged in this circumstance by the priests was
so improbable that we must necessarily regard it as insin-
cere. In a general sense, Jesus, if he had succeeded, would
have really effected the ruin of the Jewish nation. According to the principles, universally admitted by all ancient
polity, Hanan and Kaïapha were right in saying : " Better
the death of one man than the ruin of a people ! " In our
opinion this reasoning is detestable. But it has been that
of conservative parties from the commencement of all
human society. The " party of order " (I use this expression in its mean and narrow sense) has ever been the same.
Deeming the highest duty of government to be the pre-
vention of popular disturbances, it believes it performs
an act of patriotism in preventing, by judicial murder, the
tumultuous effusion of blood. Little thoughtful of the
future, it does not dream that, in declaring war against all
innovations, it incurs the risk of crushing ideas destined
one day to triumph. The death of Jesus was one of the
thousand illustrations of this policy. The movement he
directed was entirely spiritual, but it was still a movement;
hence the men of order, persuaded that it was essential for

humanity not to be disturbed, felt themselves bound to prevent the new spirit from extending itself. Never was seen a more striking example of how much such a course of procedure defeats its own object. Left free, Jesus would have exhausted himself in a desperate struggle with the impossible. The unintelligent hate of his enemies decided the success of his work, and sealed his divinity.

The death of Jesus was thus resolved upon from the month of February or the beginning of March. But he still escaped for a short time. He withdrew to an obscure town called Ephraim or Ephron, in the direction of Bethel, a short day's journey from Jerusalem. He spent a few days there with his disciples, letting the storm pass over. But the order to arrest him the moment he appeared at Jerusalem was given. The feast of the Passover was drawing nigh, and it was thought that Jesus, according to his custom, would come to celebrate it at Jerusalem.[1]

---

[1] For the order of the events, in all this part we follow the system of John. The Synoptics appear to have little information as to the period of the life of Jesus which precedes the Passion.

CHAPTER XXIII

LAST WEEK OF JESUS

JESUS did, in fact, set out with his disciples to see once more, and for the last time, the unbelieving city. The hopes of his companions were more and more exalted. All believed, in going up to Jerusalem, that the kingdom of God was about to be realised there. The impiety of men being at its height was regarded as a great sign that the consummation was at hand. The persuasion in this respect was such that they already disputed for precedence in the kingdom. This was, it is said, the moment chosen by Salome to ask, on behalf of her sons, the two seats on the right and left of the Son of man. The Master, on the other hand, was beset by grave thoughts. Sometimes he allowed a gloomy resentment against his enemies to appear; he related the parable of a nobleman who went to take possession of a kingdom in a far country; but no sooner had he gone than his fellow-citizens wished to get rid of him. The king returned, and commanded those who had conspired against him to be brought before him, and had them all put to death. At other times he summarily destroyed the illusions of the disciples. As they marched along the stony roads to the north of Jerusalem, Jesus pensively preceded the group of his companions. All regarded him in silence, experiencing a feeling of fear, and not daring to interrogate him. Already, on various occasions, he had spoken to them of his future sufferings, and they had listened to them reluctantly. Jesus at last spoke to them, and, no longer concealing his presentiments, discoursed to them of his approaching end. There was great sadness in the whole company. The disciples were expecting soon to see the sign appear in the clouds. The inaugural cry of the kingdom of God, " Blessed is he that cometh in the name of the Lord," resounded already in joyous accents in their ears. The fearful prospect he foreshadowed troubled them. At each step of the fatal road the kingdom of God became nearer or more remote in the mirage

of their dreams. As to Jesus, he became confirmed in the
idea that he was about to die, but that his death would
save the world. The misunderstanding between him and
his disciples became greater each moment.

The custom was to come to Jerusalem several days
before the Passover, in order to prepare for it. Jesus arrived
late, and at one time his enemies thought they were frus-
trated in their hope of seizing him. The sixth day before
the feast (Saturday, 8th of Nisan, equal to the 28th March)
he at last reached Bethany. He entered, according to his
custom, the house of Lazarus, Martha and Mary, or of
Simon the leper. They gave him a great reception. There
was a dinner at Simon the leper's, where many persons
were assembled, drawn thither by the desire of seeing him,
and also of seeing Lazarus, of whom for some time so many
things had been related. Lazarus was seated at the table,
and attracted much attention. Martha served, according
to her custom. It seems that they sought, by an increased
show of respect, to overcome the coolness of the public,
and to assert the high dignity of their guest. Mary, in
order to give to the event a more festive appearance,
entered during dinner, bearing a vase of perfume, which
she poured upon the feet of Jesus. She afterwards broke
the vase, according to an ancient custom by which the
vessel that had been employed in the entertainment of a
stranger of distinction was broken. Then, to testify her
worship in an extraordinary manner, she prostrated herself
at the feet of her Master and wiped them with her long
hair. All the house was filled with the odour of the perfume,
to the great delight of everyone except the avaricious Judas
of Kerioth. Considering the economical habits of the
community, this was certainly prodigality. The greedy
treasurer calculated immediately how much the perfume
might have been sold for, and what it would have realised
for the poor. This not very affectionate feeling, which
seemed to place something above Jesus, dissatisfied him.
He liked to be honoured, for honours served his aim and
established his title of son of David. Therefore, when they
spoke to him of the poor, he replied rather sharply : " Ye
have the poor always with you; but me ye have not
always." And, exalting himself, he promised immortality
to the woman who in this critical moment gave him a token
of love.

The next day (Sunday, 9th of Nisan) Jesus descended
from Bethany to Jerusalem. When, at a bend of the
road, upon the summit of the Mount of Olives, he saw the

city spread before him, it is said he wept over it, and addressed to it a last appeal. At the base of the mountain, at some steps from the gate, on entering the neighbouring portion of the eastern wall of the city, which was called *Bethphage*, no doubt on account of the fig-trees with which it was planted, he had experienced a momentary pleasure. His arrival was noised abroad. The Galileans who had come to the feast were highly elated, and prepared a little triumph for him. An ass was brought to him, followed, according to custom, by its colt. The Galileans spread their finest garments upon the back of this humble animal as saddle-cloths, and seated him thereon. Others, however, spread their garments upon the road, and strewed it with green branches. The multitude which preceded and followed him, carrying palms, cried : " Hosanna to the son of David ! Blessed is he that cometh in the name of the Lord ! " Some persons even gave him the title of king of Israel. " Master, rebuke thy disciples," said the Pharisees to him. " If these should hold their peace, the stones would immediately cry out," replied Jesus, and he entered into the city. The Hierosolymites, who scarcely knew him, asked who he was. " It is Jesus, the prophet of Nazareth, in Galilee," was the reply. Jerusalem was a city of about 50,000 souls. A trifling event, such as the entrance of a stranger, however little celebrated, or the arrival of a band of provincials, or a movement of people to the avenues of the city, could not fail, under ordinary circumstances, to be quickly noised about. But at the time of the feast the confusion was extreme. Jerusalem at these times was taken possession of by strangers. It was among the latter that the excitement appears to have been most lively. Some proselytes, speaking Greek, who had come to the feast, had their curiosity piqued, and wished to see Jesus. They addressed themselves to his disciples ; but we do not know the result of the interview. Jesus, according to his custom, went to pass the night at his beloved village of Bethany. The three following days (Monday, Tuesday, and Wednesday) he descended regularly to Jerusalem ; and, after the setting of the sun, he returned either to Bethany, or to the farms on the western side of the Mount of Olives, where he had many friends.

A deep melancholy appears, during these last days, to have filled the soul of Jesus, who was generally so joyous and serene. All the narratives agree in relating that before his arrest he underwent a short experience of doubt and trouble ; a kind of anticipated agony. According to some,

he suddenly exclaimed, " Now is my soul troubled. O
Father, save me from this hour." It was believed that a
voice from heaven was heard at this moment: others said
that an angel came to console him. According to one
widely-spread version, the incident took place in the
garden of Gethsemane. Jesus, it was said, went about a
stone's throw from his sleeping disciples, taking with him
only Peter and the two sons of Zebedee, and fell on his
face and prayed. His soul was sad even unto death; a
terrible anguish weighed upon him; but resignation to
the Divine will sustained him. This scene, owing to
the instinctive art which regulated the compilation of the
Synoptics, and often led them in the arrangement of the
narrative to study adaptability and effect, has been given
as occurring on the last night of the life of Jesus, and at
the precise moment of his arrest. If this version were the
true one, we should scarcely understand why John, who
had been the intimate witness of so touching an episode,
should not mention it in the very circumstantial narrative
which he has furnished of the evening of the Thursday.
All that we can safely say is, that during his last days the
enormous weight of the mission he had accepted pressed
cruelly upon Jesus. Human nature asserted itself for a
time. Perhaps he began to hesitate about his work.
Terror and doubt took possession of him, and threw him
into a state of exhaustion worse than death. He who has
sacrificed his repose and the legitimate rewards of life to a
great idea always experiences a feeling of revulsion when
the image of death presents itself to him for the first time,
and seeks to persuade him that all has been in vain. Perhaps some of those touching reminiscences which the
strongest souls preserve, and which at times pierce like a
sword, came upon him at this moment. Did he remember
the clear fountains of Galilee where he was wont to refresh
himself; the vine and the fig-tree under which he had
reposed, and the young maidens who, perhaps, would have
consented to love him? Did he curse the hard destiny
which had denied him the joys conceded to all others?
Did he regret his too lofty nature, and, victim of his greatness, did he mourn that he had not remained a simple
artisan of Nazareth? We know not. For all these
internal troubles evidently were a sealed letter to his disciples. They understood nothing of them, and supplied
by simple conjectures that which in the great soul of their
Master was obscure to them. It is certain at least that his
Divine nature soon regained the supremacy. He might

still have avoided death; but he would not. Love for his
work sustained him. He was willing to drink the cup to
the dregs. Henceforth we behold Jesus entirely himself;
his character unclouded. The subtleties of the polemic,
the credulity of the thaumaturgus and of the exorcist, are
forgotten. There remains only the incomparable hero of
the Passion, the founder of the rights of the free conscience,
and the complete model which all suffering souls will
contemplate in order to fortify and console themselves.

The triumph of Bethphage—that bold act of the provincials in celebrating at the very gates of Jerusalem the
advent of their Messiah-King—completed the exasperation
of the Pharisees and the aristocracy of the temple. A
new council was held on the Wednesday (12th of Nisan)
in the house of Joseph Kaïapha. The immediate arrest of
Jesus was resolved upon. A great idea of order and of
conservative policy governed all their plans. The desire
was to avoid a scene. As the feast of the Passover, which
commenced that year on the Friday evening, was a time
of bustle and excitement, it was resolved to anticipate it.
Jesus being popular, they feared an outbreak; the arrest
was therefore fixed for the next day, Thursday. It was
resolved, also, not to seize him in the temple, where he came
every day, but to observe his habits, in order to seize him
in some retired place. The agents of the priests sounded
his disciples, hoping to obtain useful information from
their weakness or their simplicity. They found what they
sought in Judas of Kerioth. This wretch, actuated by
motives impossible to explain, betrayed his Master, gave
all the necessary information, and even undertook himself
(although such an excess of vileness is scarcely credible) to
guide the troop which was to effect his arrest. The remembrance of horror which the folly or the wickedness of this
man has left in the Christian tradition has doubtless given
rise to some exaggeration on this point. Judas until then
had been a disciple like the others; he had even the title
of Apostle; and he had performed miracles and driven out
demons. Legend, which always uses strong and decisive
language, describes the occupants of the little supper room
as eleven saints and one reprobate. Reality does not
proceed by such absolute categories. Avarice, which the
Synoptics give as the motive of the crime in question, does
not suffice to explain it. It would be very singular if the
man who kept the purse, and who knew what he would lose
by the death of his chief, were to abandon the profits of
his occupation in exchange for a very small sum of money.

Had the self-love of Judas been wounded by the rebuff which he had received at the dinner at Bethany? Even that would not explain his conduct. John would have us regard him as a thief, an unbeliever from the beginning, for which, however, there is no probability. We would rather ascribe it to some feeling of jealousy or to some dissension among the disciples. The peculiar hatred John manifests towards Judas confirms this hypothesis. Less pure in heart than the others, Judas had, from the very nature of his office, become unconsciously narrow-minded. By a caprice very common to men engaged in active duties, he had come to regard the interests of the treasury as superior even to those of the work for which it was intended. The treasurer had overcome the Apostle. The murmurings which escaped him at Bethany seem to indicate that sometimes he thought the Master cost his spiritual family too dear. No doubt this mean economy had caused many other collisions in the little society.

Without denying that Judas of Kerioth may have contributed to the arrest of his Master, we still believe that the curses with which he is loaded are somewhat unjust. There was, perhaps, in his deed more awkwardness than perversity. The moral conscience of the man of the people is quick and correct, but unstable and inconsistent. It is at the mercy of the impulse of the moment. The secret societies of the republican party were characterised by much earnestness and sincerity, and yet their denouncers were very numerous. A trifling spite sufficed to convert a partisan into a traitor. But if the foolish desire for a few pieces of silver turned the head of poor Judas, he does not seem to have lost the moral sentiment completely, since, when he had seen the consequences of his fault, he repented, and, it is said, killed himself.

Each moment of this eventful period is solemn, and counts more than whole ages in the history of humanity. We have arrived at the Thursday, 13th of Nisan (2nd April). The evening of the next day commenced the festival of the Passover, begun by the feast in which the Paschal lamb was eaten. The festival continued for seven days, during which unleavened bread was eaten. The first and the last of these seven days were peculiarly solemn. The disciples were already occupied with preparations for the feast. As to Jesus, we are led to believe that he knew of the treachery of Judas, and that he suspected the fate that awaited him. In the evening he took his last repast with his disciples. It was not the ritual feast of the passover,

as was afterwards supposed, owing to an error of a day in
reckoning; but for the primitive Church this supper of
the Thursday was the true passover, the seal of the new
covenant. Each disciple connected with it his most
cherished remembrances, and numerous touching traits of
the Master which each one preserved were associated with
this repast, which became the corner-stone of Christian
piety and the starting-point of the most fruitful institutions.

Doubtless the tender love which filled the heart of Jesus
for the little Church which surrounded him overflowed at
this moment, and his strong and serene soul became
buoyant, even under the weight of the gloomy preoccupa-
tions that beset him. He had a word for each of his
friends; two among them especially, John and Peter,
were the objects of tender marks of attachment. John (at
least, according to his own account) was reclining on the
divan, by the side of Jesus, his head resting upon the
breast of the Master. Towards the end of the repast the
secret which weighed upon the heart of Jesus almost
escaped him: he said, " Verily I say unto you, that one of
you shall betray me." To these simple men this was a
moment of anguish; they looked at each other, and each
questioned himself. Judas was present; perhaps Jesus,
who had for some time had reasons to suspect him, sought
by this expression to draw from his looks or from his
embarrassed manner the confession of his fault. But the
unfaithful disciple did not lose countenance; he even
dared, it is said, to ask with the others: " Master, is it I ? "

Meanwhile, the good and upright soul of Peter was in
torture. He made a sign to John to endeavour to ascertain
of whom the Master spoke. John, who could converse
with Jesus without being heard, asked him the meaning
of this enigma. Jesus, having only suspicions, did not
wish to pronounce any name; he only told John to observe
to whom he was going to offer a sop. At the same time, he
soaked the bread and offered it to Judas. John and Peter
alone had cognisance of the fact. Jesus addressed to Judas
words which contained a bitter reproach, but which were
not understood by those present; and he left the company.
They thought that Jesus was simply giving him orders for
the morrow's feast.

At the time this repast struck no one; and apart from
the apprehensions which the Master confided to his disciples, who only half understood them, nothing extraordinary
took place. But after the death of Jesus they attached to
this evening a singularly solemn meaning, and the imagina-

tion of believers spread a colouring of sweet mysticism over it. The last hours of a cherished friend are those we best remember. By an inevitable illusion, we attribute to the conversations we have then had with him a meaning which death alone gives to them; we concentrate into a few hours the memories of many years. The greater part of the disciples saw their Master no more after the supper of which we have just spoken. It was the farewell banquet. In this repast, as in many others, Jesus practised his mysterious rite of the breaking of bread. As it was early believed that the repast in question took place on the day of the Passover, and was the Paschal feast, the idea naturally arose that the Eucharistic institution was established at this supreme moment. Starting from the hypothesis that Jesus knew beforehand the precise moment of his death, the disciples were led to suppose that he reserved a number of important acts for his last hours. As, moreover, one of the fundamental ideas of the first Christians was that the death of Jesus had been a sacrifice, replacing all those of the ancient Law, the " Last Supper," which was supposed to have taken place, once for all, on the eve of the Passion, became the supreme sacrifice—the act which constituted the new alliance—the sign of the blood shed for the salvation of all. The bread and wine, placed in connection with death itself, were thus the image of the new testament that Jesus had sealed with his sufferings—the commemoration of the sacrifice of Christ until his advent.

Very early this mystery was embodied in a small sacramental narrative, which we possess under four forms, very similar to one another. John, preoccupied with the Eucharistic ideas, and who relates the Last Supper with so much prolixity, connecting with it so many circumstances and discourses, and who was the only one of the evangelists whose testimony on this point has the value of an eye-witness, does not mention this narrative. This is a proof that he did not regard the Eucharist as a peculiarity of the Lord's Supper. For him the special rite of the Last Supper was the washing of feet. It is probable that in certain primitive Christian families this latter rite obtained an importance which it has since lost. No doubt Jesus on some occasions had practised it to give his disciples an example of brotherly humility. It was connected with the eve of his death, in consequence of the tendency to group around the Last Supper all the great moral and ritual recommendations of Jesus.

A high sentiment of love, of concord, of charity, and of

mutual deference, animated, moreover, the remembrances which were cherished of the last hours of Jesus. It is always the unity of his Church, constituted by him or by his Spirit, which is the soul of the symbols and of the discourses which Christian tradition referred to this sacred moment : " A new commandment I give unto you," said he, " that ye love one another; as I have loved you, that ye also love one another. By this shall all men know that ye are my disciples, if ye have love one to another. Henceforth I call you not servants; for the servant knoweth not what his lord doeth : but I have called you friends; for all things that I have heard of my Father I have made known unto you. These things I command you, that ye love one another." At this last moment there were again evoked rivalries and struggles for precedence. Jesus remarked that if he, the Master, had been in the midst of his disciples as their servant, how much more ought they to submit themselves to one another. According to some, in drinking the wine, he said, " I will not drink henceforth of this fruit of the vine until that day when I drink it new with you in my Father's kingdom." According to others, he promised them soon a celestial feast, where they would be seated on thrones at his side.

It seems that towards the end of the evening the presentiments of Jesus took hold of the disciples. All felt that a very serious danger threatened the Master, and that they were approaching a crisis. At one time Jesus thought of precautions and spoke of swords. There were two in the company. " It is enough," said he. He did not, however, follow out this idea; he saw clearly that timid provincials would not stand before the armed force of all the great powers of Jerusalem. Peter, full of zeal, and feeling sure of himself, swore that he would go with him to prison and to death. Jesus, with his usual acuteness, expressed doubts about him. According to a tradition, which probably came from Peter himself, Jesus declared that Peter would deny him before the crowing of the cock. All, like Peter, swore that they would remain faithful to him.

CHAPTER XXIV

ARREST AND TRIAL OF JESUS

It was nightfall when they left the room. Jesus, according to his custom, passed through the valley of Kedron; and, accompanied by his disciples, went to the garden of Gethsemane, at the foot of the Mount of Olives, and sat down there. Overawing his friends by his inherent greatness, he watched and prayed. They were sleeping near him, when all at once an armed troop appeared bearing lighted torches. It was the guards of the temple, armed with staves, a kind of police under the control of priests. They were supported by a detachment of Roman soldiers with their swords. The order for the arrest emanated from the high priest and Sanhedrim. Judas, knowing the habits of Jesus, had indicated this place as the one where he might most easily be surprised. Judas, according to the unanimous tradition of the earliest times, accompanied the detachment himself; and, according to some, he carried his hateful conduct even to betraying him with a kiss. However this may be, it is certain that there was some show of resistance on the part of the disciples. One of them (Peter, according to eye-witnesses) drew his sword, and wounded the ear of one of the servants of the high priest, named Malchus. Jesus restrained this opposition, and gave himself up to the soldiers. Weak and incapable of effectual resistance, especially against authorities who had so much prestige, the disciples took flight, and became dispersed; Peter and John alone did not lose sight of their Master. Another unknown young man followed him, covered with a light garment. They sought to arrest him, but the young man fled, leaving his tunic in the hands of the guards.

The course which the priests had resolved to take against Jesus was quite in comformity with the established law. The procedure against the " corrupter " (*mésith*) who sought to injure the purity of religion is explained in the Talmud, with details the naïve impudence of which provokes a smile.

A judicial ambush is there made an essential part of the examination of criminals. When a man was accused of being a " corrupter," two witnesses were suborned, who were concealed behind a partition. It was arranged to bring the accused into a contiguous room, where he could be heard by these two without his perceiving them. Two candles were lighted near him in order that it might be satisfactorily proved that the witnesses " saw him." He was then made to repeat his blasphemy, and urged to retract it. If he persisted, the witnesses who had heard him conducted him to the tribunal, and he was stoned to death. The Talmud adds that this was the manner in which they treated Jesus; that he was condemned on the faith of two witnesses who had been suborned, and that the crime of " corruption " is, moreover, the only one for which the witnesses are thus prepared.

We learn from the disciples of Jesus themselves that the crime with which their Master was charged was that of " corruption "; and, apart from some minutiæ, the fruit of the rabbinical imagination, the narrative of the Gospels corresponds exactly with the procedure described by the Talmud. The plan of the enemies of Jesus was to convict him, by the testimony of witnesses and by his own avowals, of blasphemy, and of outrage against the Mosaic religion, to condemn him to death according to law, and then to get the condemnation sanctioned by Pilate. The priestly authority, as we have already seen, was in reality entirely in the hands of Hanan. The order for the arrest probably came from him. It was before this powerful personage that Jesus was first brought. Hanan questioned him as to his doctrine and his disciples. Jesus, with proper pride, refused to enter into long explanations. He referred Hanan to his teachings, which had been public; he declared he had never held any secret doctrine; and desired the exhigh priest to interrogate those who had listened to him. This answer was perfectly natural; but the exaggerated respect with which the old priest was surrounded made it appear audacious; and one of those present replied to it, it is said, by a blow.

Peter and John had followed their Master to the dwelling of Hanan. John, who was known in the house, was admitted without difficulty; but Peter was stopped at the entrance, and John was obliged to beg the porter to let him pass. The night was cold. Peter stopped in the antechamber, and approached a brasier, round which the servants were warming themselves. He was soon recognised as a disciple of the accused. The unfortunate man, betrayed by his Galilean accent, and pestered by questions from the servants, one of whom, a kinsman of Malchus, had seen him at Gethsemane, denied thrice that he had ever had the least connection with Jesus. He thought that Jesus could not hear him, and never imagined that this cowardice, which he sought to hide by his dissimulation, was exceedingly dishonourable. But his better nature soon revealed to him the fault he had committed. A fortuitous circumstance, the crowing of the cock, recalled to him a remark which Jesus had made. Touched to the heart, he went out and wept bitterly.

Hanan, although the true author of the judicial murder about to be accomplished, had not power to pronounce the sentence upon Jesus; he sent him to his son-in-law, Kaïapha, who bore the official title. This man, the blind instrument of his father-in-law, would naturally ratify everything that had been done. The Sanhedrim was assembled at his house. The inquiry commenced; and several witnesses, prepared beforehand according to the inquisitorial process described in the Talmud, appeared before the tribunal. The fatal sentence which Jesus had really uttered, " I am able to destroy the temple of God and to build it in three days," was cited by two witnesses. To blaspheme the temple of God was according to the Jewish law, to blaspheme God himself. Jesus remained silent, and refused to explain the incriminating speech. If we may believe one version, the high priest then adjured him to say if he were the Messiah; Jesus confessed it, and proclaimed before the assembly the near approach of his heavenly reign. The courage of Jesus, who had resolved to die, renders this narrative superfluous. It is probable that here, as when before Hanan, he remained silent. This was in general his rule of conduct during his last moments. The sentence was settled; and they only sought for pretexts. Jesus felt this, and did not undertake a useless defence. In the light of orthodox Judaism, he was truly a blasphemer, a destroyer of the established worship. Now, these crimes were punished by the law with death. With one voice the assembly declared him guilty of a capital crime. The members of the council who secretly leaned to him were absent or did not vote. The frivolity which characterises old established aristocracies did not permit the judges to reflect long upon the consequences of the sentence they had passed. Human life was at that time very lightly sacrificed; doubtless the members of the Sanhedrim did not dream that their sons would have to render account to an angry posterity for the sentence pronounced with such careless disdain.

The Sanhedrim had not the right to execute a sentence of death. But, in the confusion of powers which then reigned in Judea, Jesus was, from that moment, none the less condemned. He remained the rest of the night exposed to the ill treatment of an infamous pack of servants, who spared him no indignity.

In the morning the chief priests and the elders again assembled. The point was to get Pilate to ratify the condemnation pronounced by the Sanhedrim, which, since the occupation of the Romans, was no longer sufficient. The procurator was not invested, like the imperial legate, with the disposal of life and death. But Jesus was not a Roman citizen; it only required the authorisation of the governor in order that the sentence pronounced against him should take its course. As always happens when a political people subjects a nation in which the civil and religious laws are confounded, the Romans had been brought to give to the Jewish law a sort of official support. The Roman law did not apply to Jews. The latter remained under the canonical law which we find recorded in the Talmud, just as the Arabs in Algeria are still governed by the code of Islamism. Although neutral in religion, the Romans thus very often sanctioned penalties inflicted for religious faults. The situation was nearly that of the sacred cities of India under the English dominion, or rather that which would be the state of Damascus if Syria were conquered by a European nation. Josephus asserts, though this may be doubted, that, if a Roman trespassed beyond the pillars which bore inscriptions forbidding pagans to advance, the Romans themselves would have delivered him to the Jews to be put to death.

The agents of the priests therefore bound Jesus and led him to the judgment-hall, which was the former palace of Herod, adjoining the Tower of Antonia. It was the morning of the day on which the Paschal lamb was to be eaten. (Friday the 14th of Nisan, our April 3rd.) The Jews would have been defiled by entering the judgment-hall, and would not have been able to share in the sacred feast. They therefore remained without. Pilate, being informed of their presence ascended the *bima* or tribunal, situated in the open air, at the place named *Gabbatha*, or, in Greek, *Lithostrotos*, on account of the pavement which covered the ground.

He had scarcely been informed of the accusation before he displayed his annoyance at being mixed up with this affair. He then shut himself up in the judgment-hall with Jesus. There a conversation took place, the precise details of which are lost, no witness having been able to repeat it to the disciples, but the tenour of which appears to have been well divined by John. His narrative, in fact, perfectly accords with what history teaches us of the mutual position of the two interlocutors.

The procurator, Pontius, surnamed Pilate, doubtless on account of the *pilum* or javelin of honour with which he or one of his ancestors was decorated, had hitherto had no relation with the new sect. Indifferent to the internal quarrels of the Jews, he only saw, in all these movements of sectaries, the results of intemperate imaginations and disordered brains. In general, he did not like the Jews, but the Jews detested him still more. They thought him hard, scornful, and passionate, and accused him of improbable crimes.

Jerusalem, the centre of a great national fermentation, was a very seditious city, and an insupportable abode for a foreigner. The enthusiasts pretended that it was a fixed design of the new procurator to abolish the Jewish law. Their narrow fanaticism and their religious hatreds disgusted that broad sentiment of justice and civil government which the humblest Roman carried everywhere with him. All the acts of Pilate which are known to us show him to have been a good administrator. In the earlier period of the exercise of his office he had difficulties with those subject to him which he had solved in a very brutal manner; but it seems that essentially he was right. The Jews must have appeared to him a people behind the age; he doubtless judged them as a liberal prefect formerly judged the Bas-Bretons, who rebelled for such trifling matters as a new road, or the establishment of a school. In his best projects for the good of the country, notably in those relating to public works, he had encountered an impassable obstacle in the Law. The Law restricted life to such a degree that it opposed all change, and all amelioration. The Roman structures, even the most useful ones, were objects of great antipathy on the part of zealous Jews. Two votive escutcheons with inscriptions, which he had set up at his residence near the sacred precincts, provoked a still more violent storm. Pilate at first cared little for these susceptibilities; and he was soon involved in sanguinary suppressions of revolt, which afterwards ended in his removal. The experience of so many conflicts had rendered him very prudent in his relations with this intractable people, which avenged itself upon its governors by compelling them to use towards it hateful severities. The procurator saw himself, with extreme displeasure, led to play a cruel part in this new affair, for the sake of a law he hated. He knew that religious fanaticism, when it has obtained the sanction of civil Governments to some act of violence, is afterwards the first to throw the responsibility upon the Government, and almost accuses them of being the author of it. Supreme injustice; for the true culprit is, in such cases, the instigator!

Pilate, then, would have liked to save Jesus. Perhaps the dignified and calm attitude of the accused made an impression upon him. According to a tradition, Jesus found a supporter in the wife of the procurator himself. She may have seen the gentle Galilean from some window of the palace overlooking the courts of the temple. Perhaps she had seen him again in her dreams; and the idea that the blood of this beautiful young man was about to be spilt weighed upon her mind. Certain it is that Jesus found Pilate prepossessed in his favour. The governor questioned him with kindness, and with the desire to find an excuse for sending him away pardoned.

The title of " Kings of the Jews," which Jesus had never taken upon himself, but which his enemies represented as the sum and substance of his acts and pretensions, was naturally that by which it was sought to excite the suspicions of the Roman authority. They accused him on this ground of sedition, and of treason against the Government. Nothing could be more unjust; for Jesus had always recognised the Roman Government as the established power. But conservative religious bodies do not generally shrink from calumny. Notwithstanding his own explanation, they drew certain conclusions from his teaching; they transformed him into a disciple of Judas the Gaulonite; they pretended that he forbade the payment of tribute to Cæsar. Pilate asked him if he was really the King of the Jews. Jesus concealed nothing of what he thought. But the great ambiguity of speech which had been the source of his strength, and which, after his death, was to establish his kingship, injured him on this occasion. An idealist that is to say, not distinguishing the spirit from the substance, Jesus, whose words, to use the image of the Apocalypse, were as a two-edged sword, never completely satisfied the powers of earth. If we may believe John, he avowed his royalty, but uttered at the same time this profound sentence : " My kingdom is not of this world." He explained the nature of his kingdom, declaring that it consisted entirely in the possession and proclamation of truth. Pilate understood nothing of this grand idealism. Jesus doubtless impressed him as being an inoffensive dreamer. The total absence of religious and philosophical proselytism among the Romans of this epoch made them regard devotion to truth as a chimera. Such discussions annoyed them, and appeared to them devoid of meaning. Not perceiving the element of danger to the empire that lay hidden in these new speculations, they had no reason to employ violence against them. All their displeasure fell upon those who asked them to inflict punishment for what appeared to them to be vain subtleties. Twenty years after Gallio still adopted the same course towards the Jews. Until the fall of Jerusalem, the rule which the Romans adopted in administration was to remain completely indifferent to these sectarian quarrels.

An expedient suggested itself to the mind of the governor by which he could reconcile his own feelings with the demands of the fanatical people, whose pressure he had already so often felt. It was the custom to deliver a prisoner to the people at the time of the Passover. Pilate, knowing that Jesus had only been arrested in consequence of the jealousy of the priests, tried to obtain for him the benefit of this custom. He appeared again upon the *bima,* and proposed to the multitude to release the " King of the Jews." The proposition made in these terms, though ironical, was characterised by a degree of liberality. The priests saw the danger of it. They acted promptly, and, in order to combat the proposition of Pilate, they suggested to the crowd the name of a prisoner who enjoyed great popularity in Jerusalem. By a singular coincidence, he also was called Jesus, and bore the surname of Bar-Abba, or Bar-Rabban. He was a well-known personage, and had been arrested for taking part in an uproar in which murder had been committed. A general clamour was raised, " Not this man; but Jesus Bar-Rabban "; and Pilate was obliged to release Jesus Bar-Rabban.

His embarrassment increased. He feared that too much indulgence shown to a prisoner to whom was given the title of " King of the Jews " might compromise him. Fanaticism, moreover, compels all powers to make terms with it. Pilate thought himself obliged to make some concession; but still hesitating to shed blood, in order to satisfy men whom he hated, wished to turn the thing into a jest. Affecting to laugh at the pompous title they had given to Jesus, he caused him to be scourged. Scourging was the general preliminary of crucifixion. Perhaps Pilate wished it to be believed that this sentence had already been pronounced, hoping that the preliminary would suffice. Then took place (according to all the narratives) a revolting scene. The soldiers put a scarlet robe on his back, a crown formed of branches of thorns upon his head, and a reed in his hand. Thus attired, he was led to the tribunal in front of the people. The soldiers defiled before him, striking him in turn, and knelt to him, saying, " Hail ! King of the Jews ! " Others, it is said, spit upon him, and struck his head with the reed. It is difficult to understand how Roman dignity could stoop to acts so shameful. It is true that Pilate, in the capacity of procurator, had under his command scarcely any but auxiliary troops. Roman citizens, as the legionaries were, would not have degraded themselves by such conduct.

Did Pilate think by this display that he freed himself from responsibility ? Did he hope to turn aside the blow which threatened Jesus by conceding something to the hatred of the Jews, and by substituting for the tragic denouement a grotesque termination, to make it appear that the affair merited no other issue ? If such were his idea, it was unsuccessful. The tumult increased, and became an open riot. The cry, " Crucify him ! Crucify him ! " resounded from all sides. The priests, becoming increasingly urgent, declared the Law in peril if the corrupter were not punished with death. Pilate saw clearly that to save Jesus he would have to put down a terrible disturbance. He still tried, however, to gain time. He returned to the judgment-hall and ascertained from what country Jesus came, with the hope of finding a pretext for declaring his inability to adjudicate. According to one tradition, he even sent Jesus to Antipas, who, it is said, was then at Jerusalem. Jesus took no part in these well-meant efforts ; he maintained, as he had done before Kaïapha, a grave and dignified silence, which astonished Pilate. The cries from without became more and more menacing. The people had already begun to denounce the lack of zeal in the functionary who protected an enemy of Cæsar. The greatest adversaries of the Roman rule were suddenly transformed into loyal subjects of Tiberius, that they might have the right of accusing the too tolerant procurator of treason. " We have no king," said they, " but Cæsar. If thou let this man go, thou art not Cæsar's friend : whosoever maketh himself a king speaketh against Cæsar." The feeble Pilate yielded ; he foresaw the report that his enemies would send to Rome, in which they would

H

accuse him of having protected a rival of Tiberius. Once
before, in the matter of the votive escutcheons, the Jews
had written to the emperor, and had received satisfaction.
He feared for his office.   By a compliance, which was to deliver
his name to the scorn of history, he yielded, throwing, it is
said, upon the Jews all the responsibility of what was
about to happen. The latter, according to the Christians,
fully accepted it by exclaiming, " His blood be on us and on
our children ! "

Were these words really uttered ? We may doubt it.
But they are the expression of a profound historical truth.
Considering the attitude which the Romans had taken in
Judea, Pilate could scarcely have acted otherwise. How
many sentences of death dictated by religious intolerance
have been extorted from the civil power ! The king of
Spain, who, in order to please a fanatical clergy, delivered
hundreds of his subjects to the stake, was more blameable
than Pilate, for he represented a more absolute power than
that of the Romans at Jerusalem. When the civil power
becomes persecuting or meddlesome at the solicitation of
the priesthood, it proves its weakness. But let the Government that is without sin in this respect throw the first stone
at Pilate. The " secular arm," behind which clerical cruelty
shelters itself, is not the culprit. No one has a right to say
that he has a horror of blood when he causes it to be shed
by his servants.

It was, then, neither Tiberius nor Pilate who condemned
Jesus. It was the old Jewish party ; it was the Mosaic
Law. According to our modern ideas, there is no trans-
mission of moral demerit from father to son ; no one is
accountable to human or Divine justice except for that
which he himself has done. Consequently, every Jew who
suffers to-day for the murder of Jesus has a right to complain, for he might have acted as did Simon the Cyrenean ;
at any rate, he might not have been with those who cried
" Crucify him ! "   But nations, like individuals, have their
responsibilities, and, if ever crime was the crime of a
nation, it was the death of Jesus. This death was " legal "
in the sense that it was primarily caused by a law which was
the very soul of the nation. The Mosaic law, in its modern,
but still in its accepted form, pronounced the penalty of
death against all attempts to change the established
worship. Now, there is no doubt that Jesus attacked this
worship, and aspired to destroy it. The Jews expressed this
to Pilate with a truthful simplicity : " We have a law, and
by our law he ought to die ; because he has made himsel

the Son of God." The law was detestable, but it was the law of ancient ferocity; and the hero who offered himself in order to abrogate it had first of all to endure its penalty.

Alas! it has required more than eighteen hundred years for the blood that he shed to bear its fruits. Tortures and death have been inflicted for ages in the name of Jesus on thinkers as noble as himself. Even at the present time, in countries which call themselves Christian, penalties are pronounced for religious offences. Jesus is not responsible for these errors. He could not foresee that people, with mistaken imaginations, would one day imagine him as a frightful Moloch, greedy of burnt flesh. Christianity has been intolerant, but intolerance is not essentially a Christian fact. It is a Jewish fact in the sense that it was Judaism which first introduced the theory of the absolute in religion, and laid down the principle that every innovator, even if he brings miracles to support his doctrine, ought to be stoned without trial. The pagan world has also had its religious violence. But, if it had had this law, how would it have become Christian? The Pentateuch has thus been in the world the first code of religious terrorism. Judaism has given the example of an immutable dogma armed with the sword. If, instead of pursuing the Jews with a blind hatred, Christianity had abolished the regime which killed its founder, how much more consistent would it have been! how much better would it have deserved of the human race!

CHAPTER XXV

DEATH OF JESUS

ALTHOUGH the real motive for the death of Jesus was entirely religious, his enemies had succeeded, in the judgment-hall, in representing him as guilty of treason against the State; they could not have obtained from the sceptical Pilate a condemnation simply on the ground of heterodoxy. Consistently with this idea, the priests demanded, through the people, the crucifixion of Jesus. This punishment was not Jewish in its origin; if the condemnation of Jesus had been purely Mosaic, he would have been stoned. Crucifixion was a Roman punishment, reserved for slaves, and for cases in which it was wished to add to death the aggravation of ignominy. In applying it to Jesus they treated him as they treated highway robbers, brigands, bandits, or those enemies of inferior rank to whom the Romans did not grant the honour of death by the sword. It was the chimerical "King of the Jews," not the heterodox dogmatist, who was punished. Following out the same idea, the execution was left to the Romans. We know that among the Romans their soldiers, their profession being to kill, performed the office of executioners. Jesus was therefore delivered to a cohort of auxiliary troops, and all the most hateful features of executions introduced by the cruel habits of the new conquerors were exhibited towards him. It was about noon. They re-clothed him with the garments which they had removed for the farce enacted at the tribunal, and, as the cohort had already in reserve two thieves who were to be executed, the three prisoners were taken together, and the procession set out for the place of execution.

The scene of the execution was at a place called Golgotha, situated outside Jerusalem, but near the walls of the city. The name *Golgotha* signifies a *skull*; it corresponds with the French word *Chaumont*, and probably designated a bare hill or rising ground, having the form of a bald skull. The situation of this hill is not precisely known. It was

certainly on the north or north-west of the city, in the
high irregular plain which extends between the walls and
the two valleys of Kedron and Hinnom, a rather uninter-
esting region, and made still worse by the objectionable
circumstances arising from the neighbourhood of a great
city. It is difficult to identify Golgotha as the precise
place which, since Constantine, has been venerated by
entire Christendom. This place is too much in the interior
of the city, and we are led to believe that in the time of
Jesus it was comprised within the circuit of the walls.

He who was condemned to the cross had himself to
carry the instrument of his execution. But Jesus, physic-
ally weaker than his two companions, could not carry his.
The troop met a certain Simon of Cyrene, who was returning from the country, and the soldiers, with the off-hand
procedure of foreign garrisons, forced him to carry the
fatal tree. Perhaps they made use of a recognised right
of forcing labour, the Romans not being allowed to carry
the infamous wood. It seems that Simon was afterwards
of the Christian community. His two sons, Alexander
and Rufus, were well known in it. He related perhaps
more than one circumstance of which he had been witness.
No disciple was at this moment near to Jesus.

The place of execution was at last reached. According
to Jewish custom, the sufferers were offered a strong
aromatic wine, an intoxicating drink, which, through a
sentiment of pity, was given to the condemned in order
to stupefy him. It appears that the ladies of Jerusalem
often brought this kind of wine to the unfortunates who
were led to execution; when none was presented by them,
it was purchased from the public treasury. Jesus, after
having touched the edge of the cup with his lips, refused
to drink. This mournful consolation of ordinary sufferers
did not accord with his exalted nature. He preferred to
quit life with perfect clearness of mind, and to await in
full consciousness the death he had willed and brought
upon himself. He was then divested of his garments,
and fastened to the cross. The cross was composed of
two beams, tied in the form of the letter T. It was not
much elevated, so that the feet of the condemned almost
touched the earth. They commenced by fixing it, then
they fastened the sufferer to it by driving nails into his
hands; the feet were often nailed, though sometimes only
bound with cords. A piece of wood was fastened to the
upright portion of the cross, towards the middle, and
passed between the legs of the condemned, who rested

upon it. Without that the hands would have been torn and the body would have sunk down. At other times a small horizontal rest was fixed beneath the feet and sustained them.

Jesus tasted these horrors in all their atrocity. A burning thirst, one of the tortures of crucifixion, devoured him, and he asked to drink. There stood near a cup of the ordinary drink of the Roman soldiers, a mixture of vinegar and water, called *posca*. The soldiers had to carry with them their *posca* on all their expeditions, of which an execution was considered one. A soldier dipped a sponge in this drink, put it at the end of a reed, and raised it to the lips of Jesus, who sucked it. The two robbers were crucified, one on each side. The executioners, to whom were usually left the small effects (*pannicularia*) of those executed, drew lots for his garments, and, seated at the foot of the cross, kept guard over him. According to one tradition, Jesus pronounced this sentence, which was in his heart if not upon his lips : " Father, forgive them, for they know not what they do."

According to the Roman custom, a writing was attached to the top of the cross, bearing in three languages, Hebrew, Greek, and Latin, the words : " THE KING OF THE JEWS." There was something painful and insulting to the nation in this inscription. The numerous passers-by who read it were offended. The priests complained to Pilate that he ought to have adopted an inscription which would have implied simply that Jesus had called himself King of the Jews. But Pilate, already tired of the whole affair, refused to make any change in what had been written.

His disciples had fled. John, nevertheless, declares himself to have been present, and to have remained standing at the foot of the cross during the whole time. It may be affirmed, with more certainty, that the devoted women of Galilee, who had followed Jesus to Jerusalem and continued to tend him, did not abandon him. Mary Cleophas, Mary Magdalen, Joanna, wife of Khouza, Salome, and others, stayed at a certain distance, and did not lose sight of him. If we must believe John, Mary, the mother of Jesus, was also at the foot of the cross, and Jesus, seeing his mother and his beloved disciple together, said to the one, " Behold thy mother ! " and to the other, " Behold thy son ! " But we do not understand how the Synoptics, who name the other women, should have omitted her whose presence was so striking a feature. Perhaps even the extreme elevation of the character of Jesus does not render such personal emotion probable at the moment when, solely preoccupied by his work, he no longer existed except for humanity.

Apart from this small group of women, whose presence consoled him, Jesus had before him only the spectacle of the baseness or stupidity of humanity. The passers-by insulted him. He heard around him foolish scoffs, and his greatest cries of pain turned into hateful jests : " He trusted in God ; let him deliver him now, if he will have him : for he said, I am the Son of God. He saved others," they said again ; " himself he cannot save. If he be the King of Israel, let him now come down from the cross, and we will believe him ! Ah, thou that destroyest the temple, and buildest it in three days, save thyself." Some, vaguely acquainted with his apocalyptic ideas, thought they heard him call Elias, and said : " Let us see whether Elias will come to save him." It appears that the two crucified thieves at his side also insulted him. The sky was dark ; and the earth, as in all the environs of Jerusalem, dry and gloomy. For a moment, according to certain narratives, his heart failed him ; a cloud hid from him the face of his Father ; he endured an agony of despair a thousand times more acute than all his torture. He saw only the ingratitude of men ; he perhaps repented suffering for a vile race, and exclaimed : " My God, my God, why hast thou forsaken me ? " But his Divine instinct still prevailed. In the degree that the life of the body became extinguished, his soul became clear, and returned by de- grees to its celestial origin. He regained the idea of his mission ; he saw in his death the salvation of the world ; he lost sight of the hideous spectacle spread at his feet, and, profoundly united to his Father, he began upon the gibbet the Divine life which he was to live in the heart of humanity throughout infinite ages.

The peculiar atrocity of crucifixion was that one might live three or four days in this horrible state upon the instrument of torture. The hæmorrhage from the hands quickly stopped, and was not mortal. The true cause of death was the unnatural position of the body, which brought on a frightful disturbance of the circulation, terrible pains of the head and heart, and, at length, rigidity of the limbs. Those who had a strong constitution only died of hunger. The idea which suggested this cruel punishment was not directly to kill the condemned by positive injuries, but to expose the slave, nailed by the hand of which he had not known how to make good use, and to let him rot on the wood. The delicate organisation of Jesus preserved him from this slow agony. Everything leads to the belief that the instantaneous rupture of a vessel in the heart brought him, at the end of three hours, to a sudden death. Some moments before yielding up his soul his voice was still strong. All at once he uttered a terrible cry, which some heard as : " Father, into thy hands I commend my spirit ! " but which others, more pre-occupied with the accomplishment of prophecies, rendered by the words, " It is finished ! " His head fell upon his breast, and he expired.

Rest now in thy glory, noble initiator. Thy work is completed ; thy divinity is established. Fear no more to see the edifice of thy efforts crumble through a flaw. Hence-forth, beyond the reach of frailty, thou shalt be present, from the height of the divine peace, in the infinite conse-quences of thy acts. At the price of a few hours of suffer-ing, which have not even touched thy great soul, thou hast purchased the most complete immortality. For thousands of years the world will extol thee. Banner of our contradictions, thou wilt be the sign around which will be fought the fiercest battles. A thousand times more living, a thousand times more loved since thy death than during the days of thy pilgrimage here below, thou wilt become to such a degree the corner-stone of humanity that to tear thy name from this world would be to shake it to its foundations. Between thee and God men will no longer distinguish. Complete conqueror of death, take possession of thy kingdom, whither, by the royal road thou hast traced, ages of adorers will follow thee.

CHAPTER XXVI

JESUS IN THE TOMB

It was about three o'clock in the afternoon, according to our manner of reckoning, when Jesus expired. A Jewish law forbade a corpse suspended on the cross to be left beyond the evening of the day of the execution. It is not probable that in the executions performed by the Romans this rule was observed; but as the next day was the Sabbath, and a Sabbath of peculiar solemnity, the Jews expressed to the Roman authorities their desire that this holy day should not be profaned by such a spectacle. Their request was granted; orders were given to hasten the death of the three condemned ones, and to remove them from the cross. The soldiers executed this order by applying to the two thieves a second punishment much more speedy than that of the cross, the *Crurifragium*, or breaking of the legs, the usual punishment of slaves and of prisoners of war. As to Jesus, they found him dead, and did not think it necessary to break his legs. But one of them, to remove all doubt as to the real death of the third victim, and to complete it, if any breath remained in him, pierced his side with a spear. They thought they saw water and blood flow, which was regarded as a sign of the cessation of life.

John, who professes to have seen it, insists strongly on this circumstance. It is evident, in fact, that doubts arose as to the reality of the death of Jesus. A few hours of suspension on the cross appeared, to persons accustomed to see crucifixions, entirely insufficient to lead to such a result. They cited many instances of persons crucified who, removed in time, had been brought to life again by powerful remedies. Origen afterwards thought it needful to invoke miracle in order to explain so sudden an end. The same astonishment is found in the narrative of Mark. To speak truly, the best guarantee that the historian possesses upon a point of this nature is the suspicious hatred of the enemies of Jesus. It is doubtful whether the Jews were at that time preoccupied with the fear that Jesus might pass for resuscitated; but, in any case, they must have made sure that he was really dead. Whatever, at certain periods, may have been the neglect of the ancients in all that belonged to legal proof and the strict conduct of affairs, we cannot but believe that those interested here had taken some precautions in this respect.

According to the Roman custom, the corpse of Jesus ought to have remained suspended in order to become the prey of birds. According to the Jewish law, it would have been removed in the evening, and deposited in the place of infamy set apart for the burial of those who were executed. If Jesus had had for disciples only his poor Galileans, timid and without influence, the latter course would have been adopted. But we have seen that, in spite of his small success at Jerusalem, Jesus had gained the sympathy of some important persons who expected the kingdom of God, and who, without confessing themselves his disciples, were strongly attached to him. One of these persons, Joseph, of the small town of Arimathea (*Ha-ramathaïm*),[1] went in the evening to ask the body from the procurator. Joseph was a rich and honourable man, a member of the Sanhedrim. The Roman law at this period commanded, moreover, that the body of the person executed should be delivered to those who claimed it. Pilate, who was ignorant of the circumstance of the *crurifragium*, was astonished that Jesus was so soon dead, and summoned the centurion who had superintended the execution, in order to know how this was. Pilate, after having received the assurances of the centurion, granted to Joseph the object of his request. The body probably had already been removed from the cross. They delivered it to Joseph, that he might do with it as he pleased.

Another secret friend, Nicodemus, whom we have already seen employing his influence more than once in favour of Jesus, came forward at this moment. He arrived bearing an ample provision of the materials necessary for embalming. Joseph and Nicodemus interred Jesus according to the Jewish custom—that is to say, they wrapped him in a sheet with myrrh and aloes. The Galilean women were present, and no doubt accompanied the scene with piercing cries and tears.

It was late, and all this was done in great haste. The place had not yet been chosen where the body would be finally deposited. The carrying of the body, moreover,

[1] Probably identical with the ancient Rama of Samuel, in the tribe of Ephraim.

might have been delayed to a late hour, and have involved a violation of the Sabbath—now the disciples still conscientiously observed the prescriptions of the Jewish law. A temporary interment was determined upon. There was at hand, in the garden, a tomb recently dug out in the rock, which had never been used. It belonged, probably, to one of the believers. The funeral caves, when they were destined for a single body, were composed of a small room, at the bottom of which the place for the body was marked by a trough or couch let into the wall, and surmounted by an arch. As these caves were dug out of the sides of sloping rocks, they were entered by the floor; the door was shut by a stone very difficult to move. Jesus was deposited in the cave, and the stone was rolled to the door, as it was intended to return in order to give him a more complete burial. But the next day being a solemn Sabbath, the labour was postponed till the day following.

The women retired after having carefully noticed how the body was laid. They employed the hours of the evening which remained to them in making new preparations for the embalming. On the Saturday all rested.

On the Sunday morning the women, Mary Magdalen the first, came very early to the tomb. The stone was displaced from the opening, and the body was no longer in the place where they had laid it. At the same time the strangest rumours were spread in the Christian community. The cry, " He is risen ! " quickly spread among the disciples. Love caused it to find ready credence everywhere. What had taken place ? In treating of the history of the Apostles we shall have to examine this point, and to make inquiry into the origin of the legends relative to the resurrection. For the historian, the life of Jesus finishes with his last sigh. But such was the impression he had left in the heart of his disciples and of a few devoted women that during some weeks more it was as if he were living and consoling them. Had his body been taken away, or did enthusiasm, always credulous, create afterwards the group of narratives by which it was sought to establish faith in the resurrection ? In the absence of opposing documents, this can never be ascertained. Let us say, however, that the strong imagination of Mary Magdalen played an important part in this circumstance. Divine power of love ! Sacred moments in which the passion of one possessed gave to the world a resuscitated God !

CHAPTER XXVII

FATE OF THE ENEMIES OF JESUS

ACCORDING to the calculation we adopt, the death of Jesus happened in the year 33 of our era. It could not, at all events, be either before the year 29, the preaching of John and Jesus having commenced in the year 28, or after the year 35, since in the year 36, and probably before the passover, Pilate and Kaïapha both lost their offices. The death of Jesus appears, moreover, to have had no connection whatever with these two removals. In his retirement Pilate probably never dreamt for a moment of the forgotten episode, which was to transmit his pitiful renown to the most distant posterity. As to Kaïapha, he was succeeded by Jonathan, his brother-in-law, son of the same Hanan who had played the principal part in the trial of Jesus. The Sadducean family of Hanan retained the pontificate a long time, and, more powerful than ever, continued to wage against the disciples and the family of Jesus the implacable war which they had commenced against the Founder. Christianity, which owed to him the definitive act of its foundation, owed to him also its first martyrs. Hanan passed for one of the happiest men of his age. He who was truly guilty of the death of Jesus ended his life full of honours and respect, never having doubted for an instant that he had rendered a great service to the nation. His sons continued to reign around the temple, kept down with difficulty by the procurators, ofttimes dispensing with the consent of the latter in order to gratify their haughty and violent instincts.

Antipas Herodias soon disappeared also from the political scene. Herod Agrippa, having been raised to the dignity of king by Caligula, the jealous Herodias swore that she also would be queen. Pressed incessantly by this ambitious woman, who treated him as a coward, because he suffered a superior in his family, Antipas overcame his natural indolence, and went to Rome to solicit the title which his nephew had just obtained (the year 39 of our era). But the affair turned out in the worst possible manner. Injured in the eyes of the emperor by Herod Agrippa, Antipas was removed, and dragged out the rest of his life in exile at Lyons and in Spain. Herodias followed him in his misfortunes. A hundred years at least were to elapse before the name of their obscure subject, now become deified, should appear in these remote countries to brand upon their tombs the murder of John the Baptist.

As to the wretched Judas of Kerioth, terrible legends were current about his death. It was maintained that he had bought a field in the neighbourhood of Jerusalem with the price of his perfidy. There was, indeed, on the south of Mount Zion, a place named *Hakeldama* (the field of blood). It was supposed that this was the property acquired by the traitor. According to one tradition, he killed himself. According to another, he had a fall in his field, in consequence of which his bowels gushed out. According to others, he died of a kind of dropsy, accompanied by repulsive circumstances, which were regarded as a punishment from heaven. The desire of showing in Judas the accomplishment of the menaces which the Psalmist pronounces against the perfidious friend may have given rise to these legends. Perhaps, in the retirement of his field of Hakeldama, Judas led a quiet and obscure life; while his former friends conquered the world, and spread his infamy abroad. Perhaps, also, the terrible hatred which was concentrated on his head drove him to violent acts, in which was seen the finger of heaven.

The time of the great Christian revenge was, moreover, far distant. The new sect had no part whatever in the catastrophe which Judaism was soon to undergo. The Synagogue did not understand till much later to what it exposed itself in practising laws of intolerance. The empire was certainly still further from suspecting that its future destroyer was born. During nearly three hundred years it pursued its path without suspecting that at its side principles were growing destined to subject the world to a complete transformation. At once theocratic and democratic, the idea thrown by Jesus into the world was, together with the invasion of the Germans, the most active cause of the dissolution of the empire of the Cæsars. On the one hand, the right of all men to participate in the kingdom of God was proclaimed. On the other, religion was henceforth separated in principle from the State. The right of conscience, withdrawn from political law, resulted in the constitution of a new power—the " spiritual power." This power has more than once belied its origin. For ages the bishops have been princes, and the Pope has been a king. The pretended empire of souls has shown itself at various times as a frightful tyranny, employing the rack and the stake in order to maintain itself. But the day will come when the separation will bear its fruits, when the domain of things spiritual will cease to be called a " power," that it may be called a " liberty." Sprung from the conscience of a man of the people, formed in the presence of the people, beloved and admired first by the people, Christianity was impressed with an original character which will never be effaced. It was the first triumph of revolution, the victory of the popular idea, the advent of the simple in heart, the inauguration of the beautiful as understood by the people. Jesus thus, in the aristocratic societies of antiquity, opened the breach through which all will pass.

The civil power, in fact, although innocent of the death of Jesus (it only countersigned the sentence, and even in spite of itself), ought to bear a great share of the responsibility. In presiding at the scene of Calvary the State gave itself a serious blow. A legend full of all kinds of disrespect prevailed, and became universally known—a legend in which the constituted authorities played a hateful part, in which it was the accused that was right, and in which the judges and the guards were leagued against the truth. Seditious in the highest degree, the history of the Passion, spread by a thousand popular images, displayed the Roman eagles as sanctioning the most iniquitous of executions, soldiers executing it, and a prefect commanding it. What a blow for all established powers ! They have never entirely recovered from it. How can they assume infallibility in respect to poor men when they have on their conscience the great mistake.of Gethsemane ?

CHAPTER XXVIII

ESSENTIAL CHARACTER OF THE WORK OF JESUS

JESUS, it will be seen, limited his action entirely to the Jews. Although his sympathy for those despised by orthodoxy led him to admit pagans into the kingdom of God—although he had resided more than once in a pagan country, and once or twice we surprise him in kindly relations with unbelievers—it may be said that his life was passed entirely in the very restricted world in which he was born. He was never heard of in Greek or Roman countries; his name appears only in profane authors of a hundred years later, and then in an indirect manner, in connection with seditious movements provoked by his doctrine, or persecutions of which his disciples were the object. Even on Judaism, Jesus made no very durable impression. Philo, who died about the year 50, had not the slightest knowledge of him. Josephus, born in the year 37, and writing in the last years of the century, mentions his execution in a few lines, as an event of secondary importance; and in the enumeration of the sects of his time he omits the Christians altogether. In the *Mishnah*, also, there is no trace of the new school; the passages in the two Gemaras in which the founder of Christianity is named do not go further back than the fourth or fifth century. The essential work of Jesus was to create around him a circle of disciples, whom he inspired with boundless affection, and among whom he deposited the germ of his doctrine. To have made himself beloved, " to the degree that after his death they ceased not to love him," was the great work of Jesus, and that which most struck his contemporaries. His doctrine was so little dogmatic that he never thought of writing it or of causing it to be written. Men did not become his disciples by believing this thing or that thing, but in being attached to his person, and in loving him A few sentences collected from memory, and especially the type of character he set forth, and the impression it had left, were what remained of him. Jesus was not a founder of dogmas, or a maker of creeds; he infused into the world a new spirit. The least Christian men were, on the one hand, the doctors of the Greek Church, who, beginning from the fourth century, entangled Christianity in a path of puerile metaphysical discussions, and, on the other, the scholastics of the Latin Middle Ages, who wished to draw from the Gospel the thousands of articles of a colossal system. To follow Jesus in expectation of the kingdom of God was all that was implied by being Christian.

It will thus be understood how, by an exceptional destiny, pure Christianity still preserves, after eighteen centuries, the character of a universal and eternal religion. It is, in fact, because the religion of Jesus is in some respects the final religion. Produced by a perfectly spontaneous movement of souls, freed at its birth from all dogmatic restraint, having struggled three hundred years for liberty of conscience, Christianity, in spite of its failures, still reaps the results of its glorious origin. To renew itself, it has but to return to the Gospel. The kingdom of God, as we conceive it, differs notably from the supernatural apparition which the first Christians hoped to see appear in the clouds. But the sentiment introduced by Jesus into the world is indeed ours. His perfect idealism is the highest rule of the unblemished and virtuous life. He has created the heaven of pure souls, where is found what we ask for in vain on earth, the perfect nobility of the children of God, absolute purity, the total removal of the stains of the world; in fine, liberty, which society excludes as an impossibility, and which exists in all its amplitude only in the domain of thought. The great Master of those who take refuge in this ideal kingdom of God is still Jesus. He was the first to proclaim the royalty of the mind; the first to say, at least by his actions, " My kingdom is not of this world." The foundation of true religion is indeed his work : after him, all that remains is to develop it and render it fruitful.

" Christianity " has thus become almost a synonym of " religion." All that is done outside of this great and good Christian tradition is barren. Jesus gave religion to humanity, as Socrates gave it philosophy, and Aristotle science. There was philosophy before Socrates, and science before Aristotle. Since Socrates and since Aristotle, philosophy and science have made immense progress; but all has been built upon the foundation which they laid. In the same way, before Jesus, religious thought had passed through many revolutions; since Jesus, it has made great conquests; but no one has improved, and no one will improve, upon the essential principle Jesus has created; he has fixed for ever the idea of pure worship. The religion of Jesus in this sense is not limited. The Church has had its epochs and its phases; it has shut itself up in creeds which are, or will be, but temporary; but Jesus has founded the absolute religion, excluding nothing, and determining nothing unless it be the spirit. His creeds are not fixed dogmas, but images susceptible of indefinite interpretations. We should seek in vain for a theological proposition in the Gospel. All confessions of faith are travesties of the idea of Jesus, just as the scholasticism of the Middle Ages, in proclaiming Aristotle the sole master of a completed science, perverted the thought of Aristotle. Aristotle, if he had been present in the debates of the schools, would have repudiated this narrow doctrine; he would have been of the party of progressive science against the routine which shielded itself under his authority; he would have applauded his opponents. In the same way, if Jesus were to return among us, he would recognise as disciples, not those who pretend to enclose him entirely in a few catechismal phrases, but those who labour to carry on his work The eternal glory in all great things is to have laid the first stone. It may be that in the " physics " and in the " Meteorology " of modern times we may not discover a word of the treatises of Aristotle which bear these titles; but Aristotle remains no less the founder of natural science. Whatever may be the transformations of dogma, Jesus will ever be the creator of the pure spirit of religion; the Sermon on the Mount will never be surpassed. Whatever revolution takes place will not prevent us attaching ourselves in religion to the grand intellectual and moral line at the head of which shines the name of Jesus. In this sense we are Christians, even when we separate ourselves on almost all points from the Christian tradition which has preceded us.

And this great foundation was indeed the personal work of Jesus. In order to make himself adored to this degree, he must have been adorable. Love is not enkindled except by an object worthy of it, and we should know nothing of Jesus if it were not for the passion he inspired in those about him, which compels us still to affirm that he was great and pure. The faith, the enthusiasm, the constancy of the first Christian generation is not explicable, except by supposing, at the origin of the whole movement, a man of surpassing greatness. At the sight of the marvellous creations of the ages of faith, two impressions equally fatal to good historical criticism arise in the mind. On the one hand we are led to think these creations too impersonal; we attribute to a collective action that which has often been the work of one powerful will and of one superior mind. On the other hand, we refuse to see men like ourselves in the authors of those extraordinary movements which have decided the fate of humanity. Let us have a larger idea of the powers which nature conceals in her bosom. Our civilisations, governed by minute restrictions, cannot give us any idea of the power of man at periods in which the originality of each one had a freer field wherein to develop itself. Let us imagine a recluse dwelling in the mountains near our capitals, coming out from time to time in order to present himself at the palaces of sovereigns, compelling the sentinels to stand aside, and, with an imperious tone, announcing to kings the approach of revolutions of which he had been the promoter. The very idea provokes a smile. Such, however, was Elias; but Elias the Tishbite, in our days, would not be able to pass the gate of the Tuileries. The preaching of Jesus, and his free activity in Galilee, do not deviate less completely from the social conditions to which we are accustomed. Free from our polished conventionalities, exempt from the uniform education which refines us, but which so greatly dwarfs our individuality, these mighty souls carried a surprising energy into action. They appear to us like the giants of an heroic age, which could not have been real. Profound error! Those men were our brothers; they were of our stature, felt and thought as we do. But the breath of God was free in them; with us it is restrained by the iron bonds of a mean society, and condemned to an irremediable mediocrity.

Let us place, then, the person of Jesus at the highest summit of human greatness. Let us not be misled by exaggerated doubts in the presence of a legend which keeps us always in a superhuman world. The life of Francis d'Assisi is also but a tissue of miracles. Has any one, however, doubted of the existence of Francis d'Assisi, and of the part played by him? Let us say no more that the glory of the foundation of Christianity belongs to the multitude of the first Christians, and not to him whom legend has deified. The inequality of men is much more marked in the East than with us. It is not rare to see arise there, in the midst of a general atmosphere of wickedness, characters whose greatness astonishes us. So far from Jesus having been created by his disciples, he appeared in

THE WORK OF JESUS

everything as superior to his disciples. The latter, with the exception of St. Paul and St. John, were men without either invention or genius. St. Paul himself bears no comparison with Jesus, and, as to St. John, I shall show hereafter that the part he played, though very elevated in one sense, was far from being in all respects irreproachable. Hence the immense superiority of the Gospels among the writings of the New Testament. Hence the painful fall we experience in passing from the history of Jesus to that of the apostles. The evangelists themselves, who have bequeathed us the image of Jesus, are so much beneath him of whom they speak that they constantly disfigure him from their inability to attain to his height. Their writings are full of errors and misconceptions. We feel in each line a discourse of divine beauty, transcribed by narrators who do not understand it, and who substitute their own ideas for those which they have only half understood. On the whole, the character of Jesus, far from having been embellished by his biographers, has been lowered by them. Criticism, in order to find what he was, needs to discard a series of misconceptions, arising from the inferiority of the disciples. These painted him as they understood him, and often in thinking to raise him they have in reality lowered him.

I know that our modern ideas have been offended more than once in this legend, conceived by another race, under another sky, and in the midst of other social wants. There are virtues which, in some respects, are more conformable to our taste. The virtuous and gentle Marcus Aurelius, the humble and gentle Spinoza, not having believed in miracles, have been free from some errors that Jesus shared. Spinoza, in his profound obscurity, had an advantage which Jesus did not seek. By our extreme delicacy in the use of means of conviction, by our absolute sincerity and our disinterested love of the pure idea, we have founded—all we who have devoted our lives to science—a new ideal of morality. But the judgment of general history ought not to be restricted to considerations of personal merit. Marcus Aurelius and his noble teachers have had no permanent influence on the world. Marcus Aurelius left behind him delightful books, an execrable son, and a decaying nation. Jesus remains an inexhaustible principle of moral regeneration for humanity. Philosophy does not suffice for the multitude. They must have sanctity. An Apollonius of Tyana, with his miraculous legend, is necessarily more successful than a Socrates with his cold reason. " Socrates," it was said, " leaves men on the earth, Apollonius transports them to heaven; Socrates is but a sage, Apollonius is a god." Religion, so far, has not existed without a share of asceticism, of piety, and of the marvellous. When it was wished, after the Antonines, to make a religion of philosophy, it was requisite to transform the philosophers into saints, to write the " Edifying life " of Pythagoras or Plotinus, to attribute to them a legend, virtues of abstinence, contemplation, and supernatural powers, without which neither credence nor authority was found in that age.

Preserve us, then, from mutilating history in order to satisfy our petty susceptibilities ! Which of us, pigmies as we are, could do what the extravagant Francis d'Assisi or the hysterical Saint Theresa has done ? Let medicine have names to express these grand errors of human nature; let it maintain that genius is a disease of the brain; let it see, in a certain delicacy of morality, the commencement of consumption; let it class enthusiasm and love as nervous accidents—it matters little. The terms " healthy " and " diseased " are entirely relative. Who would not prefer to be diseased like Pascal, rather than healthy like the common herd? The narrow ideas which are spread in our times respecting madness mislead our historical judgments in the most serious manner, in questions of this kind. A state in which a man says things of which he is not conscious, in which thought is produced without the summons and control of the will, exposes him to being confined as a lunatic. Formerly this was called prophecy and inspiration. The most beautiful things in the world are done in a state of fever; every great creation involves a breach of equilibrium, a violent state of the being which draws it forth.

We acknowledge, indeed, that Christianity is too complex to have been the work of a single man. In one sense, entire humanity has co-operated therein. There is no one so shut in as not to receive some influence from without. The history of the human mind is full of strange coincidences, which cause very remote portions of the human species, without any communication with each other, to arrive at the same time at almost identical ideas and imaginations. In the thirteenth century the Latins, the Greeks, the Syrians, the Jews, and the Mussulmans adopted scholasticism, and very nearly the same scholasticism, from York to Samarcand; in the fourteenth century everyone in Italy, Persia, and India yielded to the taste for mystical allegory; in the sixteenth, art was developed in a very similar manner in Italy, at Mount Athos, and at the court of the Great Moguls, without St. Thomas, Barhebræus, the Rabbis of Narbonne, or the *Motécallémin* of Bagdad, having known each other, without Dante and Petrarch having seen any *sofi*, without any pupil of the schools of Perouse or of Florence having been at Delhi. We should say there are great moral influences running through the world like epidemics, without distinction of frontier and of race. The interchange of ideas in the human species does not take place only by books or by direct instruction. Jesus was ignorant of the very name of Buddha, of Zoroaster, and of Plato; he had read no Greek book, no Buddhist Sudra, nevertheless there was in him more than one element, which, without his suspecting it, came from Buddhism, Parseeism, or from the Greek wisdom. All this was done through secret channels and by that kind of sympathy which exists among the various portions of humanity. The great man, on the one hand, receives everything from his age; on the other, he governs his age. To show that the religion founded by Jesus was the natural consequence of that which had gone before does not diminish its excellence, but only proves that it had a reason for its existence, that it was legitimate—that is to say, conformable to the instinct and wants of the heart in a given age.

Is it more just to say that Jesus owes all to Judaism, and that his greatness is only that of the Jewish people? No one is more disposed than myself to place high this unique people, whose particular gift seems to have been to contain in its midst the extremes of good and evil. No doubt, Jesus proceeded from Judaism; but he proceeded from it as Socrates proceeded from the schools of the Sophists, as Luther proceeded from the Middle Ages, as Lamennais from Catholicism, as Rousseau from the eighteenth century. A man is of his age and his race even when he reacts against his age and his race. Far from Jesus having continued Judaism, he represents the rupture with the Jewish spirit. The general direction of Christianity after him does not permit the supposition that his idea in this respect could lead to any misunderstanding. The general march of Christianity has been to remove itself more and more from Judaism. It will become perfect in returning to Jesus, but certainly not in returning to Judaism. The great originality of the founder remains then undiminished; his glory admits no legitimate sharer.

Doubtless, circumstances much aided the success of this marvellous revolution; but circumstances only second that which is just and true. Each branch of the development of humanity has its privileged epoch, in which it attains perfection by a sort of spontaneous instinct, and without effort. No labour of reflection would succeed in producing afterwards the masterpieces which nature creates at those moments by inspired geniuses. That which the golden age of Greece was for arts and literature, the age of Jesus was for religion. Jewish society exhibited the most extraordinary moral and intellectual state which the human species has ever passed through. It was truly one of those divine hours in which the sublime is produced by combinations of a thousand hidden forces, in which great souls find a flood of admiration and sympathy to sustain them. The world, delivered from the very narrow tyranny of small municipal republics, enjoyed great liberty. Roman despotism did not make itself felt in a disastrous manner until much later, and it was, moreover, always less oppressive in those distant provinces than in the centre of the empire. Our petty preventive interferences (far more destructive than death to things of the spirit) did not exist. Jesus, during three years, could lead a life which, in our societies, would have brought him twenty times before the magistrates. Our laws upon the illegal exercise of medicine would alone have sufficed to cut short his career. The unbelieving dynasty of the Herods, on the other hand, occupied itself little with religious movements; under the Asmodeans, Jesus would probably have been arrested at his first step. An innovator, in such a state of society, only risked death, and death is a gain to those who labour for the future. Imagine Jesus reduced to bear the burden of his divinity until his sixtieth or seventieth year, losing his celestial fire, wearing out little by little under the burden of an unparalleled mission ! Everything favours those who have a special destiny ; they become glorious by a sort of invincible impulse and command of fate.

This sublime person, who each day still presides over the destiny of the world, we may call divine, not in the sense that Jesus has absorbed all the divine, or has been adequate to it (to employ an expression of the schoolmen), but in the sense that Jesus is the one who has caused his fellow-men to make the greatest step towards the divine. Mankind in its totality offers an assemblage of low beings, selfish, and superior to the animal only in that its selfishness is more reflective. From the midst of this uniform mediocrity there are pillars that rise towards the sky, and bear witness to a nobler destiny. Jesus is the highest of these pillars which show to man whence he comes, and whither he ought to tend. In him was condensed all that is good and elevated in our nature. He was not sinless; he has conquered the same passions that we combat; no angel of God comforted him, except his good conscience; no Satan tempted him, except that which each one bears in his heart. In the same way that many of his great qualities are lost to us, through the fault of his disciples, it is also probable that many of his faults have been concealed. But never has any one so much as he made the interests of humanity predominate in his life over the littlenesses of self-love. Unreservedly devoted to his mission, he subordinated everything to it to such a degree that towards the end of his life the universe no longer existed for him. It was by this access of heroic will that he conquered heaven. There never was a man, Çakya-Mouni perhaps excepted, who has to this degree trampled under foot family, the joys of this world, and all temporal care. Jesus only lived for his Father and the divine mission which he believed himself destined to fulfil.

As to us, eternal children, powerless as we are, we who labour without reaping, and who will never see the fruit of that which we have sown, let us bow before these demi-gods. They were able to do that which we cannot do : to create, to affirm, to act. Will great orginality be born again, or will the world content itself henceforth by following the ways opened by the bold creators of the ancient ages ? We know not. But whatever may be the unexpected phenomena of the future, Jesus will not be surpassed. His worship will constantly renew its youth, the tale of his life will cause ceaseless tears, his sufferings will soften the best hearts; all the ages will proclaim that among the sons of men there is none born who is greater than Jesus.

APPENDIX

RENAN AND HIS CRITICS

It is well known that the appearance of *The Life of Jesus* was the signal for an outburst of orthodox indignation against the man who dared to reduce Jesus from a Divinity to a human being. Renan, however, calmly disregarded the flood of criticism under which a less happily poised nature would have been submerged. Renan was a scholar, a poet, a dreamer, a worshipper of the good and the beautiful. He was not a controversialist. His attitude in the " imminent deadly breach " of theological warfare was to lie still and let the storm of battle pass over him. Not until twelve editions of the book had appeared did he even notice his critics, and then he wrote for the thirteenth edition a preface full of dignity and beauty. During this period of four years Renan laboured incessantly to improve his work, and never did the abuse and calumnies of the hostile critics prevent him from profiting by such justice as their strictures contained. Everything was dispassionately weighed and tested. A finer attitude towards critical attack can scarcely be conceived.

The objections brought against *The Life of Jesus* proceeded from two opposing parties. On the one hand, Freethinkers and liberal Protestant theologians blamed Renan for lack of thoroughness in the application of his critical principles, and for retaining too pronounced a reverence for the traditional figure of his hero. With these writers Renan found himself on common ground ; they started with the same principles, and merely differed as to their application. On the other hand, the orthodox attack was delivered in greater force, but was vitiated by a fundamental misapprehension as to the reality of the supernatural incidents of the Gospel narrative. If miracles are realities, Renan's book is, as he says, a tissue of errors. If the Gospels are divinely inspired and literally true, he has done wrong in not contenting himself with piecing together the fragments of the four texts, and out of them constructing, after the approved manner of the harmonists, a redundant and contradictory whole. If, however, the supernatural element is inadmissible, he is justified in regarding the books which relate miraculous stories as containing both fictitious and historical matter, as legends full of inaccuracies and systematic expedients. The first principle of criticism is to admit at least the possibility of error in the texts which it examines : infallible texts it cannot recognise. Renan, indeed, claims that he should be ranked not as a sceptic, but as a moderate critic, since, instead of rejecting faulty documents as mere trash, he endeavours, by careful analysis, to extract from them their real historical value.

These two assumptions, that miracles do not happen, and that the Gospel writings are not divinely inspired, underlie the whole narrative of Renan's *Life of Jesus*. And that such assumptions are amply justified

Renan has no difficulty in showing. The former negation is, in fact, necessary and prior to all rational exegesis. It is the fruit of an experience which it is impossible to deny. Miracles never happen; only the credulous believe they have seen them; no miracle can be cited which has taken place in the presence of those capable of testing it; no special intervention of Deity, either in the composition of a book or in any other event, can be shown to have occurred. To admit the supernatural is to stand outside the province of science; it is to accept a non-scientific explanation: an explanation which is set aside by the astronomer, the physician, or the geologist, is not one which should be accepted without inquiry by the historian. We all disregard the supernatural, and for the same reason that we reject the existence of centaurs—because we have never seen them. To reject miracles we do not need prior disproof of the credibility of the Gospel writers. The fact that they recount miracles entitles us at once to say: "The Gospels are legends; they may contain history, but certainly all they relate cannot be historical."

There is thus no common ground between the orthodox writer and the Rationalist critic, since they start from diametrically opposite premises. To the theologian the Gospels, like the rest of the Bible, stand on a different footing from all other books; their history is truer than any other history, since it is without any admixture of error. To the Rationalist the Gospels are texts to which the ordinary rules of criticism ought to be applied. Criticism recognises the relative value of the documents submitted for its examination: they may contain errors; they may be improved by comparison with other documents. Orthodoxy, proclaiming that the sacred books contain neither contradiction nor error, resorts to the most desperate expedients in order to get out of difficulties which are created solely by its own erroneous assumption. Much orthodox exegesis becomes for this reason a tissue of subtleties. An isolated subtlety may be true; a thousand subtleties cannot all be true. If we found in Tacitus errors so pronounced as those committed by Luke in his references to Quirinius and Theudas, we should, without hesitation, say that Tacitus had been deceived. Reasonings which no one would admit in the interpretation of a Greek or Latin classic, hypotheses which no historian would dream of employing, are held to be plausible and satisfactory when it is a question of defending a Gospel writer.

Orthodoxy reproaches Rationalism with altering historical records because it does not accept word for word the documents which orthodoxy holds to be sacred. But because a statement is written down, does it follow that it must be true? The miracles of Mohammed as well as those of Jesus have been put into writing, and some of the biographies of Mohammed have a better claim than the Gospels to be considered historical documents. But do we on this account believe in the miracles attributed to Mohammed? If his biographer relates an incredible thing, we make no scruple about rejecting it. If we had four lives of Buddha partly fabulous and as mutually irreconcilable as the four Gospels, and a learned Buddhist endeavoured to purge the narratives of their contradictions, we should not charge him with falsifying the texts.

The question of the supernatural lies at the bottom of all discussion on these matters. If the miracles really happened and the Gospels are really inspired, Renan candidly admits that his method may be termed detestable. But if these beliefs are unfounded, his method is the true and right one. To the rational inquirer one simple reason settles the question: There is no room for belief in a thing of which the world can offer no experimental trace. We do not believe in miracles, just as we do not believe in the devil, in sorcery, or in astrology. There is no need to refute one by one the elaborate reasonings of astrology in order to justify our scepticism with regard to the influence of the stars on human events. It is sufficient to meet them by the simple fact that experience shows that such an influence has never been proved.

The theologian cannot be a historian. History is by its nature essentially disinterested; it deals with facts, not suppositions; its one care is with two inseparable aspects of life—art and truth. The theologian has an interest to serve—his dogma. Even where the dogma is minimised as far as possible, it is still a grievous burden to the artist or the critic. It is essential that the study of books held to be sacred should be carried on in a dispassionate spirit. Critical inquiry into the origins of Christianity will not have said its last word until it has cultivated in a purely secular spirit the method of the Hellenists, a people who were strangers to theology, who thought neither of edifying nor of scandalising, who neither defended nor overthrew the dogmas of their religion.

The foregoing observations of Renan are sufficient evidence of the gradual progress of his mind in the direction of Rationalism between the first and the thirteenth editions of *The Life of Jesus*. With increasing knowledge, and under the pressure of fact and reason, his mind took a firmer and more intellectual tone, his perception of the unity of the race strengthened, and the haze of poetic sentiment in which to him the figure of Jesus was enveloped was partially dispelled, though his sense of the beauty and grandeur of the character of Jesus and of the spiritual value of much of the Gospel writings remained as keen as that of any orthodox believer. That the progress towards a more assured Rationalism was to some extent reluctant seems clear, though this fact only confirms our impression of its genuineness and value. It was no superficial examination, but the most serious reflection, which led to the more advanced views. Renan pondered on these matters with no other prejudices than those which constitute the essence of reason itself. The most important problem which presented itself was that of the Fourth Gospel. While holding that this work had some actual connection with the Apostle John, he fully appreciated the difficulty of defining the nature of that connection. He freely avowed that in certain passages of his first edition he had inclined too much in the direction of authenticity; that he had shown a certain disposition to admit the apostolic authorship of the Fourth Gospel, which was without adequate warrant; and that he was wrong in repudiating the notion of its later origin. The second Epistle attributed to Peter affords an analogous example of a writing which must have emanated from a subsequent author, and the authenticity of which cannot be reasonably sustained. In conformity with this more advanced conception, Renan, while still holding that in the Fourth Gospel we have a fund of information equal, and in some respects superior, to that of the Synoptics, struck out from his later editions expressions which implied that the Gospel as it stands is the genuine record of the Apostle John, or of any other eye-witness of the events narrated.

That which Renan regarded as certain in the life of Jesus may be stated in a few lines. He existed. His home was Nazareth in Galilee. His preaching had a powerful charm for the multitude. His aphorisms made a deep impression on his followers. Peter and John were his principal disciples. He excited the hatred of the orthodox Jews, who arraigned him before Pontius Pilate, then Procurator of Judæa, under whom he was crucified. It was believed that, after two or three days, he had risen from the dead. Beyond this all is doubtful. As to the order of his mental development; whether he believed in the miracles attributed to him; whether he regarded himself as the Messiah; whether he was purely a Jew or definitely broke with the Mosaic law—these are questions on which persons who seek for certainty must remain silent. Little reliance can be placed on the Gospel statements on these points, since they furnish arguments equally serviceable to opposing views, and modify the character of Jesus to suit the purpose of the writers. In such matters it is permissible to make conjectures, provided they are put forward as such. The texts do not give certitude, but they give something. It is necessary neither to follow them with blind confidence, nor to reject them with disdain. We can only strive to divine their meaning, without being certain of having found it. The history of Jesus and of his Apostles has, above all other histories, to be constructed out of a vast mixture of ideas and sentiments. With such ideas and sentiments a thousand trifles and conjectures are intermingled. The details of these it is impossible now to trace with any exactness; the traditions that have come down to us may be true, but they may also be false. The best course is to follow the original narratives as closely as possible, to discard impossibilities, to sow in every direction the seeds of doubt, and to regard the diverse relations of events as matters of conjecture. Narratives dealing so largely with the supernatural cannot be true to the letter; out of a hundred accounts of supernatural occurrences probably eighty have been pieced together by popular imagination. Only in rare cases does a basis of actual fact lie behind the transformed legend. It is useless to think that a single explanation holds good from one end of the Bible to the other. That a particular explanation is repugnant to our ideas is no reason for rejecting it. History has to deal with a world which is partly good and partly evil, and in reading it we are by turns charmed and disgusted, grieved and consoled.

The method of science is in sharp contrast with the method of theology. Science alone seeks after pure truth. Science alone supports truth by convincing reasons, and subjects the methods of her convictions to severe examination. Doubtless this is one reason why, up till now, science has had so little influence on the people. In the future, when the people have received the better instruction which we hope for, they will yield their judgment only to carefully deduced proofs. But the great men of the past are not to be judged by the principles of a later development, or blamed for believing on grounds which to us would be inadequate. We should be lacking in gratitude if we did not speak kindly of Christianity. But filial recognition should never blind our eyes to the truth. We are not wanting in respect to a government when we perceive that it is unable to satisfy all man's conflicting needs; nor to a religion when we allege that it is not free from the formidable objections which science has raised against all forms of belief in the supernatural. When religions respond to the aspirations of the heart at the expense of the protestations of reason, they in their turn by slow degrees, crumble away, for no force in the world can permanently succeed in stifling reason.

THE RATIONALIST PRESS ASSOCIATION LIMITED

THE R.P.A., as it is generally styled, consists of some thousands of men and women scattered throughout the world, of many different nationalities, and of very varied social position and economic circumstance. They are pledged to no creed, to no set of dogmas; but they accept the supremacy of Reason, and aim at making this supremacy effectual in the affairs of everyday life.

In the thirty odd years of its existence the R.P.A. has printed and sold more than four million cheap reprints of the works of the great thinkers—Huxley, Darwin, Spencer, Mill, Haeckel, Renan, Paine, Winwood Reade, Lecky, Clodd, Bradlaugh, etc., in addition to hundreds of thousands of copies of new works on Science (particularly Evolution), History, Philosophy, and Biblical Criticism.

Among the Association's publications are two series of cheap books which have achieved a wide popularity. One is the Forum Series, issued at 1s. and 7d., consisting of original works by some of the leading thinkers of the day, including Sir Arthur Keith, Mr. Julian S. Huxley, Hon. John Collier, Mr. C. E. M. Joad, Major Leonard Darwin, Professor Edward Westermarck, etc. The other is the Thinker's Library, which comprises mainly reprints of famous works, attractively produced at one shilling each. Among the titles which have already appeared are Mr. H. G. Wells's *First and Last Things* and *Short History of the World*, Spencer's *Education*, Haeckel's *Riddle of the Universe*, Rt. Hon. J. M. Robertson's *Short History of Christianity*, Sir John Macdonell's *Historical Trials*, Llewelyn Powys's *Pathetic Fallacy*, Sir Leslie Stephen's *Agnostic's Apology*, James Harvey Robinson's *The Mind in the Making*, Darwin's *Origin of Species*, Winwood Reade's *Martyrdom of Man*, Sir J. G. Frazer's *Adonis*, Anatole France's *Penguin Island* and *Revolt of the Angels*, and Professor J. B. S. Haldane's *Fact and Faith*.

The R.P.A. is not satisfied with what it has done. It wants to put within the reach of the leanest purse still more of the fine intellectual product of the ages; it wants to make it possible for every one to satisfy his thirst for knowledge, to know the facts of life.

To carry out these aims the co-operation of Rationalists is essential. If you are in sympathy with its objects, if you appreciate the work it has done in the past and would like to help it to do better work in the future, you should complete the form on the next page and

JOIN THE R.P.A. NOW!

NOTE.—Members are entitled to receive publications of the Association to the full value of their annual subscriptions. Minimum Subscription, 5s.

APPLICATION FOR MEMBERSHIP

To THE SECRETARY, *The Rationalist Press Association Limited,*
  Nos. 4–6 Johnson's Court, Fleet Street, London, E.C.4.

DEAR SIR,

   I desire to become a Member [1] of the Rationalist Press Association Limited, and enclose herewith my first annual subscription [2]

of.............................; my Membership to commence with the current year.[3] I agree to abide by the Rules and Regulations of the Association as set forth in the Memorandum and Articles of Association.[4]

Please write in block letters

Name ....
        [If lady, state whether Mrs. or Miss]

Address ....

        ....

Occupation...
        [Completion Optional]

Date......................... Signature.....................................

A Subscriber who does not wish to have his or her name published in the Annual Report or any other subscription list can add here the initials or pseudonym under which the contribution is to be acknowledged.

        Initials or Pseudonym...

---

   [1] Persons under twenty-one years of age are not eligible for Membership, but may become "Non-member Subscribers."

   [2] The minimum subscription is 5s., but it is hoped that those who can afford to subscribe more liberally will do so.

   [3] Subscriptions are due in advance on the first of January of each year, so that persons who apply for Membership late in the year should cross out "the current" and substitute "next" if it be not their intention to renew the subscription in the following January. Members joining late in the year, however, are entitled to receive the Association's publications to the full value of their subscriptions.

   [4] The Memorandum and Articles of Association, or any desired information, will be forwarded free on application to the Secretary.